# HERMAN MELVILLE'S MALCOLM LETTER

Watercolor of Malcolm Melville in his uniform as a member of a "volunteer regiment" of the state militia. In a newspaper obituary his uncle, John C. Hoadley, wrote: "His new uniform received a few days before [his death?] must be tried on in the evening, to gratify his desire to see himself in the habliments of a soldier, and to amuse his sisters . . . ." The date and artist are unknown, but the watercolor may be posthumous, after a tintype of Malcolm in uniform. Berkshire Athenaeum.

# HERMAN MELVILLE'S MALCOLM LETTER
## *"Man's Final Lore"*

by
HENNIG COHEN
and
DONALD YANNELLA

FORDHAM UNIVERSITY PRESS
and
THE NEW YORK PUBLIC LIBRARY
New York
1992

**Library of Congress Cataloging-in-Publication Data**

Cohen, Hennig.
  Herman Melville's Malcolm letter : "man's final lore" / by Hennig
Cohen and Donald Yannella.
    p.   cm.
  Includes bibliographical references.
  ISBN 0-8232-1184-3
  1. Melville, Herman, 1819–1891—Biography—Family.   2. Melville,
Herman, 1819–1891—Correspondence.   3. Novelists, American—19th
century—Biography—Family.   4. Novelists, American—19th century—
Correspondence.   5. Fathers and sons—United States—Biography.
I. Yannella, Donald.   II. Title.
PS2386.C64   1991
813'.3—dc20
[B]                                                                91-28140
                                                                       CIP

The original of the "Malcolm letter" is in the Gansevoort-Lansing Collection,
Rare Books and Manuscripts Division, The New York Public Library, Astor,
Lenox and Tilden Foundations.

Printed in the United States of America

# Contents

# Preface

WE ARE PLEASED TO PUBLISH one of the most important documents from the more than six hundred Melville Family Papers acquired in 1983 by the New York Public Library, a letter by Herman Melville to his brother Allan, dated February 20, 1849. We will refer to it throughout as the "Malcolm letter."[1]

The Malcolm letter is rare indeed. It is one of only forty-eight that have been recovered since the publication of *The Letters of Herman Melville* more than a quarter century ago.[2] When read closely and in broad context, it proves to be substantial and significant. Neither a stunning literary statement nor routine business or social correspondence, it is a family letter and is, therefore, supplemental, as is the bulk of the Library's 1983 acquisition to its Gansevoort-Lansing Collection. For this reason the three new boxes of documents have been designated "Additions."[3] The Library is to be congratulated for obtaining what is clearly the most important and largest collection of Melville family papers to have been gathered anywhere thus far. The "Additions," because they include correspondence of Herman Melville's sister Augusta, provide balance to other extant family papers.

To penetrate the depths of the Malcolm letter, to "cut in" to its lower layers as the language of the whale fishery would have it, we present this essay in several sections. First we explicate the letter itself by dwelling on allusions and associations evident to the reader with knowledge of Melville's resources, concerns, and intellectual style; in so doing we ponder the significance and implications of some of the basic information cited in the glosses of the letter. This takes us beneath its surface lightheartedness, even playfulness, to profounder reaches of his thinking. These soundings lead us in the second and third sections to discuss Melville's perceptions of his own father and of the authoritarian patterns of child rearing in his family, as well as of the conception of the family within which Melville understood his own role as father and how his writings show change in this conception. In the course of discussion we inevitably touch the suicide of Malcolm some eighteen years after Melville wrote his letter to his brother Allan. Further consideration of the history and effects of the close-knit family structure and of father/son relationships is offered in the fourth part of the essay, and in the fifth section we conclude with some discussion of Melville's lifelong struggle with these matters, most notably in fiction such as *Pierre; or, the Ambiguities* (1852), his novel of family crisis and family secrets, and in the writing of his last years, his verse and *Billy Budd* (1924).

We have transcribed and annotated the Malcolm letter fully. In addition, we have attempted to show what such a letter might reveal and what conjectures it might inspire when it is read analytically and questioningly within the contexts of Melville's writing and the considerable amount of Melville commentary. We have been interested both in raising questions and offering speculations and in providing demonstrable facts and making well-supported assertions. The results of our speculations are tentative, and many of our questions are unanswered. Such is our Melvillean universe. But for us and, we dare say, for Melville, there are satisfactions that reside in the quest.

A word about our editorial principles. We present the Malcolm letter in a clear text, and we have used conventional editorial symbols to indicate the places where Melville and others deleted or inserted material in the documents quoted.[4] The instances are so few that they do not clutter the transcriptions.

Manuscript material which to the best of our knowledge is quoted or cited here for the first time is documented by reference to the classification system of the particular archive. When the manuscript has been first alluded to in whole or part by prior researchers, we have, to the best of our knowledge, so indicated.

We wish to thank William C. Morris, Alan B. Donovan, and Minna Doskow of Glassboro State College for their support of this research. We are also grateful for the assistance of the staffs of the Manuscripts Division, New York Public Library, particularly John Stinson, Anastasio Teodoro, Melanie Yolles, and especially Valerie Wingfield; the Massachusetts Historical Society, Peter Drummey, Librarian, and other staff members; Ruth Degenhardt, the Berkshire Athenæum; Dennison Beach of the Houghton Library, Harvard University; John Broderick of the Library of Congress; and the Van Pelt Library of the University of Pennsylvania.

We thank Kevin Van Anglen and the late Jay Leyda for reading this manuscript in an earlier stage of development, and Stanton B. Garner for commenting on a later version and for making available to us sections of his forthcoming monograph, *The Civil War World of Herman Melville and the Making of BATTLE-PIECES*. Their comments were helpful; however, responsibility for the essay is ours.

A number of people have been generous in supplying information, details, and other assistance: John Bryant, Mark Cohen, Mary Conaway, Andrew Delbanco, Susan Yannella Harrigan, Harrison Hayford, Thomas F. Heffernan, Lynn Horth, the Rev. Stanley E. Johnson, the late Alice B. Kenney, the Rev. Walter D. Kring, Lea Newman, Agnieszka Salska, Merton M. Sealts, Edwin S. Shneidman, Don Yannella, and Katherine Yannella. Finally, we are indebted to Joann Casey for indexing and Karen Eaves for typing the index.

# Notes

1. For an account of the circumstances surrounding the discovery and the acquisition, see "Finding the New Melville Papers," *Melville Society Extracts*, 56 (November 1983), 1–3. "More for the NYPL's Long Vaticans," *Melville Society Extracts*, 57 (February 1984), 5–7, provides an inventory of the papers by Susan Davis, former Curator of Manuscripts, New York Public Library.

The three Herman Melville letters in the Additions, including the Malcolm letter which is central to our concern here, are now located with most of his other letters in the G-L in box 310.

2. Lynn Horth, "Letters Lost, Letters Found: A Progress Report on Melville's Correspondence," *Melville Society Extracts*, 81 (May 1990), 1. Her total was updated in a conversation with Donald Yannella on August 3, 1991.

3. We designate the original Gansevoort-Lansing Collection as "G-L" and the three new boxes as "G-L Additions."

4. Insertions or additions are indicated by ↑ ↓ , and deletions by < >.

# Abbreviations

FULL BIBLIOGRAPHICAL INFORMATION is provided in the first note, and the author—or author and short title—in subsequent references with the exception of the Writings of Herman Melville in the Northwestern-Newberry Edition, cited below.

| | |
|---|---|
| *Appleton's* | *Appleton's Cyclopædia of American Biography*, New York: D. Appleton, 1887–89. |
| *Billy Budd* | *Billy Budd, Sailor: An Inside Narrative*, ed. Harrison Hayford and Merton M. Sealts, Jr. Chicago: University of Chicago Press, 1962. |
| *CAL* | *Cyclopædia of American Literature*, comp. Evert A. and George L. Duyckinck. New York: Charles Scribner, 1855. |
| *Clarel* | *Clarel: A Poem and Pilgrimage in the Holy Land*, ed. Walter Bezanson. New York: Hendricks House, 1960. |
| *Collected Poems* | *Collected Poems of Herman Melville*, ed. Howard P. Vincent. Chicago: Packard and Company and Hendricks House, 1947. |
| *Confidence-Man* | *The Confidence-Man: His Masquerade*, ed. Elizabeth S. Foster. New York: Hendricks House, 1954. |
| *DAB* | *Dictionary of American Biography*. New York: Charles Scribner's Sons, 1920–36. |
| DC | Duyckinck Collection, Herman Melville Letters, 1846–63, New York Public Library. |

| | |
|---|---|
| *DNB* | *Dictionary of National Biography*. Oxford: Oxford University Press, 1921–22. |
| Essex | Essex Institute, Salem, Massachusetts. |
| G-L | Gansevoort-Lansing Collection, New York Public Library. |
| G-L Additions | Gansevoort-Lansing Collection, New York Public Library; the new papers acquired in 1983. |
| Houghton | Houghton Library, Harvard University. |
| HWB | Henry Whitney Bellows Papers, Massachusetts Historical Society. |
| *Journal . . . London* | *Journal of a Visit to London and the Continent by Herman Melville, 1849–1850*, ed. Eleanor Melville Metcalf. Cambridge, Mass.: Harvard University Press, 1948. |
| *Letters* | *The Letters of Herman Melville*, ed. Merrell R. Davis and William H. Gilman. New Haven: Yale University Press, 1960. |
| LSP | Lemuel Shaw Papers, Massachusetts Historical Society. |
| MP | Morewood Papers, Berkshire Athenæum, Pittsfield, Massachusetts. |
| N-N | The Writings of Herman Melville, ed. Harrison Hayford et al. Evanston and Chicago: The Northwestern University Press and the Newberry Library, 1968–. These are the Melville texts cited unless otherwise indicated. |
| *OED* | *Oxford English Dictionary*, ed. James A. H. Murray et al. Oxford: Clarendon Press, 1961. |
| Sealts, no. | Merton M. Sealts, Jr. *Melville's Reading*. Columbia: University of South Carolina Press, 1988. |
| *Webster* | *Webster's Biographical Dictionary*. Springfield, Mass.: G. and C. Merriam, 1951. |

# HERMAN MELVILLE'S MALCOLM LETTER

# Introduction

ON JANUARY 2, 1849, Hope Shaw noted in her diary: "Mr and Mrs Herman Melville arrived from N York."[1] Hope Shaw was the wife of Judge Lemuel Shaw, a power among the Boston elite, and the stepmother of his daughter Elizabeth, who was married to Melville. Her diary note seems a bit stiff, given the fact that Judge Shaw was the intimate and abiding friend of the Melville-Gansevoort family, with marriage ties and other links through the generations that placed the Shaws within this close-knit fold.[2] Lizzie and Herman had come to Boston to await the birth of their first child. For Herman this was the best of times. His narrative of the South Seas, *Typee* (1846), and its sequel, *Omoo* (1847), had established him as a young writer, popular and of great promise. He had been taken up by Evert A. Duyckinck and other key figures in the New York literary world, and he was led to think that he could make his way successfully with his pen. He had just finished his third book, *Mardi* (1849), described in his preface as "a romance of Polynesian adventure." Lizzie, well-bred, amiable, and in the comfortable surroundings of the Shaw household, was shortly to have his child, and he was considering the choice of a name. In Boston Melville savored his prospects and waited.

Using Judge Shaw's membership card at the Boston Athenaeum, he sampled the latest books to arrive from London and indulged his incipient taste for painting.[3] He returned briefly to New York to take care of business connected with the publication of *Mardi*. He went to lectures and the theater. He worked on a review of Francis Parkman's *The California and Oregon Trail* (1849) for the *Literary World*.[4] He visited bookstores and corresponded with Duyckinck about his desultory literary life. On February 16, Hope Shaw wrote in her diary: "Mr Herman Melvilles son born Friday—half past 7 o'clock in the morning."[5] Not Lizzie's baby, not Judge Shaw's grandchild, but "Mr Herman Melvilles son," a choice of words that recognizes Melville's patriarchal obligation and the importance to his tribe of a son and heir.

Melville had misled Duyckinck when he described his days of waiting for the baby and those of Lizzie's slow recovery as relaxed, aimless, and a little dull. In fact, he could scarcely contain the excitement and creative energy he felt. He had a new son and a new book that overflowed with long, long thoughts, dreams, fanciful allegory, and rhapsodic discourse. (The bad reviews were yet to come.) He was reading Milton. He bought, apparently in a Boston bookstore, a set of Shakespeare and was immersing himself in the plays for the first time[6]—quibbling with Samuel Johnson's commentary, marking up the texts of the tragedies,[7] and reporting to Duyckinck on performances that pleased him, such as Fanny Kemble's Lady Macbeth, and her Desdemona, which did not.[8] He was attending Emerson's lectures, finding him "a great man," and was stirred and distressed by him as he would continue to be.[9] This was the state of his mind and his spirit when he wrote to his brother about his son.

# Notes

1. Diary of Hope Shaw, LSP, box 27; quoted in Jay Leyda, *The Melville Log* (New York: Gordion, 1969), I, 286.

2. Michael Paul Rogin, *Subversive Genealogy: The Politics and Art of Herman Melville* (New York: Knopf, 1983), p. 10, identifies Allan Melvill as "Judge Shaw's closest friend." He had been engaged to Nancy Melvill, Allan's sister, who died before they could be married, and he carried two of her love letters in his wallet for the rest of his life. See Leonard W. Levy, *The Law of the Commonwealth and Chief Justice Shaw* (Cambridge, Mass.: Harvard University Press, 1957), p. 9. The letters and the wallet survive in the Boston Social Law Library.

3. Merton M. Sealts, Jr., *Melville's Reading: Revised and Enlarged Edition* (Columbia: University of South Carolina Press, 1988), nos. 98, 198, and 199.

4. *Piazza Tales* (N-N), pp. 230–34. The review was printed in the March 31, 1849 issue.

5. Diary of Hope Shaw, LSP, box 27; quoted in Leyda, I, 288.

6. ALs, Herman Melville to Evert A. Duyckinck, February 24, 1849, DC, box 43; quoted partially in Leyda, I, 288–89, and fully in *Letters*, pp. 76–78.

7. Leyda, I, 289–91, Sealts, no. 460, and Walker Cowen, *Melville's Marginalia* (New York and London: Garland, 1987), I, 429.

8. ALs, Herman Melville to Evert A. Duyckinck, February 24, 1849, DC, box 43; quoted in *Letters*, pp. 77–78, and partially in Leyda, I, 288–89, and Metcalf, pp. 57–58.

9. ALs, Herman Melville to Evert A. Duyckinck, February 24, 1849, DC, box 43; *Letters*, p. 77, and March 3, 1849, *Letters*, pp. 78–79. See Merton M. Sealts, Jr., "Melville and Emerson's Rainbow," in *Pursuing Melville, 1940–1980* (Madison: University of Wisconsin Press, 1980), pp. 250–77.

# The Malcolm Letter

Herman Melville acquired a copy of James Macpherson's *Fingal*
*. . . Composed by Ossian* (London, 1762) in 1847. At an unknown
date he made a crossmark beside this passage:

> The grief of all arose, but most the bursting sigh of Armin. He
> remembers the death of his son, who fell in the days of his youth.

At the bottom of the same page he wrote:

> The pathos—none can speak it.

# I. The Letter

THE LETTER THAT HERMAN MELVILLE WROTE to his brother Allan from Boston on Tuesday morning, February 20, 1849, is a family communication about commonplace but clearly important events, at least to the correspondent. It is in no sense a calculated example of the epistolary art. It is unpolished, hasty, and although mannered and devious, was never intended to impress and certainly not to be scrutinized intensively. It is not a literary monument, a *Moby-Dick* (1851), and it is not comparable, for instance, with Melville's letters to Hawthorne about *Moby-Dick*. Still it tasks us. It demands that we sound its depths.

It is less a letter than an effusion. In the beginning it is a joke for the pleasure of a joke, a type of the comic more evident in his early South-Sea narratives than the books to come in which his humor is made to bear increasingly complex burdens. Letters to intimates encouraged relaxation, and sometimes his linked analogies are extravagant and irreverent. The Malcolm letter sweeps forward heedlessly, and this makes it all the more poignant and engaging. Its lack of restraint allows us to glimpse the bright prospect of Melville's imaginative landscape and the demon clouds that loom in the offing. It is ambiguous also, though a degree of ambiguity is natural enough at critical moments such as the birth of a son and heir because elation cannot entirely displace dim inklings of having given a hostage to fortune. But something more is felt. A suggestion of panic, perhaps? Melville will think in such terms as he brings his letter to a close. And our hearts are wrung because we know (or at least can anticipate) what Melville, in a moment radiant with promise, cannot possibly know. We think of the ebullient section, "Pierre Just Emerging from His Teens," with which Melville's family novel begins. But if the mood of the moment informs the character of the letter, we should remember that it is not a consciously literary production subject to the requisites of literary formulations. It is a spontaneous overflowing meant for an intimate and a brother. Nevertheless, it does have its formal qualities and its logic.

The structural framework of the letter, which we are presenting in page-for-page, line-for-line transcription, consists of a rather conventional preamble; a hyperbolic physical description of Melville's infant son, Malcolm, whom he facetiously calls "the phenomenon"; a passage in which Melville speculates on the selection of an appropriate name for his baby; a fanciful account of "a terrible commotion," extending from the streets of Boston to the Great Wall of China, that greeted his son's nativity; and, finally, a section in which Melville ostensibly marvels that "the birth of one little man" should cause "a panic" that reaches beyond the bounds of the earth itself. The letter closes with his signature, followed by a puzzling subscription to his brother.

Elizabeth ("Lizzie") Shaw Melville (1822–1906) and Malcolm as an infant. Daguerreotype, c. 1850. Berkshire Athenaeum.

Tuesday Morning
Feb 20.th

I have yours of yesterday.
I am rejoiced that Sophia
is well after her happy
delivery. Lime is doing well,
also the phenomenon, which
weighs I know not how many
pennyweight, — I would say,
hundred-weight. —— We
desired much to have him
weighed, but it was thought
that no hay-scales in town
were strong enough. It takes
three nurses to dress him;
and he is as valiant as
Julius Cæsar. —— He's a
perfect prodigy. —— If He
next comes to the worst, I
shall let him out by the

Tuesday Morning
Feb 20th

I have yours of yesterday.

I am rejoiced that Sophia[1]

is well after her happy delivery.

Lizzie is doing well,

also the phenomenon,[2] which

weighs I know not how many

pennyweight,[3]—I would say,

hundred-weight.[4]——We

desired much to have him

weighed, but it was thought

that no hay-scales in town

were strong enough. It takes

three nurses to dress him;[5]

and he is as robust [valiant?] as

Julius Caesar.——He's a

perfect prodigy.[6]——If the

worse comes to the worst, I

shall let him out by the

month to Barnum; and
take the tour of Europe with
him. I think of calling
him Barbarossa — Adolphus —
Ferdinand — Otho — Grandissimo
Hercules — Sampson — Bonaparte
— Lambert. —— If you
can suggest any thing better
or more characteristic, pray,
inform me of it by the next
post. —— There was
a little commotion here
at the time of the event.
—— I had men stationed
at all the church bells,
24 hours beforehand; &
when the Electric Telegraph
informed them of the fact —
such a ding-donging you
never heard. — All the

month to Barnum;[7] and

take the tour of Europe with

him. I think of calling

him Barbarossa[8]—Adolphus[9]—

Ferdinand[10]—Otho[11]—Grandissimo

Hercules[12]—Sampson[13]—Bonaparte[14]

—Lambert.[15]——If you

can suggest any thing better

or more characteristic, pray,

inform me of it by the next

post.——There was

a terrible commotion here

at the time of the event.

——I had men stationed

at all the church bells,

24 hours beforehand; &

when the Electric Telegraph

informed them of the fact—

such a ding-donging you

nere heard[16]——All the

engines came out. Kentucky the State-House was on fire.

Of course the news was sent on by telegraph to Washington & New Orleans. —— When old Zach heard of it — he is reputed to have said — "Mark me: that-boy will be President of the United States before he dies."

—— On New Orleans, the excitement was prodigious. Stocks rose & brandy fell. —— I have not yet heard from Europe & Pekin. But doubtless, ere this, they must have placed props against the Great-Wall. —— The harbor here is empty: — all the ships, brigs, schooners & smacks have scattered in all directions with the news for foreign parts. —— The crowd has not yet left the streets, gossiping of the event. —— The number of calls at 49 Mt Vernon Street is incalculable. Ten porters engines came out, thinking the

State-House was on fire.[17]

Of course the news was sent on

by telegraph to Washington & New

Orleans.——When old Zack

heard of it—he is reported to

have said—"Mark me: That

boy will be President of the

United States before he dies."[18]

——In New Orleans, the

excitement was prodigious. Stocks

rose & brandy fell[19]——I

have not yet heard from Europe &

Pekin. But doubtless, ere this, they

must have placed props against

the Great-Wall.[20]——The harbor

here is empty:—all the ships, brigs,

schooners & smacks have scattered in

all directions with the news for

foreign parts.[21]——The crowd has

not yet left the streets, gossiping

of the event.——The number of

calls at 49 Mt Vernon Street

is incalculable.[22] Ten porters

suffice not to receive the card;
and Canning the waiter, dropped
down dead last night thro' pure
exhaustion. —— Who would
have thought that the birth of
one little man, when ten thousand
of other little men, & little horses,
& little guinea-pigs & little rabbits,
& the Lord only knows what, are
they born — that the birth of one
little phenomenon, should cause
such a panic thro' the world: —
nay, even in heaven; for
last night I dreampt that
his good angel had secured
a seat for him above; & that the
Devil vowed tensely bethinking
him of the lusty foe to win
born into this empire world. ——

       H Melville.

The Reverend Father in Wedlock,
     Allan Melville.

suffice not to receive the cards;

and Canning the waiter, dropped

down dead last night thro' pure

exhaustion[23]——Who would

have thought that the birth of

one little man,[24] when ten thousands

of other little men, & little horses,

& little guinea-pigs & little roosters,[25]

& the Lord only knows what, are

being born—that the birth of one

little phenomenon, should create

such a panic[26] thro' the world:—

nay, even in heaven; for

last night I dreampt that

his good angel had secured

a seat for him above;[27] & that the

Devil roared terribly[28] bethinking

him of the lusty foe to sin

born into this sinful world.——

                H Melville,

The Reverend Father[29] in Wedlock,[30]

                Allan Melville.

We call Melville's letter to Allan the "Malcolm letter" even though Malcolm's name is not mentioned in it. He is its original, generative force. "Certainly, the sense of originality exists at its highest in an infant," Melville would argue in *The Confidence-Man* (1857); and to borrow an analogy from his discussion of the "original character" as a "phenomenon in fiction," Malcolm functions like the "revolving Drummond light" that surmounted Barnum's American Museum in the 1840s. Despite the fact that Malcolm's "original character" exists in little more than embryonic form, it is through him, as with the Drummond light, that "everything is lit . . . everything starts up."[31]

Since news traveled rapidly between Boston and New York—and the language of the letter supports this—it is clear that the word of Malcolm's birth had already reached the house at 103 Fourth Avenue, Manhattan, which Herman and Lizzie shared with Allan and his wife, Sophia, and other members of the family. So the immediate purpose of the Malcolm letter is to acknowledge that Sophia has been successfully delivered of her child. Melville does this at the beginning, courteously and abruptly. He does not mention that it is their first child, presumably a cause for jubilation, nor does he refer to the child's name, Maria—usually a subject of considerable remark in the Melville family—or sex—which may be a polite omission in view of a dynastic inclination toward patriarchy and primogeniture in the Melville-Gansevoort clan; and he is brief and to the point regarding Lizzie's condition. In sum, he is impatient to proceed with what is really on his mind. The perfunctory quality of the letter disappears with his initial reference to his son. He is exuberant. The child is a "phenomenon," a word Melville took seriously,[32] but here he is thinking of the "infant phenomenon," showman Crummles' daughter, comically treated in Dickens' *Nicholas Nickleby* (1838). His weight—and his value—are measured not in pence but in pounds. He is beyond measure, at least beyond the measure of the largest scales, prodigious in size, but no freak. He is a "perfect prodigy."[33] It amuses Melville to think that in a financial pinch Malcolm might be exhibited profitably by that preeminent showman, P. T. Barnum. Melville has a prototype in mind. Shortly before Malcolm's birth, Barnum's American Museum began advertising "a giant baby" said

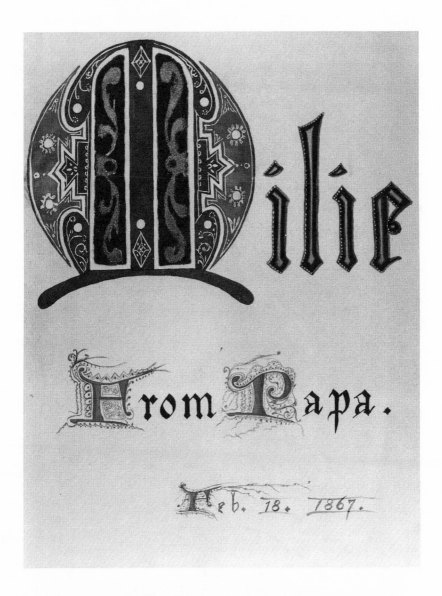

On her eighteenth birthday Allan Melville (1823–1872) gave his daughter Maria ("Milie") Gansevoort (1849–1935) an autograph album with an ornately hand-lettered opening page. Most of the signatures it contains are those of her family, including her cousin, Malcolm, and her Uncle Herman. Berkshire Athenaeum.

Pencil drawing and signature of Malcolm Melville from the autograph
album of his cousin Maria, a birthday gift of her father, Allan Melville.
Berkshire Athenaeum.

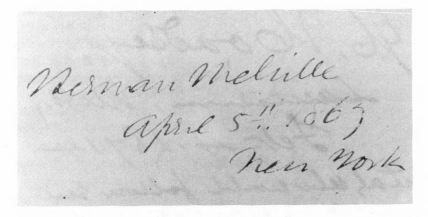

Herman Melville signed the autograph album of his niece, Maria Gansevoort Melville, on April 5, 1867. Berkshire Athenaeum.
He would write to her on October 22, 1867:

> My Dear Milie:
>     I was much gratified by your note, and was touched at the way in which you speak of Mackie. . . . We have been getting new photographs made from two tintypes—one representing him in his ordinary dress, and the other in the regimental one. . . . which we learn he had taken for you.

to be sixteen months old and weighing ninety pounds.[34] Within the family, Melville began to call his baby son "Barney," making the Barnum association an extended private joke.

The subject of Malcolm's name had received particular attention within the family circle and was already settled, but Melville compiles an epic catalogue of possibilities. He delighted in catalogues anyway, and at the time was engrossed in the wild listings of Rabelais (whose gargantuan shade hovers over Malcolm's cradle), but the impetus for his roll call was the valiant, but hardly robust, Roman emperor Julius Caesar, mentioned immediately above.[35] From Imperial Caesar he moves by association to emperors of the Holy Roman Empire, to mythic and biblical strong men, and then to the Emperor Napoleon, ending with the name Daniel Lambert, the fat man exhibited by Barnum known as "the English Mammoth."[36] Melville amuses himself and at the same time deflates his own grandiosity. Furthermore, a list that begins with authentic heroes and ends with a circus freak reflects his poor opinion of a society that equates celebrity with merit. Melville would return to this subject in *Pierre*.[37] His conclusion to the section on names is arch. He invites Allan to contribute suitable additions to the list. And indeed why not? Naming was a national pastime, a side effect of Manifest Destiny. As they populated the frontier, egalitarian Americans bestowed names expansively on their land and their children. They named as they pleased, though tacitly aware of subtle motivations within the culture. For to name was to assert primacy and power. Had not Father Adam, with divine ordination, named the creatures in Eden? Why not his progeny?

But Melville draws back from this extravagance. He uses references to Barnum, purveyor of humbug and hyperbole, to remind himself of the human tendency toward overreaching. The Barnum presence is a good-natured warning. Take care. Even in the best of bright moments, one must not expect too much. But if Barnum were a genial warning, remember that Melville was discovering Shakespeare, whose lines he did not scan lightly. Two days after the Malcolm letter, he wrote Evert Duyckinck: "Dolt & ass that I am I have lived more than 29 years, & until a few days ago, never made close acquaintance with the divine William."[38] In this bright period of his life Shakespeare "fixed" and "fascinated" him. We anticipate his usage. These words occur in his prescient poem, "The Coming Storm," though previously he had applied them to Hawthorne's somber tales. The poem was written during a time of national tragedy and personal disaffection, a time when dark thoughts of "the divine William" fixed and fascinated him. Foremost in *Hamlet*, according to Melville, Shakespeare is "probing the very axis of reality," and *Hamlet* is the core of "The Coming Storm":[39]

> All feeling hearts must feel for him
> > Who felt this picture. Presage dim—
> Dim inklings from the shadowy sphere
> > Fixed him and fascinated here.

> A demon-cloud like the mountain one
> > Burst on a spirit as mild
> As this urned lake, the home of shades.
> > But Shakespeare's pensive child

> Never the lines had lightly scanned,
>   Steeped in fable, steeped in fate;
> The Hamlet in his heart was 'ware,
>   Such hearts can antedate.
>
> No utter surprise can come to him
>   Who reaches Shakespeare's core;
> That which we seek and shun is there—
>   Man's final lore.[40]

Barnum is comic surface. Shakespearean tragedy, *Hamlet*, is the heart of the matter. The poem was published in 1866. Malcolm died the next year.

Structurally, the references to Barnum associate the name passage in the letter with the passage on the prodigious child. This connection is reinforced in other small ways. Barnum's name, for example, has phonological affinities with Barbarossa's, immediately following. The catalogue of names in the Malcolm letter is thin; it is anticipated by the burlesque inventories in *Mardi*,[41] and it foreshadows richer, more fully developed lists that will appear in *Moby-Dick* and *The Confidence-Man* that are likewise constructed on the basis of association of sound, rhythm, chronology, and literary, historical, mythic, and religious allusion directed toward a dissonant, wry, or perhaps paradoxical culmination.[42]

To some extent the subsequent sections of the Malcolm letter are also catalogues that expand in an associative way. The "terrible commotion" caused by Malcolm's nativity expands geographically. Beginning in Boston with a din of church bells such as is usually reserved for imperial arrivals, the news of his birth is proclaimed by telegraph throughout the land, and by boat (the sometime sailor Melville lists the vessels that carry the news to "foreign parts" in order of magnitude) or perhaps earlier by some mystical means, conveyed to Europe and Asia. From the distance of foreign parts we circle back to Judge Shaw's house on Mount Vernon Street, Boston, where the commotion began. Melville had written burlesques of this sort in 1847 for *Yankee Doodle*, a series of "Anecdotes" about General Zachary Taylor, hero of the Mexican War. (They include, by the way, a comic catalogue of "relics" of Old Zack's heroism to be exhibited at Barnum's Museum.)

The tone of the final section shifts from the overblown to childish prattle touched with a wit and wonder that anticipate *Moby-Dick*. The commonplace phrase, "news from foreign parts," is the cord that attaches Melville's letter to a novel that has attracted attention for the way it employs gynecological, obstetrical, and neonatal imagery. The newborn whales have "delicate side-fins and . . . flukes" that remind Ishmael of the "crumpled appearance of a baby's ears newly arrived from foreign parts" delicately unspecified.[43] But more. Tender though almost clinical memories of the infant Malcolm, his genesis even, and perhaps subconscious memories from Melville's own infancy, suffer a sea change: Melville has Ishmael look down into the transparent deep at "nursing mothers of the whales" whose sucklings like "human infants . . . will calmly and fixedly gaze away from the breast, as if leading two different lives at the time; and while yet drawing mortal nourishment, be still spiritually feasting upon some unearthly reminiscence."[44] The final section is also a list, a sequence of verbal parallels that pose the question of why "one little man" is unique among the infinite variety of other little creatures born into the world.[45] The purpose of this process of diminution is paradoxical. Melville diminishes in order to enhance. He has elevated his "little man" to the stature of a "little phenomenon," developing the phrase into an oxymoron. But while this is true, his language shows that he thinks of children as domesticated animals.[46] They are subhuman. The Dickensian joviality of the first reference to his newborn son[47] is superseded by the seriousness with which he ordinarily used the term *phenomenon*. This shift occurs at the pivotal point of the sentence, the place at which it is transformed from interrogative to declarative, from the sublunary world to the dream world, and from burlesque fantasies to a vision of a Miltonic struggle between Christ and Satan.

When Melville first read Milton has not been ascertained, but it was likely fairly early and he probably owned and marked up more than one volume of Milton's poetry in his lifetime, as he had with copies of Shakespeare. Milton is listed among the poets, philosophers, and other "worthies" that comprise the being of Melville's narrative voice, Taji, in a rhapsodic chapter of *Mardi* titled "Dreams." Melville signed the preface to *Mardi*

"New York, January, 1849" when Lizzie was in Boston awaiting the end of her term. A more telling indicator of Melville's interest in Milton in the period immediately before Malcolm's birth is the frequency of Miltonic reference in this romance. Sixteen allusions have been identified, the same number as in *Moby-Dick* and a number unsurpassed in any other Melville work. There are only two in *Typee* and one in *Omoo*.[48] In 1849, he bought a two-volume edition of *The Poetical Works of John Milton*.[49] He carried it with him on his voyage to San Francisco, and he was to wear it out with repeated reading and to mark and annotate it heavily.

"On the Morning of Christ's Nativity" was among the poems in this edition that attracted Melville. Although he nowhere quotes directly from this so-called hymn, its submerged existence in the Malcolm letter (indirectly evidenced in his reading of Plutarch) provides the letter with an audacious conclusion. Melville was especially attracted to lines 173–78, with which stanza XIX begins:

> The Oracles are dumb,
> No voice of hideous hum
>     Runs through the arched roof in words deceiving.
> Apollo from his shrine
> Can no more divine,
> With hollow shriek the steep of Delphos leaving.

He marked line 173 with a cross, and beneath it he wrote: "Plutarch on the cessation of the Oracles." The death of the gods rather than the cause of their demise was an abiding interest, and this may be what first attracted his attention to the stanza, though in the Malcolm letter he has in mind another aspect of this dialogue by Plutarch.

It seems likely that he owned a copy of the Plutarch work in some form. One of the "Extracts" that precede *Moby-Dick* was taken from "Holland's Plutarch's Morals." It is certain that he read it carefully, found it memorable, and attempted to foist it off on others. For instance, his sister Helen wrote him from Boston in 1854, and after acknowledging one of his infrequent letters to her, adds: " 'Plutarch on the Cessation of the Oracles' must be a work of deep interest, but I'll take your word for it, having no ambition to peruse the same."⁵⁰ As late as when he was writing *Clarel* (1876), the departure of the pagan gods as a consequence of the Nativity is still on his mind.⁵¹

Melville shares with Milton and Spenser an interest in Plutarch's "On the Cessation of the Oracles," from the collection usually known as the *Opera moralia*. Christian neoplatonic tradition held that the heathen oracles, who were deceptive and demonic anyway, had been silenced by the mere fact of the birth of the Christ Child.⁵² Melville seems to be following Milton's Nativity hymn, which in describing the sound and fury of Apollo on this occasion emphasizes through contrast with the dumbstruck oracles Apollo's "hollow shriek" as he fled his Delphic shrine. Was Melville particularly attracted to the word *shriek* by the suggestiveness of its modifier, *hollow*? Holler? Hallow, unhallowed? *Hollow* in the sense of vain, empty, false? In any case, his oracular Isabel greets Pierre with a "Delphic shriek"; and he remembered the shrieking, fleeing god when he wrote George Duyckinck on November 8, 1858, to thank him for the gift of a set of Chapman's *Homer*, which, Melville said, would cause "Pope's version . . . to go off shrieking, like the bankrupt deities in Milton's hymn."⁵³ Another Melville favorite, Sir Thomas Browne, likewise believed that the pagan oracles "ceased or grew mute at the coming of Christ" (*Vulgar Errors*, Book VII, Chap. xii). Melville had read Browne by 1848.⁵⁴ Echoes of Milton's shrieking deities also resound in the Devil's roar near the end of the letter, though it is more likely that Melville's primary source is biblical. St. Peter exhorted the faithful to "be vigilant; because your adversary the devil, as a roaring lion, walketh about, seeking whom he may devour."⁵⁵ The Devil's roar terrifies but it expresses the Devil's terror, too, since the Devil, like the pagan gods of the Nativity hymn, is put to route by the birth of a child.

The inferences that logically follow are extravagant, to say the least. Melville, through his hidden allusion to Milton's poem, equates Malcolm's nativity with the Incarnation. Melville's Malcolm has his seat in Heaven and is ready to confront the Adversary in the sinful world below. That he writes "I dreampt" hardly excuses his presumption. No wonder the Devil roars in rage and terror and perhaps in glee. From banter about a comic child prodigy remembered from Dickens and a giant baby such as Barnum might exhibit, Melville descends into impious inversion. And again his trope has a double edge. If Malcolm is the equivalent of the Christ Child, then Herman is the equivalent of God the Father. One of Melville's jottings on the back flyleaf of a volume of Shakespeare, some of which date from 1849 and many of them concerned with diabolic speculations he put to literary use, reflects the sardonic game he is playing: "May pious men have impious children."[56] Beneath this there is a little lower layer. In fact and when he re-created himself in fiction, and because of the way in which he had been brought up, Melville was led to regard his own father as a divine patriarch; and his response to his father was not entirely worshipful.

Nor is all this the ultimate in Melville's devious equations. Cryptically, following his signature, he subscribes the Malcolm letter to "The Reverend Father in Wedlock, Allan Melville"—his brother and his father's namesake and hence an evocation of their father. The reference is religious as well as familial. The phrase, "Our Reverend Father in God," occurs in the prayer books of the Episcopal Church as a respectful mode of address to bishops at confirmations and the ordinations of deacons and priests.[57] Melville is writing to congratulate his brother Allan, an Episcopalian,[58] on the birth of Allan's first child. It is an experience he shares, evident in his reference to the birth of Malcolm a few days before. Therefore, Melville's form of address on one level asserts facetiously that he and his brother constitute a holy fraternity of righteous men, almost prelatical in the sanctity and legitimacy of their wedded state. Yet Herman Melville is reminded here of his father, Allan, as well, and that his brother and he are privy to a shameful family secret. It is within this context that he reshapes the formula from the Episcopal prayer book into an outrageous if arcane jest. Their revered earthly father had sired a child out of wedlock, but they can congratulate themselves that their own children are legitimate. Joking aside, legitimacy was a serious consideration among the Melville-Gansevoorts. In their view, an important component of Allan Melvill's misdeed would have been that it threatened legitimate lineage.[59] There may be a still lower layer. To the extent that Melville associates not only himself but his father with the Heavenly Father, and Melville does when he employs the phrase from the prayer book, he is questioning the legitimacy of the Holy Family. While this might be an afterthought in his letter to his brother Allan, legitimacy will become a fundamental concern in *Pierre; or, The Ambiguities*.[60]

Had we lightly scanned the lines of the Malcolm letter, we would have seen only its lightheartedness, not the ambiguities at its core. Elation only, for under the circumstances elation is the expected response. Its ambiguities, however, leave a sour taste. "Presage dim— / —Dim inklings from the shadowy sphere." We know that Melville is justified in feeling a moment of panic when he realizes that the three sisters have begun their work, and this tempers his elation even as he first mentions the "phenomenon" to his brother. We are aware that the letter is steeped in fate. Nor are we utterly surprised, because what Melville could feel but dimly, we know to be categorical fact. We know that Malcolm was doomed to kill himself before he reached manhood.

# Patriarchs

Thomas Melvill (1751–1832). Engraving from *Albany Citizens' Advertiser*, an undated clipping, c. 1834. Rare Books and Manuscripts Division, The New York Public Library, Astor, Lenox and Tilden Foundations. Elizabeth Shaw Melville provided a similar illustration for Arthur Stedman's biographical article, " 'Marquesan' Melville," in the New York *World* of October 11, 1891.

General Peter Gansevoort (1749–1812) painted c. 1794 by Gilbert Stuart. Courtesy Munson-Williams-Proctor Institute, Utica, New York.

Allan Melvill (1782–1832), father of Herman Melville. Watercolor by John Rubens Smith, 1810. In *Pierre* (Bk. IV) an oil painting of Pierre's father is described: "An impromptu portrait of a fine-looking, gay-hearted, youthful gentleman. He is lightly, and, as it were, airily and but grazingly seated in, or rather flittingly tenanting an old-fashioned chair of Malacca. One arm confining his hat and cane is loungingly thrown over the back of the chair. . . ." Metropolitan Museum of Art, bequest of Charlotte E. Hoadley.

Lemuel Shaw (1781–1861), father of Elizabeth Knapp Shaw Melville. Marked "Whipple of Boston." Berkshire Athenaeum.

Peter Gansevoort (1788–1876) of Albany, Herman Melville's uncle and benefactor. Photograph c. 1875. Rare Books and Manuscripts Division, The New York Public Library, Astor, Lenox and Tilden Foundations.

## II. Family Names

READING THE MALCOLM LETTER CAREFULLY provides inklings of how the domestic aspects of Melville's life shaped his art. The Malcolm letter confirms the commanding role of the father. It is a role that Melville appears to accept joyfully though we sense his reservations soon enough. Aside from those that are normal and natural, he is haunted by the example of his own father, and this is particularly the case because of the attitude toward the concept of fatherhood and family that he inherited: the father as a kind of clan chieftain (the Melvilles doted on their Scottish ancestry); the father as a Puritan patriarch who regarded seriously his duties to church, state, and business (the Gansevoorts were of Dutch Calvinistic origin and the Melvills, like Ishmael, seem originally to have been "born and bred in the bosom of the infallible Presbyterian Church"[61]); the father on earth as a replicant of the father in heaven, at one remove, as it were, from Jehovah himself. The exaltation of their fathers followed logically from this inheritance, and it was reinforced by Victorian cultural attitudes.

There are numerous illustrations of the persistence with which Allan Melvill[62] sought to enhance the reputation of the forefathers, both Melvill and Gansevoort. One of them lies within the family penchant for composing tendentious biographical sketches. In 1829, in an attempt to preserve his father's position as Naval Officer for the Boston district, he prepared a laudatory biography of Major Melvill to be sent to President Andrew Jackson, and Melville himself wrote a life of his Uncle Thomas Melvill for inclusion in a history of Pittsfield.[63] Late in the second decade of the century and early in the third, Allan was the driving force behind efforts to publish biographical memoirs of his father-in-law, General Peter Gansevoort, the "Hero of Fort Stanwix." His wife, Maria, joined him in seeking the cooperation of her brother, Peter, who appears to have been reluctant to encourage such a public display for several reasons, not the least of which was a desire for accuracy. Allan's ardent devotion to this project might be interpreted as evidence of his having been absorbed by the substantial old

Dutch family into which he had married, to the point of disregarding his own. He was, however, profoundly concerned with the interests of the Melvills, especially those of his father, with whom his relations were warmer and close. This sense of the duty owed parents and the family, and the virtual enshrinement of the family patriarchs, appears to have been fundamental, a lesson to be taught by the older generation whenever the occasion arose. And when considering Herman's relations with his mother and his treatment of his children, the lessons of the ghost of his father must be taken into account.[64] In the family novel, *Pierre*, the title character, Pierre Glendinning, has, in his imagination, created a "shrine" to the deceased father whose name he bears: "In this shrine . . . stood the perfect marble form of his departed father; without blemish, unclouded, snow-white, and serene; Pierre's fond personification of perfect human goodness and virtue. Before this shrine, Pierre poured out the fullness of all young life's most reverential thoughts and beliefs."[65]

Fond Pierre, both loving and foolish, enshrines his father, venerating him as if he were a divinity. But "Apollo from his shrine / Can no more divine." For Melville—for Milton, too?—the word *divine* serves ulterior purposes. Apollo-Father Allan-Father, Pierre. Pierre's father is no longer godly. He is no longer divine, is no longer capable of divination, is no longer a source of "words deceiving." Is he to be thought of as lost to Satan, the Deceiver?[66] We are told in the novel that "When Pierre was twelve years old, his father had died [the same age as Melville when *his* father died], leaving behind him, in the general voice of the world, a marked reputation as a gentleman and a Christian."[67] The phrase *marked reputation* is ambiguous. As the subscription to the Malcolm letter reminds us, father Allan Melvill was less than the "personification of human goodness and virtue," but this was a well-kept secret within the family, and his public reputation as a gentleman and a Christian seems not to have suffered. He, and after his death, his family, did their best to keep it that way, Melville being an exception. In "Pierre Just Emerging from His Teens," we are told that Pierre followed "a maxim" of his father that he could not be a gentleman without being a Christian. Henry A. Murray, in his edition of *Pierre*, comments on this passage: "In Allan Melvill's mind there was no conflict between the concept of gentleman and the concept of Christian. He was a constant and enthusiastic advocate of both, or rather, of the synthesis of the two in the figure of the 'Christian gentleman.' "[68]

Like the rest of his clan, Allan Melvill held that while notable accomplishments secured the family position, a name without blemish was the fundamental imperative. When he journeyed to Scotland in 1818, the year before Herman was born, to seek his aristocratic connections, he wrote his wife, Maria, of his visit to the church where his "Great Grandfather . . . dispensed the sacred truth"; he piously added, "I entered with awe and reverence and most devoutly wished that I might leave behind as good a name."[69] In 1824 when Guert Gansevoort, his wife's nephew, received his appointment as midshipman, Allan Melvill used the financial and social resources at his command to secure for him the genteel station commensurate with "the name he bears" and anticipated with satisfaction the "honor to the family" that his promising career would bring.[70] Similarly, in 1826 he proffers avuncular advice to his nephew Midshipman Thomas W. Melvill, who is about to embark for the Pacific: "The name you bear should also inspirit you to service of the highest estimation in private society, & to deeds of noble daring in public life; . . . your great object with GOD's blessing must ever be, to preserve the Family name unsullied."[71]

The letter is extensive, with much sanctimonious emphasis on "the discharge of duty" and descent "from a Scottish hero." Allan Melvill was pleased with what he had written and made a copy for preservation in the family archives.[72]

Although its tone is comic, the Malcolm letter shows how seriously Herman Melville considered the choice of a name for his son. He understood that to name is to exercise paternal authority, and this was his duty; but at the same time he appears to have remembered paternal violation of his own individuality. His uneasiness spills over into a review he wrote within days of Malcolm's birth. The book was Francis Parkman's *The Oregon Trail*. He thought the title "ill-chosen," arguing that the "christianizing of books is very different from the christianizing of men" because "Among men, the object of a name is to individualize" while "with books . . . names or titles are presumed to express the contents."[73] As we see, he viewed names, at least those in his own family, warily. The naming of children was much discussed in the Melville-Gansevoort clan, but on the whole naming was more an act of ancestor worship than of individualizing. The appropriate name sustained family coherence by perpetuating the memory of worthy and beloved kin and important events in family history. For example, Herman's mother writes to her daughter Augusta of the birth of Herman and Lizzie's second child, Stanwix. She reports on Lizzie's health ("not so well") and the child's appearance ("small and thin, but a bright little thing"), and then asks, "how do you like the name[?]"[74] It was a name shared with a cousin of an older generation, and it commemorates, as Melville would write with historical accuracy in *Pierre*, a fort "in the Revolutionary War his grandfather had for several months defended . . . against the repeated combined assaults of Indians, Tories, and Regulars."[75] Stanwix was born at the time when *Pierre* was first emerging, and in a jovial letter to Evert Duyckinck, Melville explains that he "will probably be" named for the place "where . . . this lad's great grandfather spent his summers in the Revolutionary War before Saratoga [as a resort] came into being[.]"[76] Stanwix was likewise the name of a Gansevoort cousin and a commercial property in which the family invested heavily.[77]

When Herman and Lizzie's third child was born, Sophia Melville, Allan's wife, writes her sister-in-law Augusta: "I must congratulate Lizzie on having a girl this time, Miss Bessie, Well that is a good name but I certainly thought it would be Lucy."[78] Sophia was not famous for her tact. Lucy Melvill Nourse was a favorite aunt, and her name would be continued in the family through Sophia's fifth daughter. In due time Herman, too, would perpetuate this name. Lucy (Lizzie?) Tartan is doomed Pierre's betrothed, and her surname is another hint of the Melvilles' pride in their Scottish descent. When the Herman Melvilles' fourth and last child was born, Herman's sister Helen (Mrs. George Griggs) wrote pleasantly to Augusta, upon hearing from the Shaws "that 'its name is Fanny.' Now that is really pretty in Herman and Lizzie, and I am as much pleased, as if they had called it Georgina Helen." The namesake was Herman's sister, Frances Priscilla, but the family tree bore a respectable number of Françoises and Franceses.[79]

These comments from family correspondence suggest that the Melvilles talked among themselves more than most about what to call their children and that they favored the repetition of names of respected members of their family. There is nothing unusual in this, and certainly not in the case of daughters, who would not carry forward the Melville surname anyway. But sons were different, as the example of Stanwix indicates. Sons should bear names that memorialize family achievements, family heroes, patriarchs. The two patriarchal names that recur most often among the Gansevoorts are Herman and Peter. Harmen Harmense van Gansevoort, to use the spelling of the founder of the American line as it appears in New Netherland's legal records dated 1657, was by trade a brewer.[80] Peter Gansevoort, Harmen's great-grandson, the "Hero of Fort Stanwix," was the second and certainly the most illustrious of that name, but the family had many subsequent Peters, and its variants Petrus and Pieter.[81] Peter and Pierre are names that occur also in the Melville line (the Melvilles had a French admixture and French business connections that Herman would echo in *Pierre*). Allan Melvill, Herman's father, was Boston-born but assimilated into New York Dutch culture. A Unitarian, he joined the Dutch Reformed Church in 1824, which he continued to attend as long as the family lived in New York,[82] and he blithely referred to Herman, age seven, on his way to spend his summer vacation with his grandparents, as "an honest hearted double rooted Knickerbocker of the true Albany stamp, who I trust will do equal honour in due time to his ancestry parentage & kindred."[83] He named his first son Gansevoort, his second Herman, his third for himself, and his fourth for his father, Major Thomas Melvill, family hero of the Revolution. First Gansevoorts and then Melvills. Why does Herman Melville reject this priority when he chooses (and the decision appears to have been his) a name for his first son?

On Thursday, January 24, 1849, Augusta in New York drafted a letter to Lizzie in Boston, continuing what was evidently a late phase of the deliberations on what to name the child whose birth was three weeks away. They had the name

*Malcolm* in mind and sought justification for their preference, and for this reason Lizzie requested Augusta to search the family tree.[84] Both were presumptuous, taking for granted that the child would be male and that they were anticipating Herman's wishes. Augusta responded to Lizzie's request with enthusiasm and great care, drafting a reply that became the basis of a letter to Lizzie mailed on the following Saturday, January 27:

> My dear Lizzie, My Sweet Sister,
> And are you really, "thinking seriously" of Malcolm?—and have you actually proposed it to Herman, and has he expressed his unqualified approbation? I am more happy than I can tell you. It will sound so well with Melville, and there has never been a Malcolm Melville, and I had my heart set upon it. Kind Lizzie.
> I have been searching the Genealogical Tree, as you desired. You know the name comes from Grandma Melville's side of the house.—The Scollay family. Herewith you have the result of my investigations. To begin at the Root.—Malcolm Scollay of Thornton married Barbara Alphistone [in Scotland, often Elphistone], sister of Col. Robert Alphistone of Sofness, Sheriff Admiral of Orkney. He was born in 1646 and died in 1742 aged 96. . . . Mrs Scollay died a few years before him. They were both buried at St Peter's Kirk, Stronsey. (That settles beyond a doubt the question whether he were "a rascal, or died on the gallows or anything.") He left ten children—five sons, five daughters, none of whom bore their father's name. (He possessed no doubt the same antipathy, which his great, great, great grand-son Herman inherits at the present day.) The third son, James Scollay married Deborah Blight, and leaving their native land settled in Boston. (The first American Scollay.) He died leaving two children a son and a daughter. The son, John Scollay, resident of Boston, married Miss [Mercy] Greenleaf, and he like his great grand father left 10 children five sons and five daughters, none of whom bore the name of Malcolm. The 9th child, Priscilla Scollay married Thomas Melville [*sic*] of Boston, (our grandfather) who had 11 children, but no Malcolm. Now you see that in our branch not a single descendent has borne the name of [Malcolm].

At this point the draft ends, although a third of the page remains unused.[85] The letter Augusta mailed to Lizzie documents the rarity of the name *Malcolm* "in our own branch"[86] and the absence of any Melville named Malcolm. The letter continues:

I much fear me the old Patriarch was not over rich in flocks and
fields and healthy hills.—But now for his great-great, great-great
grand-son to do him honor.———Malcolm Melville! how easily
it runs from my pen; how sweetly it sounds to my ear; how mu-
sically it falls upon my heart.—Malcolm Melville!—methinks I
see him in his plaided kilt, with his soft blue eyes, and his long
flaxen curls. How I long to press him to my heart.

Augusta concludes her sentimental flight with the news that
*Mardi* is likewise about to be born, linking Melville's ambitious,
effusive book with the impending birth of his child, and quoting an appropriately ambivalent phrase from it: " 'Ah my own
Koztanza! child of many prayers.' Oro's blessing on thee." The
phrase is that of Lombardo, the Mardian epic bard, and he addresses it to his masterpiece, Koztanza.[87] "Oro," whose blessing
Augusta invokes, is the high god of Mardi.

The differences between Augusta's draft and the letter she
mailed are slight. She tones down her question "has he expressed his unqualified approbation" to "has he expressed himself pleased"; she adds the phrase "Malcolm Melville! What a
beautiful name. There is something noble in its very sound."
She is speaking of the name "Malcolm." Indeed there is something noble in its sound and also something Shakespearean;
Malcolm was the son of of Duncan, the king of Scotland slain
by Macbeth, and his restoration secured the throne for his family. The Melvilles liked to think of their connection with Scottish
nobility. She drops the statement that "there has never been a
Malcolm Melville," withholding this vital point until she has
cited her evidence that leads to this conclusion. And she drops
her own indication of preference, which she probably guessed
would not weigh heavily with Herman, preferring instead to ex-
ploit his known "antipathy."

*Antipathy* is a strong though inadequate word, but it is Augusta's, not Herman's. It is inadequate because it reveals only a
fragment of Melville's complex response to the name that he
had been given. Melville was both son and father, and these two
parts of him stood opposed and would remain so until one
would be sacrificed to the other. His name was an epitome of
the family, and he was ambivalent about his family, torn between pride in status and genealogy, both Gansevoort and Mel-

ville, and antipathy for the price that they exacted—the restrictions, the hypocrisies, the chilling effect on his humanities. Hawthorne had written in the preface to *The House of the Seven Gables* (1851), a copy of which he gave Melville, "that the wrongdoing of one generation lives into the successive ones." Melville was explicit in his application of Hawthorne's "moral," underscoring a phrase from the first chapter on the pride of the Pyncheons, who cherished, "from generation to generation, *an absurd delusion of family importance.*"[88] The foundations upon which his own pride in pedigree rested were divergent. The Scottish Melvilles, the forefathers, were an ancient, lofty line while the American branch established itself by becoming republican and revolutionary. His attitude toward his birth and breeding has a counterpart in his response toward his father, originally a mild acceptance and filial respect that was shattered by a surprise that led to recoil—the word he often used to describe the shock of the demon-cloud that took the innocent by surprise.[89] There would be disenchanting discoveries about other patriarchal figures as well. But on balance, at least publicly, Melville played his part as a dutiful, attentive member of his immediate and extended family.[90] So when it came time to christen his only begotten son, he sought a name that did not conspicuously bear the mark of his demanding clan but did, though almost covertly, express recognition of (pride in?) his heritage. The influence of his upbringing, despite his compassion and his honesty, was too much for anything else. Moreover, Melville knew that he lived in a world of ambiguities. "It will sound so well." Sound well? Here is another word with ramifications: the family was sensitive to how words sounded; Melville was concerned with the depths of their meanings. The fact that "there has never been a Malcolm Melville" is qualified by the phrase "in our own branch." Malcolm the individual, and Malcolm a bud on the family tree. In naming Malcolm, Herman Melville could both accept and reject his family and his father. Melville's attitude toward his literary progenitors reveals a related duality. In "Hawthorne and His Mosses," professedly about Hawthorne as an exemplary American author but implicitly about himself, he admits the preeminent authority of Shakespeare only to undercut it by suggesting that future American writers may well supplant him ("if Shakespeare has not been equalled, he is sure to be surpassed") and asserting that there is "hardly a mortal man, who . . . has not felt as great thoughts in him as any you will find in Hamlet." In *Pierre* he recognizes Shakespeare as, like himself, both son and father, "for being but a mortal man Shakespeare had his fathers too."[91]

Let us recall the names Allan Melvill, the father, chose for his sons: Gansevoort, Herman, Allan, and Thomas, all of them dynastic, and precedence given to the Gansevoorts. Recall also Allan Melvill's easy absorption into the New York Dutch milieu, to the extent that he had almost become, by a process of naturalization, a Gansevoort and would be interred in the Gansevoort burial ground. Recall Herman's New York and Albany Dutch upbringing. And add to this a complicating factor, his subordination to his accomplished elder brother, Gansevoort by name, decidedly the family favorite.[92] In some curious way it appears that for Herman the Gansevoort name came to signify more emphatically the force of the family, against which he rebelled. *Antipathy* was not too strong a word. Antipathy: "Feeling against; hostile feeling towards" (*OED*). When Melville named Ishmael, he exploited connotation and context, and when he introduced him, he wrote, ambiguously, "Call me Ishmael." In this way he will make the point that his arbitrary power to name has its limitations. In choosing a name, Melville acknowledges the uncertainty and arbitrary nature of his choice. Call me Malcolm.

For the young American who felt the need to make a move, the alternatives in the 1840s were to go to sea or to go west. There were exceptions, but in general, venturesome Gansevoorts went to sea, and Melvilles who had an eye for the main chance went west. Young Herman Melville vacillated (as his pathetic son Stanwix would do). He went to sea briefly as a ship's boy; went west to Galena, Illinois, and Uncle Thomas Melvill in the spring of 1840; and then he went whaling. The sea was the Gansevoort way of escaping the Gansevoorts. But Melville's experience at sea recapitulated in part his paternal upbringing. The captain of the ship was another father, and in his earliest books Melville's first-person narrators, the sons and his surrogates, question and rebel.[93] The narrator escapes from the au-

thority of the captain in *Typee, Omoo,* and *Mardi* on one pretext
or another. In *Redburn* (1849) he observes that "some sea-cap-
tains are fathers to their crew" and they sometimes prove to be
"severe and chastising fathers, fathers whose sense of duty over-
comes the sense of love, and who . . . play the part of Brutus,
who ordered his son away to execution."[94] Like Abraham, to
whom Melville will compare Captain Vere, who obeys without
question the orders of God the Father. In *White-Jacket* the narrator also calls Captain Claret "the father of his crew,"[95] but in
a climactic scene fantasizes "dying himself, and inflicting death
upon another," the role of "a murderer and a suicide"[96] when
Claret orders him flogged. Did Malcolm, with his pistol at hand,
harbor both murderous and suicidal fantasies?

In myths of generational rivalry, the old king dies at the
hand of the young hero, who then succeeds to the throne, the
son killing the father; but, as Melville is aware, sometimes the
reverse takes place. "Sohrab and Rustum," on the agony and
irony of the kingly father who, by chance, kills his princely son,
prompted the heaviest annotation in Melville's much annotated
copy of Matthew Arnold's *Poems . . . A New and Complete Edition*
(1856), purchased in 1862.[97] At the end of his life Melville considered the possibility that the behavior of Captain Vere (and
his own father or himself) might have been determined by circumstance. And what of Captain Ahab? His pursuit of Moby
Dick comprehends his failure as a father. Ahab sacrifices his
crew, his children; and he rejects Captain Gardiner's plea to
save Gardiner's son, who is, at one remove, Ahab's son, too (*"You*
too have a boy," Gardiner reminds him [N-N, p. 532]). And
Ishmael? Nominally, Ishmael is a cast-off son, an "orphan"
(N-N, p. 573), although he is also a son who escapes. In Ishmael's fine phrase, the sea was also for Herman Melville a "substitute for pistol and ball."[98] It substituted at once for murderous inclinations toward men and whales and for suicidal
impulses, and in the end it proved an antidote for both. But the
sea was not a denial of his Gansevoort patrimony. That would
come gradually after Malcolm's death. To look ahead, it will be
necessary soon to supply more details about how children were
brought up in the Gansevoort-Melville-Shaw households and
how the family reacted to events that besmirched the family

name. Finally, a look backward and forward. Writing to his father, Major Thomas Melvill, from New York, where he had gone to make his fortune and establish his family, Allan Melvill confides: "my children I trust will inherit an honest name."[99] Herman Melville would toy sardonically with honest names, business men, and the concept of "trust" when he came to write *The Confidence-Man.*

# The Family Circle

Herman Melville (1819–1891). Tintype in case marked "Potters Patent March 5, 1865." Dated on back "1868," the year after Malcolm's death. Berkshire Athenaeum.

Elizabeth Shaw Melville. Daguerreotype, c. 1850. Berkshire Athenaeum.

Augusta ("Gus") Melville (1821–1876), younger sister of Herman Melville. Inscribed "For Mrs. Shaw. 1864 Augusta Melville." Marked "photograph by Winslow," New York. Berkshire Athenaeum.

Allan Melville (1823–1872), younger brother of Herman Melville, from
a family album. Undated, but before 1863. Courtesy Miss Jean Melvill
and the Houghton Library, Harvard University.

Thomas Melville (1830–1884), younger brother of Herman Melville, from a family photograph album. Undated, but before 1863. Courtesy Miss Jean Melvill and the Houghton Library, Harvard University.

John Chipman Hoadley (1818–1876), Melville's friend and husband of his younger sister, Catherine. From a family photograph album. Undated, but before 1863. Courtesy Miss Jean Melvill and the Houghton Library, Harvard University.

Maria Gansevoort Melville, c. 1872; according to a note on the back, her last photograph. From the album of Charlotte Hoadley, daughter of John Hoadley and Catherine Melville, Herman Melville's sister. Rare Books and Manuscripts Division, The New York Public Library, Astor, Lenox and Tilden Foundations.

Hope Savage Shaw (1793–1879), stepmother of Elizabeth Shaw Melville, from a family photo album. Undated, but before 1863. Courtesy Miss Jean Melvill and the Houghton Library, Harvard University. The autograph is from the album of Maria ("Milie") Gansevoort Melville. Berkshire Athenaeum.

# III. Duty

IMMERSED IN THE WRITINGS OF THOMAS CARLYLE but an ever-lasting skeptic, it is likely that Melville would have mulled over Carlyle's remarks on the divine right of kings: "There is a God in this world; and a God's-sanction . . . does look-out from all ruling and obedience, from all moral acts of men. There is no act more moral between men than that of rule and obedience. Woe to him that claims obedience when it is not due; woe to him that refuses it when it is!"[100] Did Melville claim an obedience not his due? Did Malcolm unduly refuse it? In any case, by almost theocratically identifying religious and civil authority, Carlyle supplied a moral basis for a patriarchal stance, and one that could be made to serve a narrow purpose. The child-rearing practices of the Melville-Gansevoorts were designed to assure the integrity of the family. Children were expected to be dutiful and obedient, and the family elders were never reluctant to make this known to them. We have had the example of Allan Melvill, Sr., giving counsel to his nephew, Midshipman Thomas W. Melvill, on preserving the purity of the family name. In a letter of August 28, 1826, he summarized his advice: "in one emphatic sentence—perform your Duty."[101] Maria, his wife, responsible for rearing their children after his death, was equally heavy-handed. She wrote from Lansingburgh, New York, to Augusta, then age seventeen and visiting family intimates in Gansevoort, New York, on how to make herself "agreeable to those who ↑ may ↓ honor you with their notice. Remember that an earnest desire to please can hardly fail of making you agreeable." Her directions were that Augusta should be polite, helpful, and maintain a good physical appearance. But more fundamental was her warning to "Guard against selfishness," that is, to subordinate the self to the wishes of others. The basis of Maria's concept of socialization is her belief in natural depravity. She instructed Augusta to "Cultivate the ↑ best ↓ feelings of the heart & extract from it with the aid of fervent prayer, all the baser passions which are alas so natural to us, in our present state of depravity."[102] It was natural for a child to disobey, to the detriment of familial cohesion and the immortal soul. Father Mapple, in his sermon on Jonah's "sin of disobedience," explained that "if we obey God, we must disobey ourselves."[103] The same for parents and children.

A generation later Herman Melville would write to his children from aboard a ship in the Pacific, commanded by his brother Thomas, in terms that while not overtly Calvinistic are equally severe. The theme is once again the need for obedience in order to maintain the sanctity of the family. Honor thy father and thy mother; that thy days may be long upon the land that the Lord thy God giveth thee. He ends his letter to Malcolm, then eleven years old:

> I hope that, when it [his letter] arrives, it will find you well, and all the family. And I hope that you have called to mind what I said to you about your behaviour previous to my going away. I hope that you have been obedient to your mother, and helped her all you could, & saved her trouble. Now is the time to show what you are—whether you are a good, honorable boy, or a good-for-nothing one. Any boy, of your age, who disobeys his mother, or worries her, or is disrespectful to her—such a boy is a poor shabby fellow.[104]

He concludes a letter under the same cover to Bessie, who is seven, that is likewise designed to encourage obedience and family solidity:

> I hope you are a good girl; and give Mama no trouble. . . . I suppose you have had a good many walks on the hill, and picked the strawberries.
> I hope you take good care of little FANNY and that when you go on the hill, you go this way: [drawing of two figures] that is to say, hand in hand.[105]

The letter has a forced quality. It is as if Melville is rehearsing received opinion on the tuition of children, reinforced by the best authorities, for instance, his friend and family physician, Dr. Augustus K. Gardner, who wrote extensively on this subject.[106] The ordered parallelism of the rhetoric conveys rigidity. The repetition of the initial phrase, "I hope," mildly exerts parental pressure. I hope thou shalt not disobey. The retrogression from "a good, honorable boy" to "a good-for-nothing" is a patronizing turn intended to be gently humorous. It is unpleasant, and the recurrence of the word *boy* belittles his son. There is nothing here that Malcolm could possibly appreciate. Yet we see Melville trying hard to play the dutiful father. When he writes *Pierre*, Melville will bend the language of his injunctions to Malcolm to a different purpose. Initially Hamlet-like in his waverings, Pierre considers the cowardly course of denying his obligations to his supposedly illegitimate sister, Isabel, and thereby returning to the good graces of his mother: "Quit Isabel . . . ! Beg humble pardon of thy mother, and hereafter be a more obedient and good boy to her, Pierre,"[107] an inner voice counsels him. Melville teaches a repressive lesson to Malcolm. In *Pierre* he weighs the results of repression.

Other family correspondence conveys a similar view. Lizzie, on a visit to Boston, writes to Augusta, who is doing the housekeeping at Pittsfield: "Give a great deal of love to Macky [a family nickname for Malcolm], and tell him I hope he is prompt in all his duties."[108] "I hope" and "duties" again. (For Melville, things would take another turn when he thinks of Pierre as an "Enthusiast to Duty.") A battered note written by Stanwix, age eleven, on his departure from his highly regarded Aunt Augusta, an inveterate Sunday School teacher whom he had been visiting for some time at Gansevoort, New York, reveals a disciplined courtesy, deference, and docility. More intriguing is his reference to what seems to have been some kind of binding document that Augusta, whose role in bringing up the Melville boys appears to have been second only to that of their parents, had drawn up to guide his conduct. Stanwix assures her: "I will try to keep the promises you wrote on that sheet of paper. There are three particular things that I will try to do. [Letter torn] . . . to speak the tru[th], to obey Mama, and Papa, and to say my prayers. Good bye."[109] Melville's children tried very hard to keep the promises their elders articulated on their behalf.

Covenants between parents and offspring were a curious feature of the child-rearing practices of the Melville-Gansevoorts. Perhaps they were the result of Calvinist and legalistic influences that pervaded their outlook. Religion and law enforced an obedience that would maintain family strength and solidarity. They were the cement of the family, and the family was the cement of society. Herman's letter from the Pacific with its lit-

any of "I hope[s]" and Augusta's "sheet of paper" are by impli-
cation contracts insofar as unequal parties can make contrac-
tual agreements. A contract between Peter Gansevoort of
Albany and his son, Henry Sanford, regarding Henry's behavior in return for educational concessions, is explicitly legalistic
and capped with religiosity.

Peter Gansevoort, the fifth son of Peter of Fort Stanwix, was
a lawyer, politician, and businessman. It was to him that his sister Maria, Herman Melville's mother, most often turned. He
was a powerful figure in his state, his family, and his person,
and he overawed his son, the motherless child of his middle age.
Peter Gansevoort expected Henry to follow in his footsteps and
become an Albany lawyer, but he remained in the military service after the Civil War. Herman Melville was close to both father and son.

Henry wanted to enter Princeton as an upperclassman, but
this required diligent study on his own and further attendance
at the Albany Academy, from which he had graduated with
honors in 1851. He and his father drew up a contract specifying
obligations on both sides. Henry wrote (presumably from the
dictation of his father) and initialed (in accord with legal pro-
cedure) a document that states:

> That in staying home I will attend my recitations at the Al-
> bany Academy and study at my room applying myself vigorously
> to the prosecution of my studies, having an end in view and only
> a limited time to attend to it. And also if at any time, I should
> not fitly and intinsly [*sic*] apply myself to my studies and accord
> in my behavior taking fit and proper exercise in the afternoon I
> shall be compelled to attend the Albany Academy as a day
> scholar besides other proper punishment. In return I am to go
> to Princeton College to enter Sophomore. And besides I shall be
> fitted for the class in June next. (s.) H.S.G.

To this his father added some specific terms regarding his general behavior:

> First—That you are not to go out in the evening unless I know
> where you are.
> Second—If I ask you where you have been, I shall receive a
> prompt and truthful answer, not an indefinite reply.

Third. To make yourself pleasant about the house and agreeable at Table.

Fourth. That you will retire at 10 oClock and have your lamp out at that time.

Fifth. That you will attend your own Church regularly every Sabbath, with liberty to attend any other Church in the evening.[110]

Peter Gansevoort's conditions probably reflect what he viewed as lapses in his son's deportment. Henry appears to have been a mite surly and sly. He entered Princeton the following year. More to the point, it is not likely that Herman Melville would have seen anything amiss, in principle or practice, in this covenant between father and son. He treated Malcolm in much the same way, though Malcolm was thought by the family to be a gentle, agreeable young man. The family had its own reason for sustaining paternal authority and, in addition, was well within Victorian convention, although by the time of Henry Gansevoort's covenant, the convention was eroding rapidly. We should note, however, that Malcolm was as much a Shaw as he was a Melville-Gansevoort. He was reared by both his mother and his father. For this reason it is necessary to consider the sort of nurturing Lizzie received in the Shaw household, for what she learned there colored the way she approached her parental tasks. A glance at her parents, especially her father, is informative.

An atmosphere of warmth and ease appears to have prevailed within the Shaw household when the children were growing up. Without minimizing the Judge as a responsible, even a stern, parent, his exercise of authority was modified by gentleness and sophisticated humor when dealing with his family. Judge Shaw was on more pleasant terms with his children than Peter Gansevoort or Herman Melville. Perhaps part of the explanation lay in the sensitivity and tolerance he had acquired during his long career as an attorney and jurist. Rather than going to the extremes that such experience might have driven others to, Lemuel Shaw, supported at least by his wife, appears to have been an understanding, cheerful father. As a family man he seems to have been less rigid and severe than he was perceived to be on the bench.

What we have is a man willing to express his own feelings and to provide the emotional support for those dependent upon him, yet possessing a sense of duty and purpose that he was committed to passing on to his children and wards. The result, seen from another angle, is effective parental discipline made acceptable by a gentle hand, a supportive arm. This environment, a contrast to what prevailed in the homes of the Melvilles and Gansevoorts, provided Lizzie with different ways of viewing matters (*inefficient* was the word Kate Gansevoort used to describe her[111]), especially the nurturing of children. She and her brothers and sisters appear to have been spared the raw authoritarianism visited upon the children of Allan and Maria Melvill.[112]

Authoritarian methods of childrearing designed to produce dutiful, achieving children were adopted by the Melville-Gansevoorts to assure their position. It was a way of maintaining, in the words of Allan Melvill, "the Family name unsullied" and perhaps enhancing it. When there was danger that the family name might be sullied, then the family would close ranks and pretend that nothing unseemly had occurred. This is what happened when the coroner's jury reported that Malcolm "came to his Death by Suicide by shooting himself with a pistol on the 11 day of Sept. 1867."[113]

The most complete inside narrative of this tragic event is a letter from Samuel Savage Shaw, Lizzie's half brother, to his mother, written from the Albemarle Hotel in New York City the following day:

> He has also been out late at night recently, so much so that his father took away his night key from him and both his parents have talked very seriously about it but they both say that they beleive [*sic*] that there was nothing in his dissipation more than a fondness for social frolicking with his young friends. . . . On <Wednesd> Tuesday night he was out till 3 o'clock and his mother sat up for him. . . . His mother remonstrated with him kindly but she says did not scold him in the least. He kissed her good night and went to bed.

For Malcolm, caught between a kindly though inept mother and a domineering father and trapped within an atmosphere of

The "Verdict of the Jurors" following the coroner's inquest into the death of Malcolm Melville. Municipal Archives and Record Center, City of New York.

Opposite: The first page of a letter from Samuel Savage Shaw, Elizabeth Shaw Melville's half-brother, to his mother, Hope, on the death of Malcolm. By permission of the Houghton Library, Harvard University.

Dear Mother

I arrived here at a little after 5 and went with Allan and Stanny, whom I found on the train in the afternoon, coming from Pittsfield, straight to Elizabeth's house. The circumstances of Macky's death are very mysterious. He shot himself either intentionally or accidentally in his room early on Wednesday morning. They had a coroner's inquest and the verdict of the jury was *Suicide* by shooting during a temporary aberration of mind. It seems that he has been in the habit of carrying a pistol with him lately that he has talked to Stanny of sleeping with a revolver under his pillow—He has also been out late at night recently, so much so that his father took away his night key from him and both his parents have talked

(326)

S. S. Shauts

Albemarle Hotel, N. York

Sept 12. 1867

Dear Mother

I arrived here at a little after 5 and went with Allan Stacey whom I found on the train in the afternoon, coming from Pittsfield, straight to Elizabeth's House. The circumstances of Macky's death are very mysterious. He shot himself either intentionally or accidentally in his room early one Wednesday morning. They had a coroner's inquest and the verdict of the Jury was Suicide by shooting during a temporary aberration of mind. It seems that he has been in the habit of carrying a pistol with him lately and that he has talked to Stacey of keeping with a revolver under his pillow. He has also been out late at night recently, so much so that his father took away his night key from him and both his parents have talked matrimonial tension, there was no substitute for pistol and ball. Samuel Shaw's letter recounts that the next morning he overslept, replied when his sister called him, but remained in his room. His father "advised Lizzie to let him sleep, be late at the office & take the consequences." Later in the day, according to Samuel Shaw, she tried to awaken him, got no response, and found that the door to his room was locked. When Melville returned from work in the evening, "the door was broken down and Macky found in his night clothes in bed with a pistol shot in his head and apparently several hours dead."[114] There is no record that anyone heard the shot. This gap in the record is one of the more "mysterious" aspects of Malcolm's death, but also strange is the failure of Melville's biographers to notice it. The testimony of the coroner's jury, as distinguished from its verdict, has not been discovered and, for that matter, was probably unrecorded.[115] Malcolm owned a pistol because he was a member of a volunteer military company.[116] Guns fascinated him, which was curious for so gentle a boy.

In their sorrow, in their attempt to explain to themselves things that were scarcely explicable, and to others in such a way that the repute of the Melville-Gansevoorts would not suffer, members of the family brought what pressures they could. As a result, a New York newspaper reported on September 13 that the coroner's jury "came to the conclusion that deceased must have been suffering from a temporary aberration of mind."[117] This was a kind and not unusual attempt to soften the stigma attached to a self-inflicted death. After the funeral and surely at the instigation of the family, the New York *Evening Post* published two communications which were intended to mitigate, but obscured more than they clarified. The first, signed by members of the coroner's jury, but not by the coroner or medical attendant who had signed the official "Verdict of the Jurors," expressed a "desire to correct any erroneous impressions drawn from their verdict of 'suicide.'" Toward this end the jurors affirmed that Malcolm's death "was caused by his own hand, but not that the act was by premeditation or consciously done." The second communication was from Dr. Samuel Osgood, the clergyman who officiated at the funeral. He stated "that a wrong impression of the cause of death of Malcolm Mel-

ville has been given by our newspapers, though unintention-
ally," but he did not elaborate.[118] Samuel Shaw wrote his mother
that "The circumstances of Macky's death are very mysterious."[119] Honest men who wished to oblige the family could do
little more than obfuscate politely. John C. Hoadley, a prominent engineer and manufacturer who married Melville's sister
Catherine, had these afterthoughts about the tragedy of Malcolm's death: "[I]t is sad to think that his memory should lie
under the imputation either of such a crime as suicide or of
such a fearful scourge as insanity, against which all the facts of
the case revolt."[120] Suicide was not a crime in the State of New
York although it continued to be in England until 1961. It was
commonly known, however, as "self-murder," a pejorative that
communicates its stigma.[121]

Malcolm's death was indeed mysterious. It could be explained only as an accident—and there was little to prove that
it was—or as a suicide. If he committed suicide, then either the
family had to accept that he had at least temporarily lost his
mind or that he was sane, and if sane then in some way the
family might be culpable. For the family, the insanity plea was
little comfort. It was at best discreditable, and there was reason
to be hypersensitive on the subject. Allan Melvill died insane.
His son Gansevoort was given to psychosomatic illness, and at
the time of his premature death appeared to suffer from both
physical and emotional disease. Herman, on occasion, was emotionally disturbed. Lizzie tended to be "very nervous" and was
said to have suffered from hallucinations. Insanity was something that might be discreetly mentioned but only within the
family circle.[122]

Although Kate Gansevoort was not in New York City at the
time, she is probably one of the more reliable sources on the
subject of Malcolm's death. Kate was as close to various members of the Melville family, including Herman, Lizzie, and their
children, as her father and her mother were to Maria. Her intimacy with the Melvilles began in the mid- and late-1850s when
she was sent to Mrs. Sedgwick's boarding school near Pittsfield.
During her first extended stay away from home in an environment other than her most immediate family, she was homesick.
Herman and his family provided support for the young girl,

and she in turn had an opportunity to witness life at the Melville farm during a period of stress. As a result of this and other encounters with the Herman Melvilles, she could be neutral in her responses to them and their troubles, including Malcolm's suicide. Her objectivity suggests disapproval at times of what took place in Herman and Lizzie's family life, but not disaffection, and is in marked contrast to her cordial relations with Herman's brother Tom. Overall some caution should be exercised in judging her intimate knowledge of the Herman Melville family. When she went to New York in June 1868, less than a year after Mackie's death, to attend Tom's wedding, she stayed with them at 104 East 26th Street.[123] In the years to come her appreciation and affection for her cousin Herman would grow.

Given the blurred and limited information concerning the circumstances of Malcolm's death, the opinions of relatively detached observers such as Sam Shaw and Kate Gansevoort are important. They had little disposition to join in glossing over the hard fact of suicide and, besides, they knew of other things about which the less said the better.

Kate mentions Malcolm's death once in her diary and in a few letters to her brother, Henry. In her only diary reference, dated September 13, she blandly calls it a suicide. There is no mention of his death or burial in the entries for the next month. She first reports Malcolm's death to Henry on the fifteenth, after having sent him a newspaper notice, and, in keeping with the then public facts, continues to refer to it as a suicide. On the next day she follows through with a more factual than analytical rehearsal of what she still describes as a suicide, at the same time cautioning Henry to take care in handling his own firearms and commenting on Herman's rigidity and Lizzie's inefficiency as a parent.[124] There is, however, less certainty about discovering the facts of the case and a softness, a sympathy, evident in her suggestion that her brother write his cousin Herman. She provides a secondhand report of the funeral in her letter of September 19 but fails to mention Malcolm's death or the Herman Melvilles in her letter of September 22.[125]

Kate's silence regarding the tragedy and the family on East 26th Street, especially in that most personal of documents, her diary, is probably more significant than what little she said in her letters to her brother. What she wrote him, she probably felt compelled to say. One suspects that the more revealing statement of her aloofness is evident in her silences. However profound her sense of family, however warm she was toward one or another relative, her feelings and allegiances to Herman, Lizzie, and perhaps their children were reserved. She probably knew too much about the goings on in the house, the personalities that made up the household, and was put off by them. What an irony that the papers she carefully preserved should be so valuable to scholars concerned with the man and author who among all the people in her family she probably ranked at this time among the least likable.[126] And how paradoxical that this sad affair, about which she appears so distant, and which involved a kinsman about whom she had reservations, provided the impulse for a closer bond between them.

Kate Gansevoort points her finger at Cousin Herman perhaps more to explain than to accuse. But if Kate appears to have leaned toward a verdict of suicide, Malcolm's Aunt Augusta and his grandmother Maria Melville did not. Augusta voiced no doubt that Malcolm's death was an accident and told Kate, among other things, that it provided a lesson for "all who place a pistol under their pillows." (This validated Kate's warnings to Henry, but one still has to ask why a young man with Mackey's supposed military training would not have mastered the rudiments of the safe handling of weapons, among the first lessons taught any recruit.) Writing to her brother, Peter, and his wife, Susan, on September 14, the day of Mackey's burial, Maria Melville asserted, in a clear expression of will rather than judgment, "I never will believe he committed Suicide." There is no evidence to suggest that she altered this opinion. She was most open in sharing her feelings with her sister-in-law Susan, but, as might be expected from a woman of her maturity, the pain of loss was numbed by time's passing. So it was for her son Tom, who, of course, attended the funeral but then went on with his own affairs. The mettle of these people is perhaps admirable, but it borders on the insensitive, as in the instance of sister Helen, who in the first letter to Kate (dated October 6) after the funeral ignores Malcolm's death.[127]

Whatever one's belief, suicide or accident, the fact remains that, given the ways of the family, what else could Herman Melville have been but a very strict parent, if unpredictable? Not a tribal patriarch like Peter Gansevoort of Fort Stanwix, or Thomas Melvill of Boston, or Uncle Peter Gansevoort, or even father Allan Melvill, he was nevertheless a patriarch in his own household. He had accepted the role as best he could. Sometimes he had been indulgent and at other times he had been given to intemperate outbursts. Often he had been preoccupied and neglectful of his parental obligations to a degree that troubled Lizzie.[128] In the end, we learn more about how, and perhaps why, the Melville-Gansevoort family responded to a tragic event than about the event itself.

The shock and grief of a young person's death by his own hand that inspired insipid denials, rationalizations, and equivocations also encouraged the survivors to turn their attention to burial grounds and memorials (a project already under way) befitting their position, an interest consistent with Victorian mourning customs and the prevailing taste for landscaped cemeteries. In this way they were able to assert and extend their bereavement and at the same time control it. Gus, Kate, and other members of their own and the preceding generation set about refurbishing the family graves and monuments, going so far as to move Melville remains in order that they might rest with those of the Gansevoorts.[129]

# The Children

Malcolm as a young child. Undated. Berkshire Athenaeum.

Children of Elizabeth and Herman Melville: Stanwix, Frances, Malcolm,
and Elizabeth, c. 1860. Berkshire Athenaeum.

Malcolm Melville (1849–1867). Undated photograph by "Thwaites & Co.," New York. Berkshire Athenaeum.

Herman Melville made this drawing of "Arrowhead," the farm near Pittsfield, Massachusetts, where the family lived 1850–1863, while at sea during his 1860 voyage to California. He explained in an accompanying note that he is in the carriage in the right foreground and the tiny figures to the left are his wife and children welcoming him upon his return. Reproduced from a lost original published in Raymond M. Weaver's biography, *Herman Melville: Mariner and Mystic* (New York: George H. Doran, 1921).

# IV. Family Secrets

OTHER PAINFUL AND SOME DISGRACEFUL EPISODES in the family story were treated in much the same way for the sake of position, and the family's reaction to them confirms the pattern of response to Malcolm's suicide. In unspoken accord, members of the family closed ranks to protect their name and their status.[130] One detects in this a fear of failure. After all, Allan Melvill failed in business, and Thomas Melvill, Jr., was imprisoned for debt. Indeed the very fluidity of American society and its republican principles were threats to the security of the elite.[131] Signs of slackness, lack of will, moral weakness, and the risks inherent in a turbulent economy were causes of anxiety. Threats and failures were repressed, as the following examples show.

First, father Allan Melvill. Despite the outward appearance of prosperity, probity, and gentility, he engaged in shady business transactions, the last of which resulted in bankruptcy. He then retreated to Albany, the Gansevoort bastion, attempted to recoup, and failed. In 1832 he died. Maria Melville sought to preserve a respectable façade. She had some money of her own and managed to live in a fine house near the mansion of her brother Peter and to finance a business venture headed by her promising eldest son, Gansevoort. The financial panic of 1837 put an end to her pretensions. In addition, if morally dubious business dealings were not enough, there were also the morally dubious sexual misadventures of Allan's youth. When Major Thomas Melvill, Allan's father, died later in 1832, two women approached Judge Shaw, his legal adviser, to make a claim on Allan's share of his father's estate. Following Allan's death they had called on his brother in Boston, Thomas Melvill, Jr. But as Thomas Melvill informed Judge Shaw, only he, his mother, and his sister knew of the "interesting young woman," presumably Allan's illegitimate daughter, others of the family being "to this day . . . ignorant of her existence." Eventually the story of Allan's liaison became known to a wider circle within the family, and it was remembered when Melville published *Pierre*, but in Allan's lifetime and for long thereafter the secret was pre-

served.[132] Blemished parentage puts a peculiar light on fictional
children. Was it better to have a father like Pierre's, or to be,
like Ishmael, "another orphan"? Or a "foundling" like Billy
Budd?[133]

Next, Uncle Thomas Melvill, Jr. He was a charming young
man who went to France, moved with success in American business and diplomatic circles, married a French woman of station,
and due to financial reverses returned to Boston. Like his
brother Allan he overextended himself and was involved in
questionable financial maneuvers. He borrowed heavily from
his father and Judge Shaw and at one point was confined to a
debtor's prison. His misfortunes and misdeeds, however, did
not cause him to lose the regard of his neighbors in Pittsfield,
Massachusetts, where his father had set him up as a gentleman
farmer. Tempted by business opportunities, he moved to Galena, Illinois, a boom town at the time, where he lived the life
of a local aristocrat, successful businessman, and civic leader.
There he disgraced himself by embezzling from his friend and
business partner. He could not make restitution, but his partner was generous and told him, the story has it, "for the sake
of your good family and for the sake of your gray hair, I'll not
punish you." Thomas Melvill, Jr., died soon after. Herman Melville wrote a memoir of his uncle that appeared unsigned and
tactfully edited in Joseph E. A. Smith's *History of Pittsfield* . . .
(1876). Of Thomas Melvill's sad end, Smith's version had this to
say: "He finally experienced pecuniary misfortunes, and says a
relative, 'living in the plainest way, became a simple husband-
man.' " Of Galena Melville had written only that his Uncle
Thomas "went . . . there to occupy a responsible position in a
mercantile house," that Melville had visited him there, and that
there he died. The typical family response.[134] Melville recalled
the pathos of his "faded" gentility in the magazine sketch
"Jimmy Rose" (1855), named for a character he pities and de-
fends against imputations of dishonesty, and included a wry
reflection of his disastrous business career in Chapter 40 of *The
Confidence-Man*, "the story of China Aster." Again, sympathetic
and defensive. Uncle Thomas was another father who betrays
son Herman.

Brother Thomas Melville is another example. Master of a

China clipper in 1859, at age twenty-nine, he was eleven years younger than Herman, and the dashing seaman that Herman liked to think himself but never really was. They were dear to each other. In 1860 Herman sailed to California with "gallant Tom . . . beloved Tom" (so called in a poem by Melville he inspired).[135] Captain Tom, with heavy support from the family, was elected Governor of the Sailors' Snug Harbor on Staten Island in 1867, a model institution of its kind. His salary and perquisites were comfortable, and in contrast to Herman's own situation during this period, life was good. The following year he married the daughter of the staff physician of Snug Harbor, and their ample residence on the grounds became the focal point for family visits and holiday festivities. Captain Tom apparently used his office to more immediate family advantage. In 1869 he employed Allan to advise Snug Harbor on tax matters, services for which he seems to have paid considerably above the going rate. In 1872 he obtained permission from his Board of Trustees "to compile a history of the Sailors' Snug Harbor . . . from its commencement." Perhaps he was setting up something for Herman. The history was never written, for soon after the board heard evidence from the Governor's clerk that Captain Melville had misused institutional funds. In a letter to her parents, the Peter Gansevoorts of Albany, Melville's acute cousin, Kate, records the reaction of the family at Staten Island, where she had gone to attend a wedding: "The Melville Clan was strong powerful & very defensive."[136] Following an extensive investigation, the committee reported "their most emphatic disapproval of certain views of the Governor as stated in his examination in respect to extra compensation being made to him for certain services in a manner different from what is contemplated by and provided for in the existing By-Laws."

Vague words and circumlocutions. The committee failed to find "conclusive proof" of embezzlement but took away his authority to purchase supplies and transact the business of the institution. He was retained as a figurehead. The words and the decision suggest a softening and covering over of a cruel affair due to family pressure and a consideration of the family name. Captain Tom Melville did not live to a ripe old age, and when he died in 1884, there were no eulogies spread on the pages of the minute books of Snug Harbor, and the trustees did not authorize funds for funeral wreaths. These were departures from ordinary practice, a silence that has a parallel in the curious absence of his Uncle Thomas Melvill from eulogistic mention in the local histories of Galena, where he was once so prominent.[137]

And what of Herman Melville himself, the literary meteor that flashed and fell? Who lived beyond his means; whose health and mental stability were often in doubt; whose marriage brought long periods of unhappiness; whose sons were a source of anguish; whose last years as man and artist, to use a favorite word of his, were subterranean? On balance, what did *he* contribute to the position and well-being of the family?

Aside from the family's secretiveness, a plausible reaction to unpleasant moments in its history, there is the question of their effect on Melville himself and his art. Secrets, suffering, and suicide converge in the first of the many markings Melville made in Matthew Arnold's dramatic poem, "Empedocles at Etna":

> There is some root of suffering in himself,
> Some secret and unfollow'd vein of woe,
> Which makes the time look black and sad to him.[138]

Cumulatively, they contributed to the conception of fatality and tragedy he expressed, for instance, in "The Coming Storm," and they raise the possibility that a tragedy such as Malcolm's death, in the words of the Shakespearean poem, would be "No utter surprise." In addition to personal pain and a willingness to gloss over the facts for clannish reasons, his regard for what he has Ishmael call "man, in the ideal" gave him reason to cast a cloak "over any ignominious blemish" discovered in men he esteemed and loved. Of Starbuck's abasement, Ishmael tells us early that he will not have "the heart to write it; for it is a thing most sorrowful, nay shocking, to expose the fall of valor" because our "immaculate manliness . . . bleeds with keenest anguish at the undraped spectacle of a valor-ruined man."[139] Underlying this consideration is the conflict between restraint and revelation implied in the first among many markings Melville made in his copy of *Hamlet*.[140] The lines marked are spoken by the ghost:

> But that I am forbid
> To tell the secrets of my prison house,
> I could a tale unfold, whose lightest word
> Would harrow up thy soul.          [I, v, 13–16]

The blackness at "Shakespeare's core . . . which we seek and shun" Melville would secrete and disclose.

Melville's creative energies toward the end of his life were concentrated on his inside narrative, *Billy Budd*. Writing this historical novel was an occasion for self-examination and introspection. It induced reflections on his sins as a father and on his heritage. He was gradually freeing himself from the burden of patriarchy that had afflicted him and that he had inflicted on others, but he could not divest himself of his history. As a writer, he was still willing to submerge the darker side of the story. In *Billy Budd* his subject is mutiny, which, after all, has to do with the concepts of duty, obedience, and filial obligation that his family tradition instilled:

> Like some other events in every age befalling states everywhere, including America, the Great Mutiny was of such character that national pride along with views of policy would fain shade it off into the historical background. Such events cannot be ignored, but there is a considerate way of historically treating them. If a well-constituted individual refrains from blazoning aught amiss or calamitous in his family, a nation in the like circumstance may without reproach be equally discreet.[141]

So families and nations are analogous, a view that, we shall see, Melville shared with his cousin Henry Gansevoort. And their histories, he advises, might well be treated in the same way for reasons of "pride" and "policy," the usual reasons in the Melville-Gansevoort family. If it is necessary to write within the shadow of a shameful event, be considerate and discreet. Melville did not blazon family calamities, but he did write about them—casually and sympathetically in "Jimmy Rose"; and they lie obscurely within the dark heart of *Pierre* and *Billy Budd* and the gentle, elegiac verses of his last years. But Melville could treat the idea of family secrets with a lighter hand. "I and My Chimney" is a private joke in which his house, "Arrowhead," like Poe's House of Usher and Hawthorne's House of the Seven Gables, is a measure of the vitality of the family that inhabits it. Its massive, erect chimney, built by a "kinsman," is the center of its potency. One Hiram Scribe, a "master mason" presumably privy to Masonic secrets, is hired by the narrator when his wife wishes to demolish it. He informs the narrator that "there is architectural cause to conjecture that somewhere concealed in your chimney is a reserved space, hermetically closed, in short, a secret chamber." The wife wishes to discover the secret, to which the narrator replies: "if there were a secret closet, secret it should remain, and secret it shall. . . . Infinite sad mischief has resulted from the profane bursting open of secret recesses."[142] Was Melville doing more than generalizing? Could he have been thinking of *Pierre* and his profanation of his father's secret?

Lest members of Melville's family be thought unusual in their efforts to keep their secrets, we have evidence from a comparable and closely associated family, the Duyckincks. Their attitude is present in a damning review of *Pierre* in the *Literary World* which they edited. The review summarizes the dilemma of Pierre who "has two duties to perform: to screen his dead father's memory and to give his living sister her due." It emphasizes Pierre's "duty" to "conceal [Isabel's] illegitimacy and to protect his father's memory" and recognizes that in *Pierre* Melville uses the incest motif to subvert "the holy relations of the family."[143] To be precise, the vehemence of Melville's attack on the New York Dutch patrician family structure represented by the Gansevoorts and the Duyckincks, and implicitly its religious underpinnings, shocked the editors of the *Literary World*. He had betrayed his class and his origins. In her autobiography, Edith Wharton, of New York Dutch descent and impeccable social standing, reflects their view: "As for Herman Melville, a cousin of the Van Rensslaers [*sic*] and qualified by birth to figure in the best society, he was doubtless excluded from it by his deplorable Bohemianism, for I never heard his name mentioned or read one of his books."[144]

In the severity with which the family patriarchs brought up their children, acting as if they had religion and law behind them, and an obligation to society (noblesse oblige?); in the responses of Herman, Lizzie, Augusta, and the matriarch Maria Melville, as best we can ascertain them, to the suicide of Malcolm; in the protective reactions of the Melville-Gansevoorts to the discreditable behavior of individual members of the clan and an excessive show of solicitude when they were disappointed (Stanwix, a ne'er-do-well, is one example; Guert Gansevoort, whose naval career promised to be, but was not, brilliant, is another),[145] the imperatives of Herman Melville's background manifest their weight. They pressed on him heavily. For the sake of family he collaborated in the common response to the mistakes and misfortunes of his father, uncle, and brother—the smoothing over and the things left unsaid. His more personal response was reticence, to reveal as little as possible of his thoughts and to withdraw into himself. What had been a family strategy became for him a personal tactic. He reacted with a like reticence to the disappointments and hurts most immediate to him: his marital troubles; the suicide of Malcolm and the hapless life and early death of Stanwix; the dreariness of the Custom House with its atmosphere of insecurity and its notorious corruption;[146] the decline of his reputation as a writer; the knowledge that even when they sympathized, his kin thought him unbalanced, perhaps dangerously so. In the margin of Hawthorne's *Mosses from an Old Manse* (1846) he lined a passage on the isolation of Owen Warland, artist of the beautiful: "Perhaps he was mad. The lack of sympathy—that contact between himself and his neighbors, which took away the restraint of example—was enough to make him so. Or, possibly, he had caught just so much of ethereal radiance as served to bewilder him." The dates of his marginalia are uncertain, but they extend at least until 1865.[147] (Late in life he added a touching note to a manic letter addressed to his friend, fellow-poet, successful man of affairs, and brother-in-law, John C. Hoadley—"N. B. I aint crazy.") Markings in the family Bible display the depths of his alienation. He placed three checks at the beginning of Chapter 19 of the Book of Job and double lines along the right margin beside verses 13 through 19. In this passage Job laments his loneliness: "He hath put my brethren far from me. . . . My kin folk have failed, and my familiar friends have forgotten me. . . . My breath is strange to my wife, . . . and they whom I loved are turned against me." There was once writing in the margin, but it has been erased. Was it Melville's? Did he erase it because it said too much? Or some more cautious member of the family?[148]

Temperamentally, by the end of the 1860s Melville was receding into himself. He bought a copy of Matthew Arnold's *Essays in Criticism* in 1869 and marked heavily in it a quotation from the writer Maurice de Guérin (who "died without publishing anything") on the "power and beauty . . . in the well-kept secret of one's self and one's thoughts." Secrets again.[149] The pathos of this introversion, whether as artist or as anguished son, father, brother, or husband, whether as individual or as a member of a cohesive, demanding tribe, is that Melville cherished congeniality and openness and as a writer he was outgoing. The structure and substance of his first books support this. Until *Pierre* he wrote open-ended, personal narratives that emerged from an expansive ego. *Pierre*, with its movement away from the autobiographical on obvious display, suggests Melville's deepening distrust of his experienced universe. His shift from first- to third-person narrative put space between the subject and object, allowing him to scrutinize more carefully and at one remove comment upon his personal history and the Gansevoort-Melville codes. By the late 1860s one surmises that Melville no longer felt that he was a credit to the family and had his doubts about the mandates that informed its cohesion. In any event, the wind was blowing from a different direction. In the Custom House Melville felt its chill and smelled its stench.

So too did Colonel Henry Gansevoort, once a resentful young man whose father forced him into a contract assuring parental dominion. With the war over, assigned to a distant military post, he had ample opportunity for his thoughts, and they turned backward toward a more heroic and more certain past. It was an epoch in which the founding fathers of his country and of his family seemed to merge. When the Marquis de Lafayette made his triumphal tour of the United States in 1824, he called on the family of the late General Peter Gansevoort and on Major Thomas Melvill, who had taken part in the Boston Tea Party and who showed the Marquis a vial of tea leaves that

Henry Sanford Gansevoort (1835–1871), colonel commanding the 13th New York Cavalry. Steel engraving by A. H. Ritchie from a photograph c. 1864. Reproduced from a *Memorial* biography edited by John C. Hoadley, and "Printed for Private Distribution." Rare Books and Manuscripts Division, The New York Public Library, Astor, Lenox and Tilden Foundations.

had survived the occasion. This courtesy was the subject of a letter from the son of the general to the son of the major: "Your father," Peter Gansevoort wrote to Allan Melvill, "venerated for his patriotic services and his patriarchal virtues and more particularly identified with . . . our early revolutionary existence as a people, must afford Lafayette the purest gratification." (Thus one patriarch pays his compliments to another.) For his part Allan Melvill assumed a patrician pose. He declined as beneath his dignity an introduction to Lafayette that did not include the opportunity for a personal conversation and deplored the adulation Lafayette received from the crowd while at the same time he hailed Lafayette in the most extravagant language as a champion of liberty. Allan was a conservative republican gentleman, the inheritor of a Calvinism tempered by both eighteenth-century conceptions of freedom and patrician prerogative. In this respect he was like his brother Thomas, whom Melville remembered as "my plainly clad but courtly kinsman," and in another generation, "Colonel Gansevoort of Fort Stanwix."[150] The words *patriotism, paternal, patriarch, patrician*, and *patronizing* share etymological roots and rhetorical purposes. They had once been almost synonymous, and they are cognates of the New York Dutch word *patroon*. But family had diminished as an influence in government and society. Henry the boy rebel was now a nostalgic reactionary. This does not surprise. What does is how well he had learned the family lessons. He writes to his sister, Kate, and after professing his distaste for "distinctions of birth or descent" declares what had been the assumption of his clan ever since it acquired its patrician mantle.[151]

> I think more and more of family as the unit of government. . . . Our hasty and jumbled development lacks stability for it honors and rewards only individual success. . . . The custom of today unfortunately teaches us that in almost every sense a man is better off without a family at his back. Our President [Andrew Johnson] and legislators are selected . . . because they hardly know who were their Fathers, our Railroad Kings are foundlings and the society of all our great places is chaotic. . . . A foundation of Govt. on family besides the stability it secures would give us statesmen instead of politicians, scholars instead of smatterers more morality and few divorces.[152]

The old Puritan and founding father of New England, Governor John Winthrop, in making his case against the Antinomians of an earlier day, employed the analogy that Henry Gansevoort echoes: "A family is a little commonwealth, and a commonwealth is a great family."[153] The idea was a familiar one, the moral position founded on feeling, a categorical imperative. The theocratic Puritan and the eighteenth-century gentleman who did not separate the state he served as his duty and right from the society, the people, are the matrix of Henry Gansevoort's retrogressive view of the times.

The stability of the social order depends upon the stability of the patrician, patriarchal family.[154] What Henry Gansevoort states explicitly was family doctrine, the bedrock justification for the privileges claimed by the gentry. It justified the way the Melville-Gansevoorts broke the will of their children and concealed their own sins, if, indeed, they ever consciously formulated a justification. But the doctrine he subscribes to had become an anachronism, and the irony that resides in Henry Gansevoort's statement stems from its timing, its source, and its crudity. What was an unspoken assumption for Henry Gansevoort's father, whose instinctive conservatism transcended his Democratic Party politics and his commercial interests, was for his son the complaint of a lesser man out of joint with the times. Peter Gansevoort did not whimper. Nor did Herman Melville.

One more line of speculation. If Billy Budd's death were restorative, then in what way was Malcolm's? As with the story of Billy Budd, Melville left unfinished a little book of verse he tentatively called "Weeds and Wildings." He had planned it as a gift to Lizzie from whom he had been estranged in the months before Malcolm died; their love and loss of the boy in time restored them to each other and gradually led Melville to a different view of family affection and duty.[155] In the quiet autumn of his life, Melville looked back to the things that had brought him happiness when he and Lizzie lived at Arrowhead: wildflowers, woodland creatures, his wife's roses, the children, the changes of the season, birth and death as part of the flow of nature. These became the subject of his verses. One of them, "The Chipmunk," held a secret of shared memory and affection:

*The Chipmunk*[156]

*Heart of autumn!*
*Weather meet;*
*Like to sherbert*
*Cool and sweet.*

Stock-still I stand,
And *him* I see
Prying, peeping
From Beech-Tree;
Crickling, crackling
Gleefully!
But, affrighted
By wee sound,
Presto! vanish—
Whither Bound?

So did Baby,
Crowing mirth
E'en as startled
By some inkling
Touching Earth,
Flit (and whither?)
From *our* hearth!

The poem is elegiac and as such is related to the "Verses Inscriptive and Memorial" at the end of *Battle-Pieces* and the "Monody" written, probably, with Hawthorne in mind, a Victorian taste he reveals in his close attention to the elegies of Matthew Arnold and Tennyson's *In Memoriam*.[157] Lizzie would have fathomed its secret, quite different from the kind the Gansevoort-Melvilles kept. Autumn is the season of ripeness, cool and refreshing, with a hint of winter "Like sherbert." He had used this comparison in *Moby-Dick* long ago to describe "warmingly cool days" at sea like "crystal goblets of Persian sherbet," and another, a day, "Deep, blue & clear," on the Golden Horn in Constantinople, "cooled and tempered sherbet-like."[158] Malcolm died in September. A mellowed Melville feels the cool breeze of his own death in the September soon to come. For a still moment, the lively little chipmunk is "*him*," Malcolm, their baby, who like the "little roosters" with which Melville com-

The Chipmunk

Heart of autumn!
Weather meet,
Like to sherbet
Cool and sweet:

The woods shed flattering
From calm leaves
Sun-lit, ... brown-dyed
golden leaves.

Stock-still I stand,
And him I see
Prying, peeping
From Beech-tree;
Crickling, crackling
Gleefully!
(But, affrighted
By wee sound,
Presto! vanish —
Whither bound?

So did Baby,
Crowing mirth,
E'en as startled
By some inkling
Touching Earth,
Flit (and whither?)
From our hearth!

"The Chipmunk," leaves one and two, from ms.
"Weeds and wildings with a rose or two." By permission of the Houghton Library, Harvard University.

pared him in his letter to his brother Allan, is "Crowing" with joy. But the chipmunk, "startled / By some inkling" of earthly things, vanishes, as did baby Malcolm, "From *our* hearth." His and Lizzie's. From their "hearth" but not from their "Heart." *Heart* and *hearth*, close in sound and, for Melville, in meaning, envelop the poem. Its pronouns within move from *I* to *our*; he had thought about "the" hearth as a possibility, penciling in the article, but struck it, reaffirming "our" with underscoring. In his letter to his brother he had written, unaware of the storm to come, "last night I dreampt that his good angel had secured a seat for him above." Surviving manuscript drafts of "The Chipmunk" confirm its hermetic quality. The first draft apparently did not have the opening stanzas on autumn. This addition consisted of eight lines:

> Heart of autumn!
>   Weather meet,
>   Like to sherbert
>   Cool and sweet,
>   The woods shed fluttering
>     From calm eaves
> Sun-lit, sun-dyed
>   Golden leaves.

Melville revised but then deleted the second quatrain, lines that seemed obvious and inappropriate in their connotation. "Sunlit" Malcolm, the son who delighted, who lighted his parents' life; "sun-dyed" (he considered "crimson"), the son who died; "Golden leaves," the death, departure of the golden boy. Nothing gold can stay. The rhyme words *eaves* and *leaves* belong to another poem in "Weeds and Wildings," "The Little Good Fellows." It is about love and springtime.

Malcolm is present in this poem, too. Its subject is the annual return of "cock-robin" to the "orchards," putting "Old Winter" to flight, welcoming life and lovers, and showing compassion to the dead. For Melville robins, orchards, and children are linked. In his letters to Malcolm and Bessie in 1860 from the wintry coast of South America, he writes that the sea birds "never see any orchards . . . like your gay little friend in Pittsfield Robin Red Breast Esq."[159] The second stanza of "The Little Good Fellows" reads:

"The Little Good Fellows," stanzas one and two, from ms. "Weeds and wildings with a rose or two." By permission of the Houghton Library, Harvard University.

> Love for love. For ever we
> When some unfriended man we see
> Lifeless under forest-eaves,
> Cover him with buds and leaves;
> And charge the chipmunk, mouse, and mole—
> Molest not this poor human soul!

Eaves, leaves, a chipmunk, robins. Melville is thinking of Malcolm and echoing the memorable dirge from John Webster's *The White Devil* :

> Call for the robin redbreast and the wren
> Since o'er the shady groves they hover,
> And with leaves and flowers do cover
> The friendless bodies of unburied men.
> Call unto his funeral dole
> The ant, the field-mouse, and the mole,
> To rear him hillocks that shall keep him warm,
> And, when gay tombs are robbed, sustain no harm.
>
> [V, iv, 89–96]

Melville wrote Evert A. Duyckinck in 1862, asking the loan of "some of those volumes of the Elizabethan dramatists," and mentioning Webster specifically.[160] His language suggests prior acquaintance. He borrowed from Webster's dirge for a poem in *Battle-Pieces*, "The Armies of the Wilderness," which describes a forest littered with the bodies of soldiers, and again in *Clarel*, in reference to a saintly pilgrim who had drowned himself in the Dead Sea.[161] Originally Melville had written "self-slayer sad."[162] The phrase was too painful, so he provided a substitute, "some unfriended man," words from Webster's dirge, as are *leaves, mouse,* and *mole*, but not *chipmunk*, which he gives first place in his listing. Behind Webster's lines is the traditional ballad, "Babes in the Wood," preserved in Percy's *Reliques of Ancient English Poetry* (1765), praised by Addison in *The Spectator*, no. 85, and judged "perhaps the most popular of all English ballads" by Child in his authoritative volumes.[163] Lost in the forest, the children die in each others arms and

> . . . Robin Red-breast piously
> Did cover them with leaves.[164]

So "The Chipmunk" is "Baby," and if the mood is of memory and resignation, the questions of "Whither bound?" and "Flit . . . whither?" are left unanswered.[165]

Melville, in contrast to his cousin Henry, rid himself of his father. And ironically his father was the effective means of this purgation. Allan Melvill's harsh treatment of his son (a clinical psychologist has described Melville as "a psychologically 'battered child' "),[166] the favoritism he displayed for Herman's elder brother (christened a Gansevoort), and the circumstances of Allan Melvill's death (which were tantamount to his rejection of Herman) were factors that made Herman's rejection possible. To this add the trauma when Melville, like Pierre, came to know his father's flaws and corruptions. Melville did not need to kill his father.[167] His father had destroyed himself. His was the first suicide. Malcolm's was the second. But was Malcolm's death a suicide? Might it have been, at moments in Melville's eyes, a sacrificial execution, with himself as executioner? Might it have been a test of his submission to the family pieties? To family authority? A dark deed done and hidden for the family's sake? In "Daniel Orme," his late sketch of a moody, secretive old sailor who seemed haunted by "some dark deed in the past," the narrator speculates: "Even admitting that there was something dark that he chose to keep to himself, what then? Such reticence may sometimes be more for the sake of others than one's self." Or might it have been a test of obedience to the highest authority? Abraham with his knife, son Isaac, and no angel (hardly the role of the protective, ineffectual Lizzie) to stay his hand? Or a penance to cleanse Melville of his sins as a father? And hence (and as always), guilt of one kind exchanged for another? Or might Malcolm have been, as Vere saw Billy to be, a "Fated boy," and Melville, like Vere, the fatal instrument?[168] Captain Vere and Billy Budd, or "Baby Budd, as more familiarly . . . called," that is, called within the family. "*Baby* for Billy," the name given him by the old Dansker "in freak of patriarchal irony."[169] And *Baby* is a babe in the woods, too—a little goodfellow, his body covered over with "buds and leaves," like Billy Budd covered over with "oozy weeds." Herman Melville and Malcolm. In the twilight at the end, no wonder we feel such pity and fear for Vere and for Billy Budd who blessed and absolved him—and for Melville and for Malcolm who could not.

# V. Man's Final Lore

THE PROCESS OF BREAKING FREE from the sway of father and family, as his novels reflect it, rises to importance in *Redburn* and culminates in *Pierre*. *Redburn* has an obviously autobiographical, familial layer not present in the South Sea narratives that preceded it. Its subject, in the words of the subtitle, is the "First Voyage" of an orphaned "Son-of-a-Gentleman, in the Merchant Service"—orphan Herman, a ship's boy on his first voyage from New York to Liverpool in 1839. (It is, by the way, dedicated to his "younger brother, Thomas Melville, now a sailor on a voyage to China.") The sad, wise lesson that Redburn learns in his wanderings is that the "Prosy Old Guide-Book" that served his father during his travels cannot serve the son. Henry Gansevoort did not learn this lesson; or perhaps he learned another all too well. *Pierre* also is autobiographical. It is saturated with readily identifiable reference to Melville family affairs, but were it not, its self-reflexive nature would suggest such sources. Sources aside, Melville is largely concerned with the destructive effect of the concentrated, internalized family. The force and falsehood of dynasty lead to young Pierre's suicide. (One inevitably thinks of Malcolm's.) *Pierre* fuses Gansevoort and Melvill(e) elements. The surname *Glendinning* scans with the Dutch *Gansevoort*, but it is a Scottish name, as *Melville* is, and, therefore, a composite of the two.[170] To disguise the fact that he is betraying Melville family secrets and to distance the novel from its autobiographical origins, Melville uses a third-person narrator, a departure from the precedent of his six previous books, and he resorts to extravagantly artificial language and plot devices. Fact is in this way emphatically fictionalized though at bottom fiction remains fact.[171]

The tone of *Redburn* is more of regret than defiance. *Pierre; or, The Ambiguities* is a direct attack on patriarchy. A relevant function of its recurrent allusions to rock and stone, so obvious and excessive, gradually come clear. Pierre the son is crushed by the father of stone, the "perfect marble form."[172] Melodramatic, metaphysical, and mythic, with a plot that reads like a cheap romance of the day, it is a tissue of ambiguities such as we might expect in Melville's family novel. In abstract terms, the principal ambiguity and the story line have to do with a young writer who destroys his family and himself because he attempts to apply divine standards, the standards of the Father in Heaven, to the affairs of his children on earth—and Melville does not let us forget the ultimate source of the standards. The source of the story is the life of his earthly father who had fathered an illegitimate child, as well as eight children "in wedlock." Melville and Father Allan, "Young Pierre" and Pierre *père*. In *Pierre* the theme of bastardy, the sin of the father, is first confronted coincidentally with the discovery that an unmarried domestic servant is pregnant. The incident reveals the moral rigidity and cold pride of Pierre's mother, the pious hypocrisy of her minister, and the spiritual agony of Pierre. At least in part his mother's uncharitable response to the servant girl results from the fact that she defines her behavior not simply as a moral lapse and social disgrace, but as a threat to family as an institution. The legitimacy of the family, real and apparent, must be preserved regardless of the cost and at all levels.

The theme of incest, the primordial family sin, permeates the book. On their historic estate, young Pierre and his handsome, widowed mother, Mary Glendinning (Maria Gansevoort?), live out a pastoral idyll. The playful innocence of their relationship, however, has a meretricious cast that is unwholesome because it seems to mask and at the same time suggest a subsurface of tension and suppressed knowledge. They address each other as brother and sister, and banter flirtatiously, but this is less an Oedipal relationship than a forewarning of the centrality and complexity of the incest theme.[173] When Pierre is led to suspect that his father was not, as he had been brought up to believe, the "personification of perfect human goodness and virtue"[174] but had in secret sired a bastard daughter, Isabel, he feels a family duty to assume responsibility for her in order to shield his mother and to expiate the parental sin. In this last capacity he figures as Isabel's father as well as her brother. Although he both accepts and questions her claim, he responds to her in the roles of parent, brother, and lover. Furthermore, to the extent that she is wished into being by Pierre's desire for a sister, she is his daughter, fathered by his imaginings; and so she, like the mother whom Pierre treats as a sister, is joined to him in a complex and retrogressive incestuous bond. Isabel represents both the demands of domestic restraint and the freedom of passional love and of artistic creativity. The scheme that he decides upon is to reject his loving and quite suitable betrothed, Lucy, and to elope to the city and pretend to marry the mysterious, provocative Isabel. In the end Isabel is his dark mother, and he is her nursing child. His last words, uttered while "tearing her bosom loose" for the vial of poison she has there, are "in thy breasts, life for infants lodgeth not, but death-milk!"[175] Pierre's resolution recalls the subterfuge of the Melville-Gansevoorts. He seizes upon "a most deceitful way,"[176] as he recognizes, in his attempt to legitimize Isabel; he pretends to give her the name that she may be entitled to, his own, a name that her father denied her. At the same time, he is attempting to preserve the family name. To serve his double purpose, he resorts to deception as did the Melville-Gansevoorts — for the sake of the family name. Proper names were significant for Melville, whether within his family or in fiction. In the city, in the depths of his misery, Pierre has a vision of the country he left behind. He sees the Mount of Titans and below it an embedded rock formation in the shape of the giant Enceladus. In Melville's version he is "doubly incestuous Enceladus,"[177] son of brother Heaven and sister Earth and incestuous husband to his mother, a titanic counterpart of the Pierre who sportively addresses his sister/mother and deceitfully marries a woman who may be his sister. Pierre envisions the giant, once hundred-armed but now armless, as buried beneath earth and rock but struggling defiantly to break out of the thralldom of his incestuous doom. In this vision, Enceladus has the face of Pierre.[178]

The incest theme combines powerful, opposing forces. Incest is the implosion of family relationships, a centripetal force that represents the ultimate, if perverse, familial concentration and a centrifugal force that is its destruction. It is the center and circumference of *Pierre* as a novel of family crisis and the fundamental cause of the revulsion it aroused in Melville's readers. The *American Whig Review* typifies this response. It described the plot as "repulsive, unnatural, and indecent," and its protagonist as "a disobedient son, a dishonest lover, an incestuous

brother, a cold-blooded murderer, and an unrepentant suicide." In essence, according to the reviewer, Melville "strikes
with an impious . . . hand, at the very foundations of society"—
which is to say, he employs the incest theme to strike at the
foundations of the family.[179]

Metaphorically at least, incest is a way of probing a pattern of
rearing children designed to secure the status of a unified patrician family. Ever so slightly beyond metaphor, Judge Shaw,
the fraternal friend, was engaged to marry Melville's father's
sister. She died before the marriage took place. Herman Melville married Judge Shaw's daughter. Not incestuous but certainly endogamic. For incest is taboo. In the novel Pierre merely
plays at incest with his sister/mother, and although Pierre and
Isabel have their moments of passionate intensity, their marriage is a sham, and we see no unambiguous evidence that it is
consummated. Melville could not accept incest and what it signified. In the end, as the taboo demands, Pierre, his mother,
Isabel, Lucy, and the rival cousin who inherits the family estate
and shares the family name, are dead. Incest and its symbolic
equivalent, patriarchy, are at once rejected in horror, at least in
fiction.[180] For rejection, in fact, Melville must wait for the sacrificial death of Malcolm.

Earlier we referred to " 'The Coming Storm,' " Melville's
poem on Shakespearean tragedy. The poem, which appears in
*Battle-Pieces*, is anticipated in references to *Hamlet* in *Pierre*. Melville had published nothing in almost a decade, and if he had
hoped, through his poetry, to shore up his literary reputation,
he was surely disappointed. Writing verse was somewhat perverse and impulsive; at least it seemed so to the family. Lizzie,
in 1859, confided to Judge Shaw: "Herman has taken to writing
poetry. You need not tell anyone, for you know how such things
get around."[181] It is more reasonable to assume that his forsak-
ing prose was another act of withdrawal. By the end of 1866 he
had become a customs inspector, and he would publish only
verse, and that privately, for the rest of his life. " 'The Coming
Storm' " is accompanied by a headnote: "A Picture by S. R. Gifford, and owned by E. B. Included in the N. A. Exhibition,
April, 1865." In the chronological order of the volume, it follows immediately an elegy to Abraham Lincoln, who was shot

on April 14, 1865. The title, unlike most other captions in the volume, is set off by quotation marks. The catalogue of the annual exhibit at the National Academy of Design in New York for 1865 lists a landscape by Sanford R. Gifford, a painter of the Hudson River School, titled "The Coming Storm." Its owner was the Shakespearean actor Edwin Booth.[182]

A common enough subject, it depicts "an urned lake" in a pristine forest threatened by a "demon-cloud" hovering over mountains in the background. Melville found Gifford's painting prophetic of the human condition in a general way, but more than that, he was moved by the sensibility of the actor who was attracted to it and bought it.[183] To Melville it was uncanny that Edwin Booth should be fixed and fascinated by this subject unless Booth assumed that he personally must anticipate a coming storm of his own. Melville saw Edwin Booth's forebodings borne out in the assassination of Lincoln by his brother, John Wilkes Booth. From another standpoint, Melville wondered how Edwin Booth, "a spirit as mild" as the urned lake of the painting, how anyone, how he himself might withstand such terror and surprise; he perceived that Edwin Booth survived because he had reached the heart of Shakespeare's tragedy. Through *Hamlet* Booth achieved tragic understanding.

In its situation and its significances, *Pierre* portends "The Coming Storm." Isabel is the demon-cloud that darkens the pastoral landscape of Saddle Meadows, the Glendinning estate, and she casts her shadow over Pierre's mild spirit. And though young Pierre has not yet approached Shakespeare's core, he has begun the descent into the darkness that, Melville came to believe, preceded the possibility of eventual enlightenment. In a chapter titled "More Light, and the Gloom of That Light. More Gloom, and the Light of That Gloom," Pierre considers his duty to his family: to his father's memory, to his mother, to his lineage, to Isabel. Impulsively, instinctively, he reaches toward two books that lie open on his table—Dante's "Inferno," with its warning that those who would descend into the depths must abandon all hope, and a passage from *Hamlet*, a drama of family crisis and familial duty:

"The time is out of joint;—Oh cursed spite,
That ever I was born to set it right!"[184]

Pierre, like young Prince Hamlet, is steeped in fate. It is his duty to set things right, his fate to destroy.

If *Hamlet* has an obvious and applicable moral, we are told by the narrator (and his statement begins with "If"), it is "that all meditation is worthless, unless it prompt to action." Pierre is unable to act promptly, though he soon will be, nor can he grasp "the deeper significances of [*Hamlet*'s] pervading indefiniteness, which significances are wisely hidden from all but the rarest adepts." He will eventually, perhaps, but the narrator explains:

> Pierre had always been an admiring reader of Hamlet; but neither his age nor his mental experience thus far, had qualified him either to catch initiating glimpses into the hopeless gloom of its interior meaning, or to draw from the general story those superficial and purely incidental lessons, wherein the painstaking moralist so complacently expatiates.[185]

Eventually Pierre may perceive that "the deeper truths in man . . . will sometimes proceed from his own profoundest gloom. Utter darkness is then his light."[186] Eventually he may reach Shakespeare's core. Meanwhile, in misery and frustration, he tears the book apart and tramples it. Within the framework of *Pierre*, *Hamlet* is for Melville another drama of family tensions and family secrets and an opportunity to muse about the light to be found in the gloom.

These were bad times, when Melville wrote " 'The Coming Storm.' " His nation was sundered by fratricidal war; the great leader, Father Abraham, who might have brought about its healing, had been murdered. In the supplementary essay on the Civil War with which he concludes *Battle-Pieces*, Melville called the war a "terrible historic tragedy" but one that might possibly instruct "through pity and terror." Such, as Aristotle tells us, is the potential of tragedy. And these were bad times for Melville. He was well into his middle years. His literary reputation was fading away, his marriage was disintegrating, his mind, his spirit were close to breaking. In " 'The Coming Storm' " Melville continues his lifelong study of tragedy, a study that began, as if it were religious revelation, with the discovery of "the divine William" while awaiting the birth of his son. "Steeped in fable, steeped in fate." The Fates granted him Malcolm and Shakespeare at the same time. He would continue the study until it ended, in the unfinished story of Billy Budd. Malcolm/Billy. Man's final lore.

Illustration for the biographical entry on Herman Melville in *Appleton's Cyclopaedia* (1888). The engraving is after a photograph taken in 1885, the year of his retirement as an inspector of customs. The poem that grew into *Billy Budd* he conceived soon thereafter.

# Notes

1. Allan Melville, Herman Melville's brother, married Sophia Eliza Thurston of New York on September 22, 1847. Their first child, Maria Gansevoort, named for her paternal grandmother, was born on February 18, 1849. Their coming of age was observed in different ways. Malcolm, soon after reaching his seventeenth birthday on February 16, 1866, went to work for Richard Lathers' insurance company. (See Appendix A.) Millie, or Milie, as she was known within the family in childhood, made her debut at the Century Club later the same year. (ALs, Maria Gansevoort Melville to Catherine Gansevoort, December 4, 1866, G-L, box 154.) The Allan Melvilles were prosperous and pleased to show their wealth.

2. Melville is recalling an epithet from Dickens' *Nicholas Nickleby* (1838) applied by the showman, Crummles, to his daughter, purportedly a child prodigy. See the *Oxford English Dictionary* citation for *phenomenon* in the sense of "prodigy": " 'This, Sir,' said Mr. Vincent Crummles, bringing the maiden forward, 'this is the infant phenomenon.' " For the popularity and financial success of *Nicholas Nickleby* in the United States, see Peter S. Bracher, "Dickens and His American Readers, 1834–1870," Diss., Univ. of Pennsylvania 1966, esp. pp. 42–61. Note Melville's subsequent reference to Malcolm as a "little phenomenon." Melville's sister Helen, a Dickens enthusiast, uses this epithet to describe the musical performance of a ten-year-old she was subjected to. (ALs, Helen Melville to Augusta Melville, February 16, 1842, G-L Additions, box 1.)

3. A pennyweight is 24 grains and a pound is 5,760 grains, troy weight, used for precious metals and gemstones, and here, by extension, other precious objects.

4. Hundredweight: Avoirdupois weight, 112 pounds. Avoirdupois is used for gross materials.

5. In a passage that is notably Rabelaisian, three "Nurses and Governesses" play with the infant Gargantua and eventually dress him (Book I, Chaps. 11 and also 8). For Melville's early familiarity with Rabelais, see Sealts, no. 417. His writings were among the first books he borrowed from the Evert A. Duyckinck library.

Malcolm required only one nurse, at least at this point in his young life, "Mrs. Ellen Sullivan, a domestic in the Shaw household for some time." She assisted with the prodigy from the time of his birth and accompanied Herman, Lizzie, and the child to New York on April 10, and remained there until April 23. *Letters*, p. 84n3.

6. Melville appears to have infected his family with his comic exaggerations of Malcolm's prodigious qualities. See Appendix A (p. 117) for Hope Shaw's account of his phenomenal strength at age four.

7. Barnum, the showman, toured Europe, he claims, with spectacular success, 1844–47. See *The Life of P. T. Barnum Written by Himself* (New York: Red-

field, 1855), passim, and subsequent versions of his autobiography. Such allusions to Barnum were common; see, for example, ALs, Ebenezer R. Hoar (a family friend) to his wife, October 26, 1850, LSP, box 34: "I heard a good story on Chief Justice Shaw, down on all fours, playing with a baby [Malcolm], . . . If Barnum could have secured the group he would have made his fortune"; quoted in Leyda, II, 926. For an extensive burlesque of Barnum and his museum, see *Mardi* (N-N), pp. 378–81.

8. Frederick I (c. 1123–90), German Kaiser and Roman Emperor, surnamed "Barbarossa" by the Italians for his red beard.

9. Probably Gustavus Adolphus (1594–1632), king of Sweden. Among the art objects and other family possessions listed in the "Elizabeth Shaw Melville Memoranda" is a print after "The burial of Gustavus Adolphus . . . painted by Helquist." See Merton M. Sealts, Jr., *The Early Lives of Melville* (Madison: University of Wisconsin Press, 1974), p. 176.

10. The *Encyclopædia Britannica*, 11th edition, states that Ferdinand is "a name borne at various times by many European sovereigns and princes, the most important of whom are noticed below." Of the twenty-one "noticed," it is hard to imagine which Melville had in mind.

11. Probably Otto I (912–73), called "The Great," putative founder of the Holy Roman Empire.

12. The adjective *grandissimo* is not found in the *Oxford English Dictionary* and appears to be a Melville coinage. In Chapter 123 of *Mardi*, we read of "Oh-Oh's collection of ancient and curious manuscripts," which includes among its "scarce old memoirs" a "Biography of the Great and Good King Grandissimo" (N-N), pp. 382–86. Compare the substantive *grandissimus*, signifying, in *Moby-Dick*, Chap. 95, the whale's great phallus (N-N), p. 419. As late as *Billy Budd*, Melville would write of the "heroic strong man, Hercules," p. 51.

13. Melville's now unconventional spelling of the biblical judge and strong man's name. Judges, 13–16.

14. Napoleon Bonaparte (1769–1821), the legendary French emperor who captured the imagination of many of his contemporaries. The momentum of the list perhaps overcame Melville's dislike of Napoleon, evident in *Mardi* (N-N), p. 553, *Redburn* (N-N), p. 276, and *Moby-Dick* (N-N), p. 143.

15. Melville is continuing his hyperbolic references to Malcolm's weight and size. According to George C. D. Odell, *Annals of the New York Stage* (New York: Columbia University Press, 1927–49), V, 390, Barnum's new show of June 19, 1848, included the "Lambert Family," more often billed as "the Highland Mammoth Boys." The Lamberts were exhibited regularly during the 1846–49 seasons. Advertisements for Barnum's American Museum in the *New York Herald* in the month of January 1849 state that "The Highland Mammoth Boys may . . . be seen at all hours of the day." The notice for January 31, 1849, bills them as "the fattest pair this side of Greece." Phineas T. Barnum (*The Catalogue or Guide Book of Barnum's American Museum*), New York: Printed and Published for the Proprietor, 186[?], p. 58, lists among the "Wax Figures" on display "Daniel Lambert [1770–1809], the English Mammoth,

who when living weighed 739 lbs., and measured 9 ft. 7 inches around the waist." See also Melville's allusions in *Mardi* (N-N): "In the palisade was a mighty breach . . . wide enough to admit six Daniel Lamberts abreast" and "fat Lamberts" (pp. 286 and 516). Baby Malcolm's phenomenal size and strength have parallels in infants Hercules (note 12) and Davy Crockett, mentioned in *Moby-Dick*, N-N, p. 363.

16. See John Brand, *Observations on Popular Antiquities* (London: Chatto & Windus, 1913), pp. 422–34, first published in 1777, for his disquisition on bells "to drive away demons" and "evil spirits" who are "much afraid of Bells" (pp. 423–29n), and for the "custom of rejoicing with bells . . . from which we seem to have derived the modern compliment of welcoming persons of consequence by a cheerful peel" (p. 431). See also Theresa C. Brakeley, "Bells," *Dictionary of Folklore*, ed. Maria Leach (New York: Funk & Wagnalls, 1972), pp. 132–34.

17. The State House, at the intersection of Beacon and Park Streets, is in the immediate vicinity of and was visible from Lemuel Shaw's residence at 49 Mount Vernon Street. A landmark, it was designed by Charles Bulfinch, and the cornerstone was laid in 1795.

18. Zachary Taylor was twelfth president of the United States, 1849–50. In 1847 Melville contributed a series of "Authentic Anecdotes of 'Old Zack' " to the New York humorous weekly *Yankee Doodle*, edited by Cornelius Mathews. See Luther Mansfield, "Melville's Comic Articles on Zachary Taylor," *American Literature*, 9 (1938), 411–18, and *Piazza Tales*, (N-N), pp. 212–29, 636–39.

19. There is a humorous touch here. Melville often referred to ascent and descent for different purposes, some of them complex and ironic. See, for example, "The Paradise of Bachelors" where he alludes to "the rise of bread and the fall of babies" and *Israel Potter* (N-N), p. 163, where he notes "the sad prospects of a rise in bread, or the tide." Behind Melville's phrase are the studies of Thomas Malthus (1766–1834), author of *Essay on Population* (1798) and *Observations on the Effect of the Corn Laws, and the Rise or Fall in the Price of Corn* . . . (1814). Also see *Billy Budd*, p. 132, where in "Billy in the Darbies" he writes, "I must be up too, / Early in the morning, aloft from alow."

20. Pekin and the Great Wall of China are important in the brick kiln metaphor in *Israel Potter* (N-N), p. 257. See also *Mardi* (N-N), p. 366, *Redburn* (N-N), p. 292, and *Pierre* (N-N), p. 167. See *Piazza Tales* (N-N), p. 231, for "Mr. Parkman's Tour," a review written at the time of Malcolm's birth.

21. *Moby-Dick* (N-N), p. 5, has a similar comic list "of ships, barques, brigs, and what not." Both suggest a burlesque of a Homeric catalogue of ships. Edward Rosenberry, *Melville and the Comic Spirit* (Cambridge, Mass.: Harvard University Press, 1955), pp. 36–37, calls attention to "A mock-Heroic chapter entitled 'The Great Massacre of the Beards' " (*White-Jacket* [N-N], Chap. 85) which employs expansive lists and parallels, as does the preceding chapter.

22. "In her copy of the Constable edition of *Pierre*, now in the Berg Collection of the New York Public Library, Mrs. Eleanor Melville Metcalf, HM's granddaughter, noted that Glen Stanly's house in New York (*Pierre* [N-N], p. 332) was like the Shaw home in Mount Vernon Street, Boston." See Amy Puett Emmers, "Melville's Closet Skeleton: A New Letter about the Illegitimacy In-

cident in Pierre," *Studies in the American Renaissance*, ed. Joel Myerson (Boston: Twayne, 1977), p. 341. See also note 132.

23. More exaggeration. Samuel Canning was one of several Irish-born domestics in the employ of the Shaws. He is listed as forty years old in National Archives Microfilm Publications, Microcopy no. 432, Population Schedules of the Seventh Census of the United States, 1850, roll 336 (Washington, D.C.: N[ational] A[rchives], 1963), ward 6, p. 33. Melville did not cross the *t* in what is evidently *waiter*, thus leaving transcription susceptible to the erroneous reading *mailer*.

24. "Little men are sometimes very potent," Melville writes of a "baby god" who lorded it over the larger, much more impressive idols in *Typee* (N-N), p. 175.

25. In the folklore of the frontier, from Davy Crockett and Mike Fink to Mark Twain's Mississippi raftsmen, the rooster signified American ebullience and bravado. Melville's more memorable roosters include Ahab, who identified himself with the "crowing cock" emblazoned on the doubloon (*Moby-Dick* [N-N], p. 431) and Beneventano in "Cock-A-Doodle-Doo!"

26. Panic resounds in Spenser, Milton, Plutarch, and Sir Thomas Browne. See notes 52 and 53.

27. Melville's dream of the good angel seems to anticipate the passages in *Moby-Dick* where friends of the Sub-Sub Librarian clear out the angels to make a place for him in "the seven-storied heavens" (N-N, p. xviii) and the dream vision of "long rows of angels in paradise, each with his hands in a jar of spermaceti" (N-N, p. 416).

28. See note 55, which quotes St. Peter on the roaring lion. Melville had toyed with this quotation in *Omoo* (N-N), p. 132, *Mardi*, (N-N), p. 40, and *Redburn* (N-N), p. 284.

29. See pp. 25–26 where the suggestiveness of "Reverend Father" is discussed, and consider the subversive irony of Pierre's "reverential thoughts and beliefs" regarding his father's character on p. 34.

30. The word *wedlock* seems to have amused Melville. In "Rip Van Winkle's Lilac" he writes humorously of Rip, a young husband "new to the complexities of the lock wedlock." *Collected Poems*, p. 284.

31. (N-N), pp. 238–39.

32. Consider the use of this word in moments of high drama or descriptions of preternatural objects and events in *Moby-Dick*, Chaps. 42, 59, 68, 124, and 134 (N-N, pp. 193, 276, 305–307, 517, and 557).

33. Melville revitalizes a formulaic expression by using *perfect* in its original and primary meaning, a practice seen occasionally in his more consciously controlled writing.

There is also a suggestion of Virgil's "Messianic Eclogue" (see esp. Ec. 4. 6–7): "iam redit et Virgo, redeunt saturnia regna; / iam nova progenies caelo demittitur alto" ("Now comes the virgin, Saturn reigns again; / Now from high heaven descends a wondrous race"; trans. C. S. Calverley). In general, however, the word *prodigium* bears a negative connotation, a "monster," the sort of exhibit Barnum would have in his freak show. But see the "prodigious" excitement in New Orleans, mentioned below.

34. On May 1, 1848, Barnum advertised a new show which numbered among its featured attractions "a Giant Baby." It continued to be exhibited through December 1849. See Odell, V, 390 and 484. The "giant baby" seems to have emerged as one of the categories of "living curiosities" regularly exhibited. Phineas T. Barnum, *The Catalogue or Guidebook of Barnum's American Museum*, p. 109, has a description and illustration of another "Giant Baby." See pp. 25–26.

35. Sealts, no. 417. For Melville's use of Rabelais in *Mardi* (1849), then his most recent book, see Merrell Davis, *Melville's MARDI: A Chartless Voyage* (New Haven: Yale University Press, 1952), passim, and Rosenberry, pp. 65–79.

36. See note 15. For a typical allusion see the list of "the Giants" from whom Rabelais's Pantagruel was descended (Book II, Chapter 1).

37. For example, Pierre, the young patrician, declines to have his daguerreotype made for publicity purposes because "in former times a faithful portrait was only within the power of the . . . aristocrats of the earth," whereas in egalitarian America "true distinction lies in not having yours published at all" (N-N, p. 254). Melville declined a request for a daguerreotype from Evert Duyckinck in similar terms (ALs, Herman Melville to Evert A. Duyckinck, February 12, 1852, DC, box 43; *Letters*, pp. 120–21).

38. ALs, Herman Melville to Evert A. Duyckinck, February 24, 1849, DC, box 43; in *Letters*, p. 77, and in Leyda, I, 288, and Metcalf, p. 57. See also his ALs to Evert A. Duyckinck, March 3, 1849, DC, box 43, in *Letters*, p. 79, in which he refers to his "jubillations [*sic*] <at discovering> over Shakespeare."

39. See "Hawthorne and His Mosses" (N-N), pp. 244–46 and 252–53, in which he treats Hawthorne's tragic vision and compares him (and vicariously himself) with Shakespeare. For the subjective and fictional facets of "Mosses," see Marvin Fisher, *Going Under: Melville's Short Fiction and the American 1850s* (Baton Rouge: Louisiana State University Press, 1977), pp. 1–11. Cf. *Moby-Dick* (N-N), p. 136: "To grope down into . . . the very pelvis of the world."

40. *Battle-Pieces and Aspects of the War* (New York: Harper & Brothers, 1866), p. 143. We quote the entire poem but call special attention here to the last four lines. "Such hearts can antedate," Melville writes in the line preceding the final quatrain. According to the *Oxford English Dictionary* the etymology of *core* is "uncertain" but ascribed to the French *coeur* and Latin *cor*, meaning "heart." This is the etymology in a copy of *Webster's Dictionary* Melville owned. See Sealts, nos. 550–52. Note the recurrent references to heart in "The Coming Storm" and also in "The Chipmunk," p. 80.

41. For example, the museum "relics" and "curious manuscripts" in Chaps. 122 and 123 (N-N), pp. 378–86.

42. For examples, see the "Etymology" and the "Extracts" that preface *Moby-Dick*, and Chapter 2 of *The Confidence-Man* (N-N), pp. 7–9, with the beginning list of verbal responses to the "stranger," the list of "pilgrims," and, at the end, the analogy to the trees.

43. (N-N), p. 388.

44. (N-N), pp. 387–88. On breast feeding, see Martin Bickman's summary of suppositions in "Melville and the Mind" in *A Companion to Melville Studies*, ed. John Bryant (Westport, Conn.: Greenwood Press, 1986), p. 529f.: "because of his many younger siblings young Herman was thrust away from the breast early and had to endure repeatedly the role of onlooker as his mother's milk and love were deflected to others." For more on sibling rivalry see note 92. For Isabel and breast feeding, see p. 88.

45. See *Mardi* (N-N), pp. 603–609, for a similar and much more extensive list of verbal parallels: the "many ancient and illustrious examples" of suppers, beginning "old Jove gave suppers; the god Woden gave suppers; the Hindoo deity Brahma gave suppers."

46. For an analogous opinion, see note 106. Chattel slaves at the time were commonly thought of in the same way. See, for example, the animal metaphors in *The Narrative of the Life of Frederick Douglass, an American Slave* (1845).

47. See note 2.

48. Henry F. Pommer, *Milton and Melville* (Pittsburgh: University of Pittsburgh Press, 1950), p. 129.

49. (Boston: Hilliard, Gray, and Company, 1836), 2 vols. Melville's edition of Milton's *Works* was sold in New York on March 27, 1984, by the auction house Phillips. Prior to sale, Phillips graciously allowed scholars to inspect the volumes. They are now in private hands. Sealts, no. 358b. See also "Melville's Milton," *Melville Society Extracts*, 57 (February 1984), 7.

50. ALs, Helen Melville Griggs to Herman Melville, May 29, 1854, G-L Additions, box 1. Philemon Holland published his translation of "Plutarch's Morals" in 1603.

51. *Clarel*, ed. Walter E. Bezanson (New York: Hendricks House, 1960), p. 430; Part IV, Canto viii, lines 1–7, reads:

> When rule and era passed away
> With old Sylvanus (stories say),
> The oracles adrift were hurled,
> And ocean moaned about the world,
> And wandering voices without name
> At sea to sailors did proclaim,
> *Pan, Pan, is dead!*

See also Rolfe's "threnodies of Pan" (*Clarel*, III, xxix, 82), a lament for lost Arcadia but also the death of the gods. In one of the "Weeds and Wildings" verses, unpublished at the time of his death, "When Forth the Shepherd leads the Flock," Melville refers to the "Golden Age" before Pan was "hearsed." Sir Thomas Browne (*Vulgar Errors*, Book VII, Chap. xii) cites as an example of an oracle after the birth of Christ the "record by Plutarch, of a voice that was heard to cry unto Mariners at the sea, Great Pan is dead." A more detailed reference to the oracular announcement of the death of Pan occurs in Spenser's gloss for "May" in "The Shepherd's Calendar." See note 52. Plutarch is referred to here also. See the phrase "panic through the world" from the last sentence of the Malcolm letter.

52. A note by Spenser to "May" in "The Shepherd's Calendar" explains that the kingdom of Satan "at that time was by Christ conquered [and] all Oracles surceased, and enchaunted spirits, that were wont to delude the people, thenceforth held theyr peace." Melville presented the copy of Spenser's *The Poetical Works* . . . (Boston: Little, Brown, 1855), which he acquired in 1861 (Leyda, II, 640), to his sister Helen (Leyda, II, 651). See Sealts, no. 483.

53. *Pierre* (N-N), p. 48. ALs, Herman Melville to George L. Duyckinck, November 8, 1858, Duyckinck Family Papers, box 43; *Letters*, p. 191; Pommer, pp. 25–26, and Metcalf, p. 171. Spenser, too, might have helped him remember. The gloss to "May" in "The Shepherd's Calendar" states upon the announcement "that Pan was dead: wherewithall there was heard suche piteous outcryes and dreadfull shriking, as hath not bene the like."

54. Sealts, nos. 89 and 90.

55. I Peter 5:8. For other terrific, roaring lions, see Psalm 22:31 and Proverbs 21:13. Melville combined these biblical lions in the zodiacal sign, "Leo, a roaring lion," explicated by Stubb in "The Doubloon" chapter of *Moby-Dick* (N-N), p. 433. See note 28.

56. Walker Cowen, *Melville's Marginalia* (New York and London: Garland, 1987), II, 484. Cf. *Pierre* (N-N), p. 66: "I will be impious, for piety hath juggled me, and taught me to revere, where I should spurn."

57. Until the 1928 revision of *The Book of Common Prayer*. Even so, the formula is still well known. Cf. Pierre's "most reverential thoughts and beliefs" regarding his deceased father. See note 56.

58. Allan was married on September 22, 1847, to Sophia Thurston at the Episcopal Church of the Ascension (Leyda, I, 259–60). The church was situated in Bond Street, a little to the south and west of the house, at 103 Fourth Avenue, occupied by Allan and Herman and their wives, as well as other members of the Melville family. The Allan Melvilles were still attending the Church of the Ascension the next spring when Sophia accompanied Herman's father-in-law, Lemuel Shaw, to worship there. ALs, Lemuel Shaw, Jr., to Hope Savage Shaw, January 30, 1848, LSP, box 14; quoted in Metcalf, p. 52. Allan's funeral services were held on Sunday, February 11, 1872, at the Episcopal Zion Church, Madison Avenue and East 38 Street. *The* [N. Y.] *Evening Post*, February 10, 1872, p. [3].

59. Pierre's mother displays a comparable concern. She is not merely priggish and devoid of compassion in "the wretched affair of Delly," the pregnant servant (N-N, pp. 100–103). As the Glendinning "Dowager" (see N-N, p. 14) she manages the estate, prepares her son for the succession, and otherwise seeks to assure the legitimacy of the dynasty. Her disinheriting Pierre and designating Glendinning Stanly as her heir is further evidence of her efforts to maintain dynastic integrity. Emphasis on dynastic legitimacy persists until the end of the novel. When Pierre kills Glen Stanly, the narrator observes that Pierre by "his own hand had extinguished his house in slaughtering the only unoutlawed human being by the name of Glendinning" (N-N, p. 360). Nota bene the words "house" and "unoutlawed."

60. Emmers, pp. 339–43. See note 132.

61. Melville was baptized on August 19, 1819, into the South Reformed Dutch Church of New York City, according to his father Allan's entry in the family Bible, reproduced in Leyda, I, 4. For the religious backgrounds of the Gansevoorts and Melvills and Herman Melville's childhood exposure to religion, see T. Walter Herbert, Jr., *MOBY-DICK and Calvinism: A World Dismantled* (New Brunswick, N.J.: Rutgers University Press, 1977), pp. 26–37. His observations about the religious views of Melville's paternal grandfather, Thomas, are based in part on William H. Gilman, *Melville's Early Life and REDBURN.* (New York: New York University Press, 1951), p. 38, who describes Thomas's studies for the ministry at the Presbyterian College of New Jersey—Princeton University—and later joining the Unitarian Church. For the strong Scottish roots of Presbyterianism and the sect's early development in America, see Sydney H. Ahlstrom, *A Religious History of the American People* (New Haven: Yale University Press, 1972), pp. 265–79, esp. pp. 272–75.

The Reverend Thomas Melvill (1692?–1766) of Scoonie, Fife, Scotland, "a clergyman of the Scotch kirk" (*CAL*, II, 672), was one of the many Protestant clergymen among Melvill's ancestors. See note 69. *Moby-Dick* (N-N), p. 52.

62. Maria Gansevoort added an *e* to the surname after Allan Melvill's death. Her aristocratic pretensions may have encouraged her since it conformed to the spelling of their titled Scottish kin. As a Gansevoort and not a Melville, she would not have been changing her surname by birthright but that of her deceased husband, an easier matter. For him a change might have raised questions of respect for his father and for American egalitarianism, which he balanced against his concern for his ancient, noble Scottish ancestral connections. Maria does not appear to have been moved by democratic sentiments. If nothing else, the change is further evidence of name consciousness.

63. Stanton Garner, "Allan Melvill to Martin Van Buren on Major Melvill's Removal," *Melville Society Extracts*, 47 (September 1981), 4–5. See also note 134.

64. See Appendix B.

65. (N-N), p. 68.

66. References to Satan as deceiver are concentrated in Revelation. See, for example, 12:9, 20:3, 20:8, and 20:10.

67. (N-N), p. 68.

68. (N-N), p. 6; and (New York: Hendricks House, 1949), p. 433.

69. ALs, Allan Melvill to Maria Gansevoort Melvill, May 18, 1818, G-L, box 30; quoted in Herbert, p. 27, and Rogin, pp. 31–32. For the Melville genealogy see Merton M. Sealts, Jr., "The Melvill Heritage," *Harvard Library Bulletin*, 34 (1986), 337–38.

70. See Appendix B for a discussion of Allan Melvill's role in the launching of Guert Gansevoort. The phrases quoted are from the ALs, Allan Melvill to Peter Gansevoort, October 25, 1824, G-L, box 34; quoted partially in Rogin, p. 296.

71. Houghton, 85M–7 bMS Am 188.6; quoted in Leyda, I, 26. Subjects such as the name Guert bears and the family's honor are discussed in Allan Melvill's letter to Guert Gansevoort of October 27, 1824, G-L, box 33, and in Appendix C.

72. ALs, Allan Melvill to Thomas W. Melvill, August 28, 1826, G-L, box 34; quoted in Leyda, I, 26.

73. *Piazza Tales* (N-N), p. 230. The review is titled "Mr Parkman's Tour" and was published in the *Literary World*, 4 ( March 31, 1849), 291–93.

74. ALs, Maria Gansevoort Melville to Augusta Melville, November 5, 1851, G-L Additions, box 1. Stanwix was born in Pittsfield on October 22, 1851, and died in 1886.

75. (N-N), p. 6. The General Pierre Glendinning of the novel is based on General Peter Gansevoort (1749–1812), the "Hero of Fort Stanwix," Herman Melville's maternal grandfather. Fort Stanwix is recalled in the name of Pierre's cousin, Glendinning Stanly, who displaces him as heir to the family estate. Rome, N.Y., was laid out on the site of the fort.

76. ALs, Herman Melville to Evert Duyckinck, November 7, 1851, DC, box 43; *Letters*, p. 140–41, and partially in Leyda, I, 431–32, and Metcalf, p. 127.

77. An important commercial venture of the Gansevoorts, a business building completed in 1833 on the site of the original Gansevoort homestead in Albany, was named Stanwix Hall. Alice P. Kenney, *The Gansevoorts of Albany: Dutch Patricians in the Upper Hudson Valley* (Syracuse, N.Y.: Syracuse University Press, 1969), pp. 200–203, and 206. Rogin, pp. 30–31, interprets Stanwix Hall as an assertion of family position.

78. Elizabeth Melville was born at Pittsfield on May 22, 1853, and died in 1908. Sophia Melville's letter to Augusta Melville was written from New York, probably in early June, 1853, G-L Additions, box 2.

79. Frances was born March 2, 1855, at Pittsfield and died in 1938. Helen Melville Griggs' letter to Augusta Melville is dated March 13, 1855, from Longwood, near Boston, the residence of Helen and her husband, George (G-L Additions, box 1). For others with this name, see the genealogy on the flyleaf of Metcalf. For more information, see Appendix C.

80. Kenney, pp. [x-xi] and 9.

81. Kenney, pp. [x-xi] and 98–105.

82. Gilman, pp. 22–24; and Herbert, pp. 32–33.

83. ALs, Allan Melville to Peter Gansevoort, August 10, 1826, Houghton, Document no. MS. Am. 188, item 103; quoted in Leyda, I, 25, and Metcalf, pp. 4–5.

84. Allan Melvill compiled a "Genealogical Tree" that traced the Melvilles back to a thirteenth-century Scottish knight. See Raymond M. Weaver, *Herman Melville: Mariner and Mystic* (New York: George H. Doran, 1921), p. 34. Weaver's second chapter, "Ghosts," is devoted to Melville's illustrious ancestors and the satisfaction the family took in them, and he suggests that Allan Melvill encouraged this pride in his children. But regarding the accuracy of Weaver's information, see Sealts, "The Melvill Heritage," 337–61, especially 338n, which includes the most thorough family tree published to date.

85. The draft is in the G-L Additions, box 1; misdated "1848" by Augusta.

86. This slightly different quotation is from ALs, Augusta Melville to Elizabeth Shaw Melville, January 27, 1849, Houghton, document no. MS. Am. 188, item 124 ; excerpts from it appear in Leyda, I, 286–87.

87. The passage from *Mardi,* presented in the letter in slightly different form, is from (N-N), p. 601.

88. Cowen, I, 593.

89. Allan Melvill described him at age ten to his own father as "a most amiable & innocent child." ALs, Allan Melvill to Thomas Melvill, May 20, 1830, G-L, box 39; quoted in Leyda, I, 43.

90. See Appendix D.

91. *The Piazza Tales* (N-N), pp. 245–46; and *Pierre* (N-N), p. 135.

92. For early evidence of the family favoritism shown Gansevoort, see Henry A. Murray, "Another Triumph for Maria's Firstborn," *Melville Society Extracts,* 58 (May 1984), 1–3, a printing and a discussion of a letter from Maria Melvill to her mother, Mrs. Peter Gansevoort, dated December 28, 1826, in the Berkshire Athenaeum. The letter describes with great pride how the ten-year-old Gansevoort won a crown of evergreens for his recitation at the "annual examination of the Scholars at the high school." In a typical gesture, "the Crown was hung from his Grandfather's Picture to remain untill after the Holidays." The "Picture" was a copy of the Gilbert Stuart portrait of General Peter Gansevoort. For evidence that Melville rankled from the recollection of his subordinate position to his promising brother, see Melville's late poem "Timoleon," which includes a bitter reference to Timoleon's civic crown. For a discussion of "the violent and personal elements of the fratricidal myth" of Cain and Abel, with reference to "Timoleon," *Pierre,* and other works, see Wyn Kelley, "Melville's Cain," *American Literature,* 55 (1983), 25.

93. Robert K. Martin, *Hero, Captain, and Stranger: Male Friendship, Social Critique, and Literary Form in the Sea Novels of Herman Melville* (Chapel Hill: University of North Carolina Press, 1986), p. 28.

94. N-N, p. 67.

95. N-N, p. 90.

96. N-N, pp. 280–81.

97. Cowen, I, 77–81. See, for example, Chap. 24, "The Killing of the Divine King," in the abridged edition of James G. Frazer, *The Golden Bough* (New York: Macmillan, 1922).

98. *Moby-Dick* (N-N), p. 3.

99. ALs, Allan Melvill to Major Thomas Melvill, May 2, 1816 and June 27, 1818, G-L, boxes 29 and 30; cited in Rogin, pp. 23–24.

100. *On Heroes, Hero-Worship and the Heroic in History* (1841), Lecture VI; Sealts, no. 122.

101. Houghton, 85M bMS Am 188.6; quoted in Leyda, I, 26.

Melville's Civil War poem "In the Turret" is an ode to duty. He gave the heroic captain of the *Monitor* these lines:

> "Duty be still my doom,
> Though drowning in liquid gloom;
> First duty, duty next, and duty last;
> Ay, Turret, rivet me here to duty fast!"

See Appendix E.
102. October 17, 1838, G-L Additions, box 1.
103. *Moby-Dick*, (N-N), p. 45.
104. September 16, 1860, Houghton, document no. MS. Am. 188, item 176; *Letters*, p. 203; and partially in Leyda, II, 626.
105. September 2, 1860, Houghton, document no. MS. Am. 188, item 177; *Letters*, pp. 204–5; Metcalf, p. 188; and partially in Leyda, II, 625.
106. Gardner was a member of the Duyckinck circle and a contributor to the *Literary World*. He specialized in gynecology, mental diseases, and child rearing, publishing widely on these as well as on literary subjects. He gave Melville a copy of his *Old Wine in New Bottles; or, The Spare Hours of a Student in Paris* (New York: C. S. Francis & Co., 1848), Sealts, no. 222, and advice on where to stay and what to do in that city. When Melville returned, he sent Gardner a set of *Redburn* (ALs, Herman Melville to Augustus K. Gardner, February 4[?], 1850, Essex Institute; *Letters*, p. 105; *Journal . . . London*, pp. xix, 138, 172–73). For his authoritarian attitudes toward women and children, see G. J. Barker-Benfield, *The Horrors of the Half-Known Life: Male Attitudes toward Women and Sexuality in Nineteenth-Century America* (New York: Harper & Row, 1976), in which Gardner figures prominently and Melville is often mentioned. Melville was indebted to *Old Wine in New Bottles* for details of the Parisian episode in *Israel Potter* and Surgeon Cuticle in *White-Jacket*. Gardner also seems a presence behind the obstetrical and masturbatory references in *Moby-Dick*. In his reticent way, Leon Howard describes him as "perhaps the most stimulating of all the young author's acquaintances at the time," in part for his "store of curious information" (p. 110).

Gardner thought of children in terms of animals that must be lashed into obedience, and this was the business of men. In *Old Wine in New Bottles*, he writes:

> In the *punishment of misbehavior*, I think the French are not severe enough. One thorough correction . . . is more effective than many slight ones. . . . The lower animals afford illustrations of the same principle. A horse soon becomes insensible to perpetual slight cuts of the whip, especially when administered with the characteristic gentleness of lady equestrians, whose most efficient *lashes* are those of their eyes. [p. 225]

In a letter to his brother Thomas, Melville jokes "about spareing [*sic*] the strap & spoiling the child" and quotes his adaptation of a facetious passage from Byron's *Don Juan* (Canto II, ll.1–4) on the merits of chastising the young (ALs, Herman Melville to Thomas Melville, May 25, 1862, Houghton, document no. MS. Am. 188, item 180; *Letters*, pp. 213–15; Leyda, II, 652). Within the context of Gardner's opinions on child rearing, which Melville must have taken seriously, this does not amuse.

In *Omoo* Melville grudgingly approves the use of the whip in the Navy to discipline unruly ship's boys: "The boy becomes, in time, a thorough-bred tar, equally ready to strip and take a dozen on board his own ship, or, cutlass in hand . . . board the enemy's" (N-N, pp. 108–9.) But note his use of the word *boy.*

Yet Melville's opposition to flogging, most evident in *White-Jacket* but present elsewhere (for example, "The House-Top," [1866], "Bridegroom Dick" [1891]), is well known. The distinction in his mind appears to be that whipping is an appropriate means with which to discipline children because children are lesser beings, but it dehumanizes adults because it reduces them to the level of children, slaves, and animals.

Dr. Gardner was called in when Malcolm killed himself.

There is a further complication: Gardner's theories on the discipline of children and Melville's actual treatment of Malcolm. He may have spared the whip, but he applied the threat of shame and the reward love merited. Melville's own schooling lies somewhere in the background. In 1825, at the age of seven, he was enrolled in the New York Male High School, where he was a student until 1829. The school followed the Lancastrian method of instruction, employing more advanced students as monitors and rewarding performance. The system was hierarchical, sought "to instill obedience to authority," and "utilized public shame" rather than corporal punishment to instill discipline. Henry A. Murray and Eugene Taylor, "The Lancastrian System of Instruction," *Melville Society Extracts*, 69 (February 1987), 6.

107. (N-N), p. 171.

108. March 21, 1863, G-L Additions, box 1.

109. April 24, 1862, G-L Additions, box 1.

110. Contract, Peter Gansevoort to Henry Sanford Gansevoort, December 4, 1851, G-L, box 32; quoted in Kenney, p. 229. Neither the New York Public Library staff, the late Alice B. Kenney, nor we were able to locate the manuscript. For a more conventional legal contract between Henry Sanford Gansevoort and his father, Peter, see Appendix F.

111. ALs, Catherine Gansevoort to Henry Sanford Gansevoort, September 16, 1867, G-L, box 161, Henry Sanford Gansevoort/Letterbooks 1866–67; quoted in part in Leyda, II, 691.

112. See Appendix G.

113. City of New York, Municipal Archives and Records Center. We are indebted to Edwin S. Shneidman, M.D., for this information and a photocopy of the document. See also Leyda, II, 688, for a slightly different report, also in the City of New York, Municipal Archives and Records Center.

114. ALs, Samuel S. Shaw to Hope Savage Shaw, September 12, 1867, Houghton, document no. MS. Am. 188, item 326; quoted in Leyda, II, 687–88.

115. Both Leon Howard in his carefully factual *Herman Melville: A Biography* (Berkeley: University of California Press, 1951) and Edwin Haviland Miller in his psychoanalytically oriented study *Melville* (New York: George Braziller, 1975) are silent on this subject. So is Edwin S. Shneidman, "Some Psychological Reflections on the Death of Malcolm Melville," *Suicide and Life-Threatening Behavior*, 6 (1976), 231–42, who is concerned with the "mode" of Malcolm's death and focuses on psychological rather than physical facts. An-

other odd psychological fact is that a family not only psychically close-knit but physically in close proximity to each other, and, presumably, to the scene of the tragedy, heard nothing.

116. We have been unable to retrieve any of Malcolm's military records. According to Roger Ritzmann of the New York State Archives, Albany, the service records for 1866–68 have been lost. Conversation with Donald Yannella, August 1, 1991. However, written on the back of the watercolor of Malcolm in uniform (see frontispiece) are notations which indicate that he was a member of "Company B 2nd [22nd?] Regt. of Infantry/ First Brigade,/ N[ew] Y[ork] S[tate] N[ational] G[uard]." Eleanor Melville Metcalf states that Malcolm was "a member of the New York Twenty-second Regiment of the National Guard." *Herman Melville: Cycle and Epicycle* (Cambridge, Mass.: Harvard University Press, 1953), p. 208. We do not know her source.

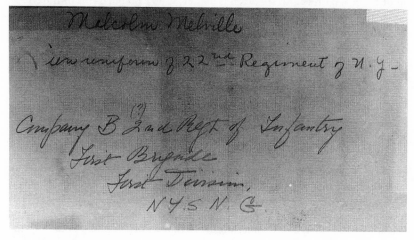

117. Leyda, II, 688.

118. Leyda, II, 690. Evert A. Duyckinck, who had known William Cullen Bryant from at least as early as the 1840s, had written reviews for the *Post* then, and was later to collaborate with him on an edition of Shakespeare, may have been helpful to the Melvilles here.

119. ALs, Samuel S. Shaw to Hope Savage Shaw, September 12, 1867, Houghton, document no. MS. Am. 188, item 326; quoted in Leyda, II, 688.

120. *Boston Weekly Advertiser*, September 18, 1867, p. 5; quoted in part in Leyda, II, 691.

121. "*Self murder* or *felo de se*, is not noticed in the revised statures [*sic*], except so far as it affects third persons"—that is, those who assist the suicide. Nevertheless, the following qualification helps one understand the stigma the Melvilles felt: in such a case "the person killed is not looked upon as *felo de se*, inasmuch as his assent was merely void, being against the laws of God and man." Oliver Lorenzo Barbour, *Treatise on the Criminal Law of the State of New-*

*York; and upon the Jurisdiction, Duty and Authority of Justices of the Peace, and Incidentally, of the Power and Duty of Sheriffs, Constables, &c. in Criminal Cases,* 2nd ed. (Albany: Gould, Banks, and New York: Banks, Gould, 1852), pp. 31–32. Perhaps the question for the family was more moral or emotional than legal.

In July 1870 Melville bought a copy of Henry Crabb Robinson, *Diary, Reminiscences, and Correspondence* . . . (Boston: Fields, Osgood, 1869), which reprints a defense of suicide addressed "To the Coroner and Gentlemen who will Sit on my Body" by Elton Hamond. Sealts, no. 428. Melville drew a double line in the margin beside the opening paragraph, which begins: "Gentlemen,—To the charge of self-murder I plead not guilty. For there is no guilt in what I have done. Self-murder is a contradiction in terms. If the king who retires from his throne is guilty of high treason; if the man who takes money out of his own coffers and spends it is a thief; if he who burns his own hayrick is guilty of arson; or he who scourges himself of assault and battery, then he who throws up his own life may be guilty of murder, if not, not" (Cowen, II, 273). The year following he bought Matthew Arnold's *New Poems* (1867) in which he marked extensively "Empedocles on Etna," another justification of suicide provoked by despair. Sealts, no. 20, and Cowen, I, 68–69. Melville also owned a set of George Cruikshank's prints, *The Drunkard's Children* (1848). Plate 8 shows the "Self Murder" of the drunkard's daughter. It is reproduced in Robert K. Wallace, "Melville's Prints and Engravings at the Berkshire Athenaeum," *Essays in Arts and Sciences,* 15 (June 1986), fig. 14.

122. ALs, Peter Gansevoort to Thomas Melvill, Jr., January 10, 1832, G-L, box 311; quoted in Leyda, I, 51. Allan Melvill, Sr. "presents the melancholy spectacle of a deranged man —."

ALs, Gansevoort Melville to Herman Melville, April 3, 1846, Houghton, document no. MS. Am. 188, item 163; quoted in Leyda, I, 208–9 and in Metcalf, pp. 34–35: ". . . I sometimes fear that I am gradually breaking up. . . . I think I am growing phlegmatic & cold. Man stirs me not, nor woman either. . . . A degree of insensibility has been long stealing over me, & now seems permanently established." Louis McClane, who headed the American legation in London, reported in an ALs to James Buchanan, then Secretary of State, that on May 4, 1846, Gansevoort Melville was suffering from a "disorder in some degree connected with the brain, and in a state of nervous derangement, which if it should now come would not surprise me." Correspondence of James Buchanan, Historical Society of Pennsylvania, Philadelphia, in Leyda, I, 213. For McClane's animosity toward Gansevoort Melville and their political differences, see *Gansevoort Melville's 1846 Journal,* ed. Hershel Parker (New York: New York Public Library, 1966), pp. 12–14.

ALs, Samuel Shaw to Henry Whitney Bellows, May 6, 1867, Henry Whitney Bellows Papers, MHS, [box for] 1867, April-December: "I think that the safest course is to let her [Lizzie's] real position become apparent from the first, namely that of a wife, who, being convinced that her husband is insane *acts* as if she were so convinced and applies for aid and assistance to her friends and acts *with* them"—quoted in Walter D. Kring and Jonathan S. Carey, "Two Discoveries Concerning Herman Melville," *Proceedings of the Massachusetts Historical Society*, 87 (1975), 140; rpt., *The Endless, Winding Way in Melville: New Charts by Kring and Carey*, ed. Donald Yannella and Hershel Parker (Glassboro, N.J.: The Melville Society, 1981). The Rev. Dr. Bellows was the minister of All Souls Unitarian Church, New York, with which Elizabeth Melville was affiliated. She sought his advice at a time of marital "griefs" (Kring and Carey, p. 141). He baptized Malcolm.

ALs, Maria Gansevoort Melville to Augusta Melville, November 5, 1851, G-L Additions, box 1: "Lizzie [shortly after the birth of Stanwix] is not so well. . . . She is very nervous being constitutionally so, and now being so weak, with loss of appetite, that a sheet had to be placed on the wall to cover the paper the figures of which seem'd to her in motion[.]"

In every case, further evidence might be adduced.

123. See Appendix F.

124. See note 111.

125. See Appendix I.

126. These are the Gansevoort-Lansing Papers, deposited at the New York Public Library. See Appendix I.

127. See Appendix J.

128. For example, she wanted to visit her family in Boston but was afraid "to leave home again without someone here to over look things" since she could not trust her husband to manage the household and control the "goings-on" of the boys. ALs, Elizabeth Melville to Augusta Melville, February 11, 1863, and March 4, 1863, G-L, box 216.

129. See Neal L. Tolchin, *Mourning, Gender, and Creativity in the Art of Herman Melville* (New Haven and London: Yale University Press, 1988), pp. xi–xii, and, for the examples of Queen Victoria and Maria Gansevoort Melville as representative Victorian mourners, pp. 12–13. See Appendix K.

130. See Appendix L.

131. Barbara Ehrenreich, *Fear of Falling: The Inner Life of the Middle Class* (New York: Pantheon, 1989), passim.

132. The disastrous climax of Allan Melvill's business career is summarized in Herbert, pp. 45–53. He was a silent partner in a business venture. Herbert clarifies the moral issues:

> Since his associates had no source of money apart from himself, Allan's signature on their notes would create an illusion of greater financial substance than the firm really enjoyed. This deceit would permit his associates to secure an extra degree of the credit so necessary to the speculations of a jobbing firm. But since Allan himself had to borrow [from Peter Gansevoort, his brother-in-law] what real funds were available to back the venture, he was moving into a position that was financially vulnerable as well as morally untenable. [pp. 48–49]

Rogin, pp. 23–31, has valuable information on the commercial context in which Allan conducted his business affairs and details on his questionable operations.

For information on the case of the illegitimate daughter, see Emmers, pp. 339–41. The discovery of the letter indicating that Allan Melvill had an illegitimate daughter was made but not used by Charles Olson. He gave a transcript of the letter to Henry A. Murray, who, with Eugene Taylor and Harvey Myerson, published "Allan Melvill's By-Blow," in *Melville Society Extracts*, 61 (February 1985), 1–6. It identifies the daughter and is the fullest account of the case available. The letter was first published, with a comment associating it with *Pierre*, by Emmers, pp. 339–43. For further information on Melville's half sister, see Philip Young, "Small World: Emerson, Longfellow, and Melville's Secret Sister," *New England Quarterly*, 60 (September 1987), 382–402. Harrison Hayford, at Melville symposia (NYPL and University of California, 1991), argued that the case of the illegitimate daughter lacks incontrovertible proof. See *Melville Society Extracts*, 87 (November 1991), 9, 11. Family secrets were indeed well preserved, as is apparent from the fact that the existence of Allan Melvill's illegitimate daughter and Herman Melville's "unhappy marriage" (see note 148) and his emotional crackup did not become common knowledge until recently.

Eleanor Melville Metcalf, Herman Melville's granddaughter, reflects family tradition and protective attitudes regarding *Pierre* and its author: "Here is a sick man writing of some matters known to be true, some entirely untrue, combined in such a way that the family feared its members and their friends might assume all to be true—that is, factual." Mrs. Metcalf then raises a question that apparently disturbed the family: Would outsiders "be able to separate fact from invention?" Metcalf, p. 135. There is little evidence Melville was ill physically or mentally at the time, according to Leon Howard, "Historical Note," *Pierre* (N-N), p. 391.

133. *Moby-Dick* (N-N), p. 573; *Billy Budd*, p. 52.

134. Stanton Garner, "The Picaresque Career of Thomas Melvill, Junior," *Melville Society Extracts*, 60 (November 1984), 1–10; and *Melville Society Extracts*, 62 (May 1985), 1, 4–10. See also G. Thomas Tanselle, "Herman Melville's Visit to Galena in 1840," *Journal of the Illinois Historical Society*, 53 (1960), 376–88, esp. p. 384 for "the story that Thomas was mixed up in a scandal. . . . there was something strange about his position in the town that cannot be explained but which must have been the basis for the stories still current." Melville's memoir was titled "Sketch of Major Thomas Melville [*sic*] by a Nephew." A transcription based on a manuscript copy in G-L is reprinted in Merton M. Sealts, Jr., "Thomas Melvill, Jr., in *The History of Pittsfield*," *Harvard Library Bulletin*, 35 (Spring 1987), 208–16. Elizabeth S. Foster in a note to her edition of *The Confidence-Man* (New York: Hendricks House, 1954) suggests that Melville's sketch "recalls the language and to some extent the theme of his story of China Aster" who was, quoting from the sketch, "betrayed by a false friend—Hope by name . . ." (p. 360).

135. "To Tom," and "To the Master of the 'Meteor,' " *Collected Poems*, pp. 407 and 196.

136. ALs, Catherine Gansevoort to Peter and Susan Gansevoort, June 10, 1874, G-L, box 219; quoted in Leyda, II, 737. A curious coincidence: *Harper's*

*Magazine* published a laudatory article on Snug Harbor and its Governor in January 1873.

137. See J. J. Boies, "Melville's Staten Island 'Paradise,' " *Staten Island Historian*, 27 (July-September 1966), 24–28. For further details regarding the troubles of Captain Thomas Melville, see *Sailors' Snug Harbor: Investigation into Charges Preferred against the Officers & Management* (New York: Slote and Jones, 1883). A speculation: Was the name *Tommo*, in *Typee*, suggested by one of the Thomas Melvill(e)s who were to sully their name?

138. Cowen, I, 68. For suicide and Arnold's "Empedocles on Etna," see note 121.

139. *Moby-Dick*, (N-N), p. 117.

140. Cowen, II, 475.

141. *Billy Budd*, p. 55.

142. *Piazza Tales* (N-N), pp. 369 and 376.

143. *Literary World*, August 21, 1852, pp. 118–20. For the description of Pierre's dilemma, the review utilizes Melville's language and otherwise follows his text closely. See (N-N), p. 171.

144. *A Backward Glance* (New York and London: D. Appleton, 1934), p. 68. Rensselaer, not Rensslaer, would be the correct spelling. The term *bohemian* was originally applied to Gypsies and later to "one . . . cut off from society for which he is otherwise fitted" (*OED*).

145. Lieutenant Guert Gansevoort had a crucial part in suppressing the notorious mutiny aboard the United States Brig *Somers* in 1842, an important source for *Billy Budd*. He was suspended from his command in 1856 for being intoxicated (Leyda, II, 522). In "Bridegroom Dick" (1891), Melville refers to him as "Tom Tight," a punning name that alludes to his drinking and his secretiveness regarding the *Somers* affair. A poem of nautical recollection, it lauds Lieutenant Gansevoort for being "True to himself and loyal to his clan." He was a captain when he retired in 1867 and died a year later. See *Letters*, p. 215n.2.

146. Stanton Garner, "Melville in the Custom House, 1881–1882: A Rustic Beauty among the Highborn Dames of Court," *Melville Society Extracts*, 35 (September 1978), 12–14.

147. Cowen, I, 625.

148. For information on Melville's state of mind and on his marital difficulties, and for the reflections by Melville scholars on pertinent letters they discovered, see Kring and Carey, pp. 139–41. Harrison Hayford summarizes: "Certainly this view of 'an unhappy marriage' was a family tradition passed on, plainly enough, by Mrs. Metcalf to Weaver, Murray, Mumford and later inquirers" (*Melville's "Monody": Really for Hawthorne?* [Evanston, Ill.: Northwestern University Press, 1990], p.14). See also Metcalf's refutation of Weaver's statement "that Melville was happily married" (quoted from his personal notes in Hershel Parker, *Reading Billy Budd* [Evanston, Ill.: Northwestern University Press, 1990], p. 45). ALs, Herman Melville to John C. Hoadley, March 31, 1877, Melville Family Papers, box 310; in *Letters*, p. 260, and Metcalf, p. 250. See also Cowen, I, xxi, 286–87, 617, and 625.

149. Sealts, no. 17; and Cowen, I, 27 and 30.

150. ALs, June 14, 1825; quoted in Rogin, pp. 33, 322n57. No doubt Peter Gansevoort was gratified by the respect paid his father when Lafayette was in Albany. The Albany *Commercial Advertiser* of August 21, 1824, reported that the Senate Chamber of the state capitol, decorated for his reception, featured "the standard of Brigadier General Gansevoort's Regt. of N. Y. Militia" that had "waived [sic] in triumph at Yorktown, when that regiment was under the command of Fayette"(quoted in Edgar Ewing Brandon, *Lafayette: Guest of the Nation* [Oxford, Ohio: Oxford Historical Press, 1950], I, 241). See also Sealts, "Thomas Melvill, Jr.," p. 214.

151. Henry Gansevoort betrays the ambivalence of the American who wishes to be both patrician and democrat. In this he is closer to Allan Melville.

152. ALs, Henry Sanford Gansevoort to Catherine Gansevoort, June 30, 1867, G-L, box 23; quoted in Kenney, pp. 250–51.

153. *A Defense of an Order of the Court Made in the Year 1637*; quoted in Alan Heimert and Andrew Delbanco, *The Puritans in America* (Cambridge: Harvard University Press, 1985), p. 166.

154. The concept of the family as a source of social "stability" and hence "A foundation of Govt.," enunciated by Henry Gansevoort, is cogently analyzed and placed in a historical perspective by Lawrence Stone in *The Family, Sex and Marriage, 1500–1800* (New York: Harper & Row, 1979), the abridged edition of his much longer work. Among the relevant ideas he discusses are the family as a microcosm of the state and the prevalence of the authoritarian head of the family during periods of social, political, and religious change. Stone emphasizes that the "pursuit of individual happiness" is a "modern preconception" (p. 70), that alternations between periods of patriarchal absolutism and personal autonomy are the rule, and that important exceptions due to class, locale, economic interest, religious persuasion, and other causes are common. Thus, the pursuit of happiness in the mid-eighteenth century was followed by revival of patriarchy in the Victorian period and its subsequent decline (pp. 421–22). This gave way, in turn, to "affective individualism in the twentieth century" (pp. 424–25). The Melville-Gansevoorts had their own reasons for adhering to an authoritarian pattern. Still, they were within the Victorian convention, which, by the time of Henry Gansevoort's letter, was eroding rapidly.

155. For a possible allusion to their marital crisis of May 1867 and reconciliation following Malcolm's death, see Appendix H, note 33.

156. Weeds and wildings with a rose or two, Houghton, MS. Am. 188, item 369.1.5.

157. Walter E. Bezanson, "Melville's Reading of Arnold's Poetry," *PMLA*, 69 (June 1954), 379–80. Sealts, nos. 503a, 504, and 505. See also Harrison Hayford, *Melville's "Monody."*

158. December 13, 1856, *Journals* (N-N), p. 60. Melville spelled the word "sherbert" and also "sherbet."

159. ALs, Herman Melville to Elizabeth Melville (daughter), September 2, 1860, Houghton, document no. MS. Am. 188, item 177; quoted in Metcalf, p. 188; *Letters*, p. 204; and Leyda, II, 625.

160. ALs, Herman Melville to Evert A. Duyckinck, February 1 [?], 1862, DC, box 43; *Letters*, p. 213; and Metcalf, pp. 196–97. In 1873 Melville acquired a copy of *Songs from the Dramatists* . . . (London: Parker, 1854), which reprints the Webster dirge. Sealts, no. 56. He put a check in the margin beside the opening line. Cowen, I, 252.

161.

> "Ah, whither gone?"
> Clarel, and bowed him there and kneeled:
> "Whither art gone? thou friendliest mind
> Unfriended—what friend now shalt find?
> Robin or raven, hath God a bird
> To come and strew thee, lone interred
> With leaves, when here left far behind?"
> ["Obsequies," II, xxxix, 60–66.]

162. See note 121 on self-murder and Hamond's statement.

163. *English and Scottish Ballads*, ed. Francis James Child (Boston: Little, Brown, 1854–57), III, 129. Sealts, no. 143.

164. *Reliques of Ancient English Poetry*, ed. Henry B. Wheatley (London: Bickers & Son, 1877), III, 169–76. See *Brewer's Dictionary of Phrase and Fable* (New York and Evanston: Harper & Row, 1965), p. 199, for its popularity and literary influence.

165. William Bysshe Stein, in *The Poetry of Melville's Late Years: Time, History, Myth, and Religion* (Albany: State University of New York Press, 1970) suggests that "The Chipmunk" was "written for a child as an explanation for the death of another member of the family" (p. 173). William H. Shurr, in *The Mystery of Iniquity: Melville as Poet, 1857–1891* (Lexington: University of Kentucky Press, 1972), notes astutely that its "meaning and all the emotional drama are compressed into the short parenthesis" (p. 188): "(and whither?)." See " 'Ah, whither gone?' . . . 'Whither art gone?['] " (*Clarel*, II, XXXIX, 60–62); quoted in note 161. The replies to Clarel's questions are inconclusive. See also the phrase "Gone whither?"—a lament for the once "new / And primal" Greek isles remembered in the late poem "The Archipelago."

166. Shneidman, 231–42. This paper describes a "psychological autopsy" that sought to determine the "mode of death" of Malcolm Melville. The judgment arrived at was "probable suicide." Shneidman argues "that Herman Melville himself had been a psychologically 'battered child' and, in a way typical for battered children, psychologically battered his own children when it came to be his turn to be a parent." Though Shneidman employs the terms of another discipline, they seem quite appropriate to the emphasis of this essay on the force of the inherited child-rearing practices of the Melville-Gansevoorts. Like father, like son.

Shneidman reports that at a meeting in preparation for the "psychological autopsy" Henry A. Murray "talked about Melville's children's terror of their father and the apparent absence of love in the home" (p. 237).

167. Nor does Pierre in a parallel situation, since his father's sins are posthumously discovered.

168. *Billy Budd*, p. 99.

169. *Billy Budd*, pp. 44 and 70.

170. Glendinning was originally a place name in Westerwick, Dumfries-shire (George F. Black, *The Surnames of Scotland* [New York: New York Public Library, 1946], p. 313). Henry A. Murray notes that the name might have been taken from Scott's *The Monastery* and *The Abbot* which Melville must have read (notes on *Pierre* [New York: Hendricks House, 1962], p. 431), a further Scottish dimension.

Isabel tells Pierre about the handkerchief left behind by a "good gentle-man" on which she "found a small line of fine faded yellowish writing" with "the talismanic word—Glendinning." She puzzles it out, "Glen-din-ning;—just as many syllables as *gentleman;* and—G—it begins with the same letter; yes, it must mean *my father*" (*Pierre*, N-N, p. 146–47). *Gansevoort* has the same initial sound and the same number of syllables as Glendinning, and significantly for both surnames, as *gentleman*. See Othello's allusions to the magical and pro-phetic qualities of his fatal handkerchief (*Othello*, III, iv, 50–69) and his state-ment "Sure, there's some wonder in this handkerchief . . ." (III, iv, 101).

171. For a family response to *Pierre* as fact and fiction, see Mrs. Metcalf's comments in note 132.

172. (N-N), p. 68. Or rather, by the weight of family epitomized in the fathers. In any event, patriarchy crushes Pierre.

173. The death of Pierre's father has removed him in any literal sense as Pierre's Oedipal rival, though his living memory continues to haunt Pierre. In a ritual of immolation just prior to his elopement with Isabel, he burns family letters and his father's portrait, exclaiming: "Henceforth, cast-out Pi-erre hath no paternity, and no past" (N-N, p. 199). For another view of incest, parricide, and the Oedipal factor, see Eric J. Sundquist, *Home As Found: Au-thority and Genealogy in Nineteenth-Century American Literature* (Baltimore: Johns Hopkins University Press, 1979), pp. 143–85.

174. (N-N), p. 68.

175. *Pierre*, (N-N), p. 360. On breast feeding, see note 44.

176. (N-N), p. 192.

177. (N-N), p. 347.

178. (N-N), pp. 346–47.

179. *American Whig Review*, 16 (November 1852), 446–54. See especially pp. 446, 448–49. The review is unsigned. An unidentified reviewer for the *Literary World*, 11 (August 21, 1852), 118–20, edited by his friends, the Duyck-inck brothers, among others, expressed equal outrage in less forthright terms: "We cannot pass without remark, the supersensuousness with which the holy relations of the family are described. Mother and son, brother and sister are sacred facts. . . . in what we have termed the supersensuousness of description, the horrors of an incestuous relation between Pierre and Isabel seem to be vaguely hinted at." Both reviews, and others, asserted that Melville must have lost his mind.

180. The compelling force of the "most touching, but most awful of all feminine heads," Guido Reni's portrait of Beatrice Cenci, described at length by Melville's narrator in the last book of *Pierre*, originates in the artist's success in capturing the effect of her history in her countenance. It included her

notorious involvement in "the two most horrible crimes . . . possible to civilized humanity—incest and parricide" (N-N, p. 351). See also note 173.

181. Quoted from Weaver, p. 360.

182. Gifford and Edwin Booth were friends and moved in the same artistic circles. Mrs. Thomas Bailey Aldrich remembers a gathering in the studio of Launt Thompson, the sculptor, about 1864 that included Edwin Booth, his brothers Junius and John Wilkes, Albert Bierstadt, and Gifford. She records Booth's remark to the two landscape painters, "that they must lose all sense of being save in the painted ripple of a lake, or the peaks of a snow-capped mountain." *Crowding Memories* (Boston and New York: Houghton Mifflin, 1920), pp. 56–57.

183. See "The Coming Storm," line 11, "The Hamlet in his heart was ware" and Emerson's comment that "Shakespeare . . . can tell nothing except to the Shakespeare in us." *Representative Men: Seven Lectures* (Boston: Phillips, Sampson, 1850), p. 205. Sealts, no. 206a.

184. (N-N), p. 168.

185. (N-N), p. 169.

186. (N-N), p. 169.

# Appendix A
# Malcolm: "A Beautiful Boy . . . Perfect & Healthy"

TO COMPOSE A SKETCH OF MELVILLE'S SON MALCOLM, the biographer of Melville and his family must piece together remnants. In the main essay we attempted to achieve a richly layered and suggestive statement. But hard information for even an *outer life* of Malcolm is sparse. We offer here, then, some of the more vivid fragments of his portrait and we suggest its cloudy background. They are essentially the lines, shapes, and colors of its surface.

Melville's elation about Malcolm's birth early in February 1849 was shared by the rest of the family, especially by his baby's paternal great uncle, Peter Gansevoort, and his maternal grandfather, Lemuel Shaw. Writing to Judge Shaw six weeks later, Uncle Peter conveyed his and his family's "best love to Elizabeth & Herman & kisses for the young stranger; . . . & sincerely hop[ed] that the young gentleman may prove a source of real comfort & happiness to all the family—particularly to his parents & grandparents[.]" About two weeks later, on April 11, Judge Shaw responded, describing the infant as "a beautiful boy, about eight weeks old, apparently perfect & healthy in all his senses & faculties, & as far as countenance can indicate, bright & intelligent." And he, too, asserted the virtual obligation of the little prodigy to "be a source of comfort to [his parents] & to all his connections."[1] Both family patriarchs welcomed the new heir; both had high expectations for him. His mother reported to Hope Shaw on the last day of April that he was "very well, and improving daily in size and intelligence. . . . he is a great pet in the house [103 Fourth Avenue, New York City], and behaves himself as a prince should do."[2] The child's deportment was critical to her as well, even at that age. In September 1849, as Herman prepared for his trip to England and the Continent, his sister Augusta replied in kind to a witty letter from the Judge. Adopting tones of mock humility, her pseudolegal response, signed by the new parents and others in the crowded household, certified "that the debt to which the Chief Justice stands creditor, has been cancelled by the payment of thirty five good and substantial kisses, satisfied, imposed upon, and delivered to one Malcolm ↑ Melville ↓ " who was to be baptized a Unitarian, in the Shaws' church, on the last day of the month.[3] The child was firmly and lovingly established in the bosom of the family.

Before the end of the year we have a relatively detailed report on Malcolm (as well as his cousin and contemporary, Allan's daughter) and life generally at 103 Fourth Avenue. Writing to her Aunt Susan Gansevoort on November 20, 1849, as one of the house full of Melvilles in which Malcolm lived the first years of his life, Fanny Melville begins her letter by summarizing the events of the two weeks she had been in Lansingburgh, a "most delightful visit," and apologizing for having visited her only once, despite the fact that Albany is such a short distance from Lansingburgh. But our interest centers on the report she offers about life in New York City. Her description is useful not only for what it reveals of the infant Malcolm's progress, but for what it says about the nurturing atmosphere in the home: "We found the family all very well, and almost <one or part of one deleted word> smothered the babies alive with kisses, we were so glad to see them, they have grown a great deal I think, Malcolm particularly, what a great big boy he is." But she knew the joy of the child's presence was soon to be missed: "I don't know what we will do without him this winter; Lemuel Shaw is here now, and they will leave for Boston early Thursday morning[.] Lizzie is very busy getting ready to go, how we shall miss them all, we shall really feel lonely."[4]

Family pride and concern did not abate. Augusta reported to Hope Shaw in the first week of 1851, shortly before the boy's second birthday: "A nobler little fellow, I feel very confident, Boston can not boast."[5] By September 1852, not yet four years old, he was able to lift "three barrels of potatoes,—David [Herman's and Lizzie's servant boy], is a particular *friend of his*—He is training Malcolm & the old lady (Mrs Melville) is educating David."[6] There was little coddling and the demands for propriety were always there to balance the pride and warmth of the family. The Judge, for example, reported to his son Lemuel that "The four children are, or it appears to me, greatly improved, in appearance and conduct."[7] Behavior anything less than the best would not be countenanced, must be corrected— not only that of the now nine-year-old Malcolm, but of seven-year-old Stanwix, five-year-old Elizabeth, and three-year-old Frances.

Such expectations were integral to the family fabric, though balanced by affection and playfulness. For instance, Hope Shaw wrote her son Lemuel from Arrowhead in September 1855 that the Judge, then seventy-four, was "making a kite for Malcolm today—I cannot imagine, it will be like the one for twenty years to my knowledge he has been wishing to make—as it would be larger than Lizzie & her four children all together."[8] At this point in Melville's life there is little if any evidence to suggest alienation from Barney, as he then called Malcolm, or the other children, beyond the ordinary stress and strain of domestic life.

Consider Herman's relationship with Malcolm during the child's first year. In mid-October Melville departed for England and the Continent on what was to be a trip lasting slightly more than four months. In the eighty-five small pages of the travel journal his granddaughter was to edit and publish, he mentions young Malcolm—Barney,[9] as he consistently refers to him—almost ten times, recording what were evidently among his first words, "Where dat ole man?" three times, once adding to it, "Where books?" his homesickness and yearning for Lizzie some half dozen times; his purchase of a fork for his son—this to help ease him into the manly sport of dining? his pleasure at the boy's being described to him as a bouncer; and his enjoyment in sending or receiving at least seven letters to and from Lizzie, and other family members.[10] He even turns down an invitation from his distant kinsman, "The Duke of Rutland . . . to

visit Belvoir Castle. . . . Can not go—I am homeward-bound, &
Malcolm is growing all the time."[11] Most of these allusions appear as non sequiturs, arising in Melville's mind as he jots notes
and impressions about his business concerns and travels.
Three-and-a-half thousand miles and the recession of time did
not lessen Melville's sense of marital or paternal affection and
responsibility.

Which makes it all the more remarkable that some biographers (Edwin Haviland Miller, for instance) paint so unrelent-
ingly grim a portrait of Melville as husband and father.[12]

Still an only child and hence the focus of special concern,
Malcolm was reported to be suffering an illness in late 1850,
which resulted in "lameness,"[13] but by the beginning of the new
year, 1851, when *Moby-Dick* would be published, his Aunt Augusta described him as "wonderfully improved."[14] He appears
to have been healthy for the most part.

His formal schooling commenced in the late summer of
1853, when his mother wrote Judge Shaw that he "made his
debut as a scholar at the white school-house by Dr. [Oliver Wen-
dell] Holmes'—I was afraid he would lose the little that he already know[s] 'of letters,' and as I could not find the time to
give him regular instruction, I sent him to school rather earlier
than I should have done otherwise." Joining a troop of neigh-
borhood children, his lunch pail in one hand, his book in the
other, "The grand feature of the day to him seem[ed] to be the
'eating his dinner under the trees.' "[15] Shortly before his tenth
birthday, Malcolm himself wrote his cousin Maria, Allan's
daughter, two days his junior, and told her of studying "arithmetic, with cyphering, geography, spelling and reading, and
every Friday we have to speak a piece." He went on to describe
childhood frolics in the Berkshire snow and ice and "reading
the Rollo Books all through" and "the Aimwell stories," as well
as "the Childs Paper every month," a gift from Aunt Augusta.[16]
By May 1862 Herman wrote his brother Tom that Malcolm
was "studying Latin——'Hic—haec—hoc'—'horum, horum,
horum,' he goes it every night."[17]

But the school in Pittsfield was not adequate, perhaps a major
reason for the Melville's return to New York City.[18] The two
boys were sent to boarding school, Malcolm to one in Newton

Center near Boston—and the Shaws. How long he remained there is not clear. But there was to be no college for him as far as we know. Malcolm's higher education, like his father's, was to be gained through practical experience. By March 6, 1866, his grandmother Maria was able to report to her niece, Catherine Gansevoort, that "Malcolm has a fine position in the Great Western Marine Insurance Co," earning "$200 a year" at age seventeen. (His father had just begun at the Custom House at a salary of about $1,000 a year.) Its president, Melville's longtime friend and distant relative, was Richard Lathers, in Maria's view "an active industrious man—Prompt, energetic, & Just the Man for Malcolm or any other boy."[19] Malcolm was employed at the Great Western when he committed suicide.

Anyone studying the Melville family soon encounters the gaps in the available record. The family burned letters, obscured unpleasant details, kept private what it deemed inappropriate for outsiders to know. This is a condition of research for Melville scholars. Nevertheless, we should consider what evidence we have about Malcolm's boyhood and his relations with the family, for it is all we know of his outer life. The picture, at least on its surface, had its pleasant side, as a few instances will show.

In September 1855 he joined his mother, Sarah Morewood, and Aunt Augusta, among others, in a "fancy dress pic nic" near Melvill Lake, appearing "as Jack the Giant Killer, with sword and buckler [and] marched about bravely, bearing on his belt the inscription, 'I am the gallant Cornishman / Who slew the giant Cormogan.' "[20] And he was a frequent visitor in Boston[21] and Gansevoort, New York. In the summer of 1864, for example, he, his brother, and his father visited Gansevoort, and the boys ended up staying fully eight weeks, about six more than planned.[22] Writing to her niece Kate in August 1864, Maria reported that John Hoadley as well as Herman and some of the family had joined them: "M$^r$ Hoadley left us this morning for Boston, after a weeks sojourn. Herman, Augusta, & Hermans two boys, Malcolm & Stanwix, also took the car's [sic] for Glens Falls to spend the day."[23] So their little excursion extended beyond the homestead. Nor were Lizzie and the two girls left behind, as Maria informed Kate in another letter early the next month: "Lizzie will leave us on Friday next with her four children for New York."[24]

In her letter to Kate, Grandmother Maria offered a spirited account of Malcolm struggling through the crowd at a revival to see "a woman it was said 'got religion' she lay on her back . . . with hands upraised & screaming with all her might."[25] The camp meeting, attended by some thousand fashionably dressed folk, was held on grounds owned by Uncle Peter, the father of Maria's correspondent, Catherine Gansevoort. In September 1865 the Melville boys vacationed together, visiting the Hoadley relatives in New Bedford[26] and probably other places "East" such as Boston, as Malcolm was to do alone the following year.[27] In late July and early August of 1867, midway between the climax in marital tension between Herman and Lizzie and Malcolm's suicide, there was a gathering of the clan, including Herman and the boys, at the home in Gansevoort.

All of this compounds the mystery of Malcolm's death. It smothers obvious causes, but it is a means of control in its own way. There is little evidence of his estrangement from father and family, and much evidence of family affection and pleasures. On the other hand, there is stifling closeness and a hint of death by suffocation, as if Malcolm were unable in the end to draw a breath of fresh, free air of his own. The assertion of freedom and manhood implied by his smart and dashing military uniform and revolver and the promise of new opportunities that his position in the insurance office held forth might have provided the space he needed. They could have, but they did not do so in time.

# Notes

1. ALs, Peter Gansevoort to Lemuel Shaw, March 28, 1849, LSP, box 14; and ALs, Lemuel Shaw to Peter Gansevoort, April 11, 1849, G-L, box 17; quoted in Leyda, I, 294, 297; and in Metcalf, p. 61.

2. ALs, Elizabeth Shaw Melville to Hope Savage Shaw, April 30, 1949, Houghton, document no. MS. Am. 188, item 143 ; quoted in Leyda, I, 301–2; and partially in Metcalf, p. 61.

3. ALs, Augusta Melville to Lemuel Shaw, September 27, 1849, Houghton, document no. MS. Am. 188, item 125 ; quoted in Leyda, I, 314. The letter is signed by Herman, Allan, Sophia, Elizabeth, Helen, and Fanny Melville.

4. ALs, Frances Melville to Susan Lansing Gansevoort, November 20, 1849, G-L, box 154.

5. ALs, Augusta Melville to Hope Savage Shaw, January 7, 1851, LSP, box 14; quoted in Leyda, I, 402. See p. 38: "Malcolm Melville! . . . There is something noble in its very sound." Augusta reflects the satisfaction the family found in its links with Scottish nobility. Allan Melvill, writing of Guert Gansevoort in 1824, lists some of the attributes that will make him a "noble officer" (pp. 130–32).

6. ALs, Hope Savage Shaw to Lemuel Shaw, Jr., October 4, 1852, LSP, box 15; quoted in Leyda, I, 459.

7. ALs, Lemuel Shaw to Lemuel Shaw, Jr., September 19, 1858, LSP, box 16; quoted in Leyda, II, 595.

8. ALs, Hope Savage Shaw to Lemuel Shaw, Jr., September 17, 1855, LSP; neither we nor the MHS staff has been able to locate this letter; quoted in Leyda, II, 508; and in Metcalf, p. 154.

9. *Journals* (N-N), pp. 10, 12.

10. Melville uses the name *Barney* some nine times in *Journal of a Voyage from New York to London 1849*, in *Journals* (N-N), pp. 7, 8, 10, 12, 21, 39, 41, 43, and 45.

11. *Journals* (N-N), p. 39.

12. Miller, pp. 175–81. For example, Miller ignores references to Malcolm in the journal. He argues that Melville had no affection for his first-born son and suggests Melville's journey was largely an abandonment of—escape from—Lizzie. This forced her into the position of buffer between him and the children, a martyr dedicated to the protection of her young (pp. 318–21). We do not wish to quarrel with Miller's assertions about Melville's authoritarianism (p. 302) but suggest that it sprang from sources different from those he identifies.

Leon Howard is considerably closer to presenting an accurate picture of Melville's relations with the family, recording, for example, the intelligence offered in the 1849 *Journal* with fidelity and generally presenting a cautious account substantiated by information available in Leyda's "documentary life."

As our discussion demonstrates, until recently little work has been done on Melville's family context, especially on his relations with Malcolm.

13. ALs, Mary A. A. Melvill to Lemuel Shaw, October 16, 1850, LSP, box 14; quoted in Leyda, I, 398.

14. ALs, Augusta Melville to Hope Savage Shaw, January 7, 1851, LSP, box 14; quoted in Leyda, I, 402.

15. ALs, Elizabeth Shaw Melville to Lemuel Shaw, August 10, 1853, Houghton, document no. MS. Am. 188, item 142; quoted in Leyda, I, 478; and in Metcalf, pp. 148–49.

16. ALs, Malcolm Melville to Maria Melville, February 13, 1859, MP ; quoted partially in Leyda, II, 602.

17. ALs, Herman Melville to Thomas Melville, May 25, 1862, Houghton, document no. MS. Am. 188, item 180; quoted in Leyda, II, 652; Metcalf, pp. 197–99; and Rogin, p. 297.

18. Sealts, Early Lives, pp. 35, 108, 135, 152, 160, 222n20, and 234n44.

19. ALs, Maria Gansevoort Melville to Catherine Gansevoort, March 6, 1866, G-L, box 216; quoted in Leyda, II, 678–79.

20. J. E. A. Smith[?], Berkshire County Eagle, September 7, 1855; quoted in Leyda, II, 507.

21. Samuel Shaw's Diary, May 1, 1862, LSP, Samuel S. Shaw, Diaries, 1851–1912 box; and Catherine Gansevoort to Henry Sanford Gansevoort, July 20, 1864, G-L, box 161; quoted in Leyda, II, 651, 670.

22. ALs, Maria Gansevoort Melville to Catherine Gansevoort, August 9, 1864, G-L, box 215; quoted in Leyda, II, 670–71.

23. ALs, Maria Gansevoort Melville to Catherine Gansevoort, August 4, 1864, G-L, box 215.

24. ALs, Maria Gansevoort Melville to Catherine Gansevoort, September 5, 1864, G-L, box 215.

25. ALs, Maria Gansevoort Melville to Catherine Gansevoort, August 19, 1864, G-L, box 215; quoted in Metcalf, p. 204.

26. ALs, Frances Priscilla Melville to Catherine Gansevoort, September 12, 1865, G-L, box 215; quoted in Leyda, II, 675.

27. ALs, Catherine Gansevoort to Henry Sanford Gansevoort, July 23, 1866, G-L, box 245; quoted in Leyda, II, 681.

# Appendix B
# Paternalism and Authority:
# The Case of Allan Melvill

ONE OF THE MORE PROVOCATIVE FILES in the Gansevoort-Lansing Papers concerns promoting the reputation of the "Hero of Fort Stanwix" (Peter Gansevoort, so called for having held the fort against a British and Indian invasion directed toward Albany, New York, in August 1777) and thereby the reputations of his progeny by publishing a biographical memoir. Several such sketches were discussed, proposed, or written. We shall concentrate on a completed one which is representative. It appeared in the third edition of Thomas J. Rogers, *A New American Biographical Dictionary, or, Remembrancer of the Departed Heroes . . . ,* comp. Thomas J. Rogers (Easton, Pa.: Rogers, 1824).[1] What became a device to enhance the fame of the "Hero of Fort Stanwix" had begun as a business scheme in which Melville's father was invited to take part.[2]

Allan Melvill initiated the memoir early in 1822, and it was about three years before the volume containing it appeared. Allan wrote Peter Gansevoort on March 1 that Thomas Rogers, the compiler or editor, had evidently contacted him and Allan had promptly answered, transmitting a copy of his response to his brother-in-law the day before, February 28. He was asking Peter to "*return*" the "Proposals for the Work . . . *without delay*" to Rogers "after obtaining as many Subscribers as possible, that I may have time to add to the number here, and transmit it to M$^r$ Rogers as requested the 1$^{st}$ April[.]" He continues: "Perhaps the best method would be to procure *personally* a respectable list

of names, from among the old revolutionary Worthies & leading members of the Legislature, without distinction of Party, &
then place it conspicuously for a week or ten days, in the Reading Room at the Capitol, engage Cooke [*sic*] the State Librarian[3]
to subscribe officially & to exert his influence among his literary
& political friends to obtain further patronage[.]" Clearly, Melville's father was not one to miss an opportunity to turn a dol-
lar. But perhaps of more importance is his purpose for promoting this project. He continues: "I feel much interest in the
success & circulation of this Work, independent of its intrinsic
merit & usefulness, as a medium of rescuing the fame of your
gallant Father from unmerited neglect, & of preserving it for
the consideration of future Biographers & Historians, and I
trust the motive will justify the earnestness with which I entreat
you, to prepare in season a sketch of his life & services, (which
would come with peculiar grace & effect from your pen) from
the materials at hand, that when ↑ Mr ↓ Rogers applies, you
may be in full readiness to furnish at once the desired information, it being obvious he is a Man of Business from his epistolary promptitude."[4] (One is reminded of Melville's attempts
to rescue his Uncle Thomas's reputation and Elizabeth Melville's to preserve her husband's after his death.)[5] For whatever
reasons, Peter did not respond to Rogers with the sort of
promptitude Allan was exhibiting, as we shall point out below.
Of principal concern is that there can be no doubt that Allan
was thoroughly sincere and, as the subsequent written ex-
changes on this subject demonstrate, acting according to what
he regarded as the highest motives. The chance to make a
profit does not compromise his integrity in the matter of enhancing—frankly, promoting—his father-in-law's reputation,
not only to benefit the family, but to assure the accuracy of the
historical record.

He pursues the business dimension of the question: "It is yet
uncertain whether Mr Walsh[6] assumes the Editorship of the
Universal Biography, if not, some other eminent Writers will
probably undertake it, in either case let me urge this subject on
your immediate attention, that the opportunities w$^h$ now offer,
& may never again occur, of enrolling the heroism & virtues of
your Father among the departed 'Giants of those days.' " As far
as we have discovered there are no passages in Allan's known

correspondence that surpass this in displaying his sense of the past, his allegiance to the tradition that was his and his family's. He was not alone in pursuing the subject with such vigor. Before offering the customary closing to his correspondence with Peter, in which he almost invariably reports on the good health of the family, he adds, "Maria most heartily participates, & enjoins upon you the enviable office of perpetuating his memory[.]"[7]

In a letter of February 1823 to Peter, who appears to have been at best unresponsive, Allan again wrote of the importance of having the accomplishments of the General, his father-in-law, recognized.[8] He offers much more detail in the next letter, dated March 11, in which the first two paragraphs make the case for the Revolutionary War hero's inclusion in yet another compilation being planned. He even includes on the same sheet a copy of a letter he has written to Robert Walsh of Philadelphia advocating inclusion of an entry for his father-in-law.[9] Allan's campaign bore fruit during the summer. Writing to Peter on July 10, he announced that "The Publishers of the Universal Biographical Dictionary [had] yesterday applied to me to furnish a sketch or materials for the life of your lamented Father." The lengths to which he had gone to realize his project—pressing his brother-in-law to participate and to provide the sketch with the stamp of family authority—may well have been extreme; in the end he even "promised to become a Subscriber." He requests that Peter "attend to this interesting subject *immediately,* as after the 10 August, it will be too late to improve a suitable occasion to do justice to the memory of the 'Hero of Fort Stanwix,' who so justly deserves to be enrolled among his distinguished Countrymen[.]"[10]

Given the ordinary speed of the mails, there is what appears to be a telling lapse of several days before Peter responded to what Allan called his "good news." In the second sentence, Peter said, "I am highly gratified by the anxiety you feel that the present opportunities should be embraced to have 'Justice done['] to" his and Maria's father. He then details the problems he confronts in gathering the documents the biographical sketch would be built upon. For example, papers have been lost or borrowed and not returned. Peter reports of his unsuccessful attempts to retrieve them and also complains that those which are in his possession are in disarray. Nevertheless, he promises that "this week" he "will devote . . . all the time which I can conveniently spare from my professional business." Ever the practical man, first things first, whatever the enthusiasms, energies, and time Allan had put into the project. The rest of the letter has more thought-provoking material. Peter admits, "I <always have been desirous> ↑ was inclined ↓ to postpone the publication of a sketch of my father's life until after the Death of Col. Willett[11]—for many reasons which I intended to have stated ↑ explained ↓ to you when I was last at New York . . . particularly lest from the barrenness of the materials, some error might be made, which would have been seized upon with acidity by the friends of Willet [sic] & . . . operated to the injury of the subject of the memoir[.]"

The point is that Peter was cautious because of the perils publication might bring, not only to the reputation of his father, but to the reputation of his descendants. As he comments in the next sentence: "Many a fair fame has been tarnished by the zeal &c of its biographer." Nevertheless, he "will prepare a short notice on the <plan> ↑ model ↓ of Lemprière[12] & will forward ↑ it ↓ to you in season . . . before 10th of next month[.]" He also reveals that Rogers and he have been in touch directly about these and other matters concerning publication, adding that he has not been altogether punctual about keeping up his end of the correspondence.[13]

Allan's zeal to promote his father-in-law's memory remained undiminished, despite Peter's reticence. But we should not overemphasize Peter's reserve. On July 24, he wrote Thomas J. Rogers about a few matters, including a suggestion for an author for the sketch of William Floyd;[14] and he again repeated what he had written to Rogers[15] on July 21, which had included an explanation about the state of disarray of the General's papers.[16] Both letters provide fairly detailed outlines of the shape of the sketch he was to compose.

By August Peter was apparently making headway. He had written Allan on July 31, and Allan had answered on August 9, to congratulate him on "the progress made in the sketches of your heroic father's life, prepared for the various biographical works," all of "which afford an excellent medium to perpetuate his fame & to do justice to his memory[.]"[17] On a sheet marked "copy," Rogers' letter to Allan of March 20, 1824, survives. In it he reports that he is preparing a sketch for the biographical dictionary and that he had written Peter but never got an answer. The second half of this sheet bears Allan's response to Rogers, dated March 30; he acknowledges receipt of Rogers' letters of the past month and apologizes for Peter's not having come through, pointing out that Peter has been ill.[18] We might infer that the documents dated July 21 and 24, 1823, in the Gansevoort-Lansing Collection were not copies of materials sent but drafts of items Peter never mailed. But as subsequent correspondence substantiates, Peter transmitted, in however unfinished a form, some material to Rogers.

By early the next year the project had receded from Allan and Peter's concerns. On June 18, Allan wrote Peter that "I endeavored ↑ to obtain ↓ a copy of Rogers last edition[.]"[19] The book Allan is speaking of was probably published in either early June or late May of 1825, but as of June 14, when Peter wrote Allan, one can detect anxiety and even a certain regret about an evidently lost (at least not fully utilized) opportunity: "Have you seen Rogers last Edition of his 'American Biography' containing a short sketch on fathers life—Please to purchase one for me & send it up by an early opportunity—The sketch was prepared in great haste and intended only as memoranda for Mr. Rogers."[20] In the light of the prospects for doing honor to the "Hero of Fort Stanwix" that Allan saw when the project was conceived, the result was, if not a failure, at least not all it might have been. We might also infer from Peter's words that there is a measure of guilt about having missed the opportunity, hence the defensiveness flying under the flag of explanation in his statement that what he had provided Rogers were, at least in his judgment, "memoranda."

Allan and Peter were not alone in their desire to preserve the memory of General Gansevoort. More than four years before the project with Rogers commenced, General H. A. S. Dearborn had expressed interest in a similar undertaking.[21] Dearborn contacted Allan Melvill, who passed along his request to Peter Gansevoort, observing that Dearborn "seems to regret in common with ourselves & the discerning part of the Publick, that no Historian has yet done justice to the heroick defence of Fort Stanwix." Allan draws on language that for the reader of the Gansevoort-Lansing Papers becomes a cliché: the defense was "by that brave & patriotick Soldier of the Revolution whose name you have the honour to bear, & with whose fame I deem it an honour to be allied." One almost hears a lament by Allan that he himself did not have the "honour" of being a Gansevoort, so thoroughly had he been absorbed into the Gansevoort family.

Allan's filial respect, his commitment to honoring the memory of the men of earlier generations, extended to the Melvills as well. The same fidelity is apparent in his regard for his own father, Thomas Melvill; their relations were warmer than those between his brother-in-law, Peter, and the "Hero of Fort Stanwix, as well as those between Peter and his own son, Henry Sanford Gansevoort. Allan's feelings about his father are captured nicely in his December 1818 letter to Peter. Neither Allan's mood nor his circumstances are good, and he is waxing philosophical to console himself. In a long rumination he says, "I have an invaluable friend in my father, on whom I can rely with confidence in any absolute emergency."[22]

When writing to his father, Allan usually closed by referring to himself as a "dutiful" or "affectionate" son, or both.[23] He was clearly willing to share his views with his father, as he did in a letter in September 1819, which expressed his contempt for the excessive materialism and social ambition of his countrymen.[24] Pride informs his letter of March 1822, celebrating Thomas Melvill's political appointment as Naval Officer for the Port of Boston. Not only is there commitment to duty, but a real sense of satisfaction for having been of service in bringing this about.[25] The son's involvement when his father successfully fought the threat to his political appointment (in part the result of the family's pulling together) is finally manifest in another letter to Thomas a month later; there is a bit of crowing here: the son has done battle on behalf of the father and has won. There is evidence that Melvills will take care of Melvills in Allan's suggestion that he does not trust the asserted or implied role played by one or a few of the Gansevoorts (probably Peter) in achieving the victory for Major Melvill, a Revolutionary War veteran, if not hero.[26] Perhaps Thomas himself described the ground on which parental relationships are built, in a letter to Allan about eight years later: "Im glad for you that your Children, are so promising, it is one of the greatest Comforts to a *Parent* when they Conduct well, it is our part to *Guard,* and *guide, them* with a firm and *Steady Step*—and to look to the *Parent* of all for Direction."[27] In short, while it appears that the Melvills were as concerned as the Gansevoorts about the responsibilities of childrearing, their approach was not so harsh, nor were their relationships with their children so cold, distanced, and formal.

The Gansevoorts and Melvilles concerned themselves not only with their own offspring, but with members of the family at large. Young Guert Gansevoort is a case in point. When Peter's nephew entered the Navy as a midshipman aboard the U.S.S. *Constitution* in 1824, Peter wasted no time in communicating with Commander Thomas Macdonough.[28] In a letter of October 23, he advised Macdonough that young Guert was arriving armed with references from such prominent citizens as Governor DeWitt Clinton[29] and Judge John Duer.[30] He added that he wished to "beg leave to unite with them in asking your indulgent feelings in favor of this lad in the full confidence, that you will find him worthy of your benevolence."[31] The next day his friend and associate James Stevenson[32] reported to Peter that he had accompanied Allan Melvill on board the *Constitution* for a visit and that "Guert behaved like a man on Board, he has got into an excellent mess, all young Gentlemen[.]"[33] If the Melville-Gansevoorts were demanding of their children, they were also supportive of them when they were striking out into the world. Although Guert received an advance of two months' salary, $40.00, the additional $257.11 he required was advanced by Allan, who was reimbursed by Peter.[34] One can only wonder what sort of support the young Herman would have received, whatever route he may have chosen, had his father not died so young.

On the 24th, Allan also gave his version of the visit to Guert's ship, a visit which gave evidence of the family's position and the courtesies it engendered: "Guert & myself accompanied by Col Stevenson proceeded on board the Constitution at anchor in the Hudson early this morn^g we saw the Commander & officers & met with a flattering reception—our young Midshipman seemed quite at home, behaved with admirable propriety & I dare say will become a great favorite—We obtained admission for him among the Midshipmen of the starboard mess—'all fine young Gentlemen'—to use the Commodores own phrase." Allan admitted that the total cost of $297.11 for the "Out fit" to launch Guert on his career would be more than Peter had "imagined, but I thought it my duty as it regarded himself, & the name he bears, to put him afloat in his Country's service as a Gentleman." The father of the five-year-old Herman judged that the investment was worthwhile, for "with GOD's blessing I am proud to anticipate from his general deportment that he will be an honor to the family, & to the stars & spangled banner he is destined to defend." With our foreknowledge we sense the same irony that we hear in the words Melville wrote his brother Allan upon the birth of Malcolm. The end would be very different for both of them. But at the time, just before the sailing of the *Constitution*, Allan reported that "Guert seems in high spirits, & all alive to his duty—his eye seems keen & his heart bold, & I will answer for him, that he will make a noble officer—& in due time serve with distinction, & fight bravely his way to a pair of Epaulettes[.]"[35] Neither he nor Malcolm fulfilled the promise of his youth.

Allan Melvill's letter of October 27, 1824, to Guert Gansevoort is among the most eloquent statements on some of the subjects we are exploring, the themes of family authority and filial duty. He obviously wrote it out of a sense of family obligation. He exhorts Guert to be mindful of issues such as close family ties and obligations; the virtues of religion, including a rather conventional Christian morality that smacks of a Franklinian ethic which would have appalled Herman; the necessity of gentlemanly behavior; obedience to the authority of one's superiors and the dictates of one's country, which logically leads to an emphasis on patriotism; and, finally, an insistence on pride in the family name and the elevation of its honor, in which cause the "hero of Fort Stanwix" as well as the lad's deceased father, not to mention his mother, are invoked. The letter encapsulates many of the values we are discussing:

New York 27 Oct$^r$ 18<u>24</u>

My dear Nephew—

Having embarked on a three years Cruise in the service of your Country, on board of a noble Frigate, under the auspices of a gallant Commander, you are now fairly launched at an early age upon the great Ocean of life—with a cheering prospect in <full> view, but you must permit <one word> ↑ an ↓ Uncle anxious for your fame & welfare to offer <undeciphered word> ↑ some ↓ parting words of advice, which if received with "Kindred affection, may with GOD's blessing, prove useful——

You leave behind my dear boy many warm friends & kind relatives, who have done much & will do more for you, but their best efforts & good wishes will avail nothing, unless strengthened by your own exertions, upon which under Providence *almost everything depends*,——be mindful of reputation as a Gentleman, & true to duty as an officer; be respectful & obedient to your superiors, frank & polite to your messmates & Companions, civil manly & obliging to the whole Crew—reverence Religion & Morals; adhere to truth & honesty; avoid idleness, gaming, profanity, intemperance, dissipation, & all evil examples—cultivate habits of order & cleanliness, sobriety, vigilance, industry, attention and cheerfulness;—thus with Honour for a compass, & Glory for a watch word, you may in peace or war, become a brave & accomplished naval officer, defend "the star spangled banner" of your Country with courage & fidelity, & add lustre to a name distinguished in the Revolution by your paternal Grandfather, as "the Hero of Fort Stanwix"—

Recollect my dear Nephew that the heart of a beloved & widowed Mother will watch your career with intense solicitude, & that the fond thoughts of your Sisters & Brothers will often be directed towards you—remember what you owe to the memory of a dearly lamented Father;—but above all, my little sailor Boy, let me conjure you, *forget not your Creator in the dawn of youth,* for in him alone, can you safely provide for protection, at sea or as here, in storm or sunshine; therefore neglect not the Bible, regard it as *your polar star,* its religious precepts & moral doctrines are alike pure & sublime, & equally inculcate obedience, patriotism, fortitude, & through merit to gain promotion——Being much pleased with your conduct & will[?] you arrived in town, I fondly trust you will justify the best hopes of your family, deserve    the    approbation    of    your    Commander—but as I have already said, it depends [undeciphered word] the smiles of Providence, <u>entirely upon yourself</u>——

Kind heaven grant you a safe & happy return to your Mothers arms, improved in mind & manners, with a fair character & sound health, & with the fervent prayers of your Aunt & myself for your welfare & prosperity, in which all your little Cousins most heartily unite, I remain

> my dear Boy
> Your affectionate Uncle
> & sincere friend
> Allan Me<u>lvill</u>

Copy[36]

Covering this letter was a one-page note that stated its purpose and also mentioned the more pedestrian concerns Allan, and presumably other members of the family, had in mind. The copy in the Gansevoort-Lansing Collection begins with evidence of just how serious and sincere Allan was in parceling out such advice to the young midshipman: "I enclose a Letter of advice which you will read when at leisure, & often refer to as a guide to your conduct, it comes warm from the heart of your Uncle, & I hope will be of service to you[.]" Then practical matters— analogous to the detailed accounting with which Allan provided Peter of the costs incurred in getting Guert off to a good start—become the focus: "I have now further to request that you will take good care of your Clothes, Bedding, Papers, Books, Instruments & Equipments——be careful of your money, & draw no pay without absolute necessity——you have herewith a bit of effects brought from Albany & of those procured in New York." The note continues with more specifics.[37]

Hopes for Guert and his career at the beginning were to be betrayed. He died in 1868 following the disappointing conclusion of his career in the Navy.[38]

Allan Melvill cared about his family and its reputation, his wife and, more to the point here, his children. A problem lay, however, in how he manifested it. If his heavy-handed, pompous advice to Guert did not serve the young man well, and if it can be taken as an example of Allan's parenting of his son, then it served Herman no better.

# Notes

1. Pp. 147–53. Editions had also been printed in 1813, 1823, 1829, and 1834, according to the *National Union Catalogue* and the *N.Y.P.L. Research Libraries Dictionary Catalog*, but the sketch of Peter was only in the 1824 printing, as far as we know; the entry was deleted from the considerably shorter 1829 edition. We have not seen a copy of the 1834 edition.

2. ALs, Peter Gansevoort to Thomas Rogers, July 24, 1823, G-L, box 33.

3. John Cook (1764[?]–1823), the first New York State Librarian, was appointed by Governor Clinton in 1818. Cecil R. Roseberry, *For the Government and People of This State: A History of the New York State Library* (Albany: New York State Library, the University of the State of New York, the State Education Department, 1970), pp. 5 and 9.

4. ALs, Allan Melville to Peter Gansevoort, March 1, 1822, G-L, box 32.

5. "Sketch of Major Thomas Melville [*sic*] Junior, by a Nephew," in Joseph Edward Adams Smith, *The History of Pittsfield (Berkshire County), Massachusetts, from the Year 1800 to the Year 1876* (Springfield, Mass.: C. W. Bryan & Co., 1876), II, 398–400. (See also Sealts, "Thomas Melvill, Jr.," pp. 201–17, esp. 208–16.) Sealts, *Early Lives*, pp. 47–64; Kathleen E. Kier, "Elizabeth Shaw Melville and the Stedmans: 1891–1894," *Melville Society Extracts*, 45 (February 1981), 3–8; and Dorothy V. B. D. R. McNeilly, "The Melvilles and Mrs. Ferris," *Extracts: An Occasional Newsletter*, 28 (November 1976), 1–9.

6. The reference is to a project other than Rogers'. Walsh is probably the journalist and literary man Robert Walsh (1784–1859), who had early in the century settled in Philadelphia and edited the short-lived, Federalist-biased *American Register* during 1809 and 1810, founded the *American Review of History and Politics* in 1812, and wrote a biographical sketch of Franklin for *Delaplaine's Repository of the Lives and Portraits of Distinguished American Characters* (1815). He was also professor of English at the University of Pennsylvania from 1818 to 1828. *DAB*. He was treated in the Duyckincks' *CAL*, II, 37–39, and in its *Supplement*, II, 40.

7. ALs, Allan Melvill to Peter Gansevoort, March 1, 1822, G-L, box 32.

8. ALs, Allan Melvill to Peter Gansevoort, February 23, 1823, G-L, box 33.

9. ALs, Allan Melvill to Peter Gansevoort, March 11, 1823, G-L, box 33. Leyda quotes only a small part of this document useful for his purposes and does not include the passage we allude to.

10. ALs, Allan Melvill to Peter Gansevoort, July 10, 1823, G-L, box 33.

11. Marinus Willett (1740–1830), second-in-command to the "Hero of Fort Stanwix" during the siege in 1777. *DAB*.

12. John Lemprière (1765?–1824), the classical scholar known for his *Bibliotheca Classica; or, A Classical Dictionary Containing a Full Account of All the Proper Names Mentioned in Antient Authors*, first published in 1788 and then enjoying subsequent editions and abridgments, and for a *Universal Biography*

... of *Eminent Persons in All Ages and Countries* (1808, 1812, and 1825), composed of short, undocumented entries. *DNB*.

13. Draft of ALs, Peter Gansevoort to Allan Melvill, July 16, 1823, G-L, box 33.

14. The sketch of William Floyd (1734–1821) appeared in the third edition of Rogers, *A New American Biographical Dictionary* (1824), pp. 130–32. He was a member of the Continental Congress from New York and a signer of the Declaration of Independence. *DAB*.

15. Draft of ALs, Peter Gansevoort to Thomas J. Rogers, July 24, 1823, G-L, box 33.

16. Draft of ALs, Peter Gansevoort to Thomas J. Rogers, July 21, 1823, G-L, box 33.

17. ALs, Allan Melvill to Peter Gansevoort, August 9, 1823, G-L, box 33.

18. ALs, Allan Melvill to Thomas J. Rogers, March 20, 1824, G-L, box 34.

19. ALs, Allan Melvill to Peter Gansevoort, June 18, 1825, G-L, box 34.

20. ALs, Peter Gansevoort to Allan Melvill, June 14, 1825, G-L, box 34. The volume referred to is the third edition (1824) of Rogers, pp. 147–53. See note 1.

21. In a letter of January 20, 1818, to his brother-in-law Peter, Allan transmitted the request, written on the fifteenth, from Henry Alexander Scammell Dearborn (1783–1851), the son of Henry Dearborn (1751–1829), veteran of the Revolution and the War of 1812; H. A. S. Dearborn was a politician and author who wrote, among other works, *Defence of General Henry Dearborn against the Attack of General William Hull* (1824). *DAB*. For the elder Dearborn's connections with Thomas Melvill, Jr., and his father, as well as Peter Gansevoort, see Stanton Garner, "The Picaresque Career of Thomas Melvill, Junior," *Melville Society Extracts*, 60 (November 1984), 1, 6–8. Dearborn, according to Allan's transcription of Dearborn's letter, was "collecting materials for a work which at some future period may be published, relative to some of the events of the revolutionary War;——the gallant defence of Fort Stanwix by the brave & patriotic Colonel Gansevoort being of such vital consequence to the U States, at that dark & eventful period." Dearborn was "very solicitous to obtain all the information possible in connexion with that splendid affair; particularly as there is not a correct account of the measures adopted by Colonel Gansevoort to enable him to resist the powerful force sent by General Burgoyne to sweep with the [undeciphered word] of destruction the settlements on the Mohawk River." The materials Dearborn sought included specifically

> a statement of facts such as [Peter, the son] has collected from his venerable Father or other Persons who may have shared the dangers & privations of that campaign–Copies of the Letters which he may have written to Generals [George] Washington [(1732–99)], [General Philip John] Schuyler [(1733–1804), who early in the Revolution was stationed in northern New York], [General Horatio] Gates [(1728/29–1806), who replaced Schuyler after the loss of Fort Ticonderoga and went on to command the Northern and Southern Departments of the Army],

[General Benedict] Arnold [(1741–1801), who in 1775 captured Ticon-
deroga], Governor [DeWitt] Clinton [(1769–1828) *DAB*] or other Persons while commanding Fort Stanwix—Letters from the Persons above
named, as well as even more detailed information. After a brief ampli-
fication about the significance of the then Colonel's actions at the time,
Allan again reveals that the Colonel's daughter, Maria, was also involved
in the campaign to preserve her father's memory: "Maria tells me that
your Cousin Anthony has probably some materials of your fathers military career which might be an important acquisition, I can only add
that you will do me a personal favor by zealously promoting the views
of my friend Genl Dearborn." ALs, Allan Melvill to Peter Gansevoort,
January 20, 1818, G-L, box 30.

Clearly, the preservation of the place in history of Allan Melvill's
father-in-law, as well as that of the descendants, was almost a family
passion.

22. ALs, Allan Melvill to Peter Gansevoort, December 11, 1818, G-L, box
30; quoted partially in Rogin, pp. 52 and 250.

23. ALs, Allan Melvill to Thomas Melvill, April 20, 1824, G-L, box 34; and
ALs, Allan Melvill to Thomas Melvill, March 8[?], 1826, box 34, which is in-
correctly filed.

24. ALs, Allan Melvill to Thomas Melvill, September 14, 1819, G-L, box
30; quoted in part in Leyda, I, 4–5, and in Metcalf, pp. 1–2.

25. ALs, Allan Melvill to Thomas Melvill, March 11, 1822, G-L, box 30;
quoted in part in Leyda, I, 10, and in Metcalf, pp. 1–2.

26. ALs, Allan Melvill to Thomas Melvill, April 16, 1822, G-L, box 30;
quoted in part in Leyda, I, 10.

27. ALs, Thomas Melvill to Allan Melvill, September 30, 1830, G-L, no.
39 in unnumbered volume; quoted in part in Leyda, I, 45.

28. Thomas Macdonough (1783–1825), who had distinguished himself
during the War of 1812 by his maneuvers against the British on Lake Cham-
plain. *DAB*. He was appointed commander of the *Constitution* on May 31, 1824,
became ill, left his command in the Mediterranean, and died the following
November. Rodney Macdonough, *Life of Commodore Thomas Macdonough, U.S.
Navy* (Boston: The Fort Hill Press, 1909), pp. 248–54.

29. DeWitt Clinton (1769–1828), politician, statesman, philanthropist,
and man of letters, whom Peter Gansevoort had served as private secretary;
in 1819 he was appointed by the Governor Judge Advocate General of the
State of New York. *DAB* and Kenney, p. 154.

30. John Duer (1782–1858), the distinguished and powerful jurist, was a
native of Albany, N. Y., who, among other contributions, was a member of
"the commission to revise the New York statutes" from 1825 to 1827. *DAB*.

31. ALs, Peter Gansevoort to Thomas Macdonough, October 23, 1824,
G-L, box 34.

32. According to Kenney, James Stevenson was Peter Gansevoort's second
"cousin and closest friend."

33. ALs, James Stevenson to Peter Gansevoort, October 24, 1824, G-L, box
34.

34. ALs, Allan Melvill to Peter Gansevoort, October 25 and November 1, 1824, G-L, box 34.

35. ALs, Allan Melvill to Peter Gansevoort, October 24, 1824, G-L, box 34.

36. ALs, Allan Melvill to Guert Gansevoort, October 27, 1824, G-L, box 177; quoted in part in Leyda, I, 19.

37. ALs (copy or draft), Allan Melvill to Guert Gansevoort, October 27, 1824, G-L, box 177. Inserted within these two items is an inventory of possessions Guert was bringing to sea.

38. ALs, Abraham Lansing to Catherine Gansevoort, July 16, 1868, G-L, box 216. Guert had died on the 15th. It was Allan Melville's task to go to Schenectady "to prove Cousin Guert's will." What he possessed he left "to his sister Kate." ALs, Augusta Melville to Catherine Gansevoort, July 30, 1868, G-L, box 216.

# Appendix C
# Pride in Family: Genealogy
# and Preservation

FAMILY PRIDE SUFFUSES A GREAT DEAL of the correspondence in the Gansevoort-Lansing Collection. This is the reason Kate Gansevoort Lansing preserved and deposited her family papers. Let us focus on Allan's pride in his ancestry, which is evident in his reports of his trip to Scotland in 1818. Writing to his father at the end of May, he was unblushing about how thrilled he was at the prospect of meeting his Scottish relatives in Edinburgh.[1] The whole volume in which these documents were collected was a testament to family pride. It was rich in Melvill family history and in letters Allan wrote on this and related subjects to his father and wife.[2] And it included accounts of what was probably one of the finest demonstrations of filial duty that Allan ever performed for his father: helping him secure the political appointment he needed in 1822 as Naval Officer of the Port of Boston. The son's letter of March 11 to Thomas is shot through with sentiments about these matters.[3]

Interest in genealogy is an obvious manifestation of family pride which Herman Melville, his forebears, and his contemporaries pursued. Consider Melville's reflections on his Uncle Thomas, which were carefully crafted so as to place the best face on what was not an altogether happy situation.[4] This ongoing concern with the family record appears, for example, in an 1867 letter of his brother Tom to their cousin Kate Gansevoort Lansing in which he tells her, among other matters, that the " 'Genealogical Trees' " are "ready for" her.[5] Almost a year later his other brother, Allan, sends her a package and cover letter for a genealogical volume which was actually three pamphlets bound together, two on the Thurstons (the family of his first wife, Sophia) and one on the Pitmans, which had been prepared by Charles M. Thurston. He also advised her that he was depositing a copy in the New York State Library.[6]

# Notes

1. ALs, Allan Melvill to Thomas Melvill, May 31, 1818, G-L, Box 30.

2. As it was arranged before being dismantled recently due to the poor condition of the binding, and the resulting impossibility of reading portions of the documents or having them photocopied, this was a large book of letters and other documents (bound in a volume with a red spine on which was printed in gilt lettering: "Gansevoort / Lansing / Collection / Melville / Family Papers / 1649–1915"); the first fifteen items (each document in the volume was numbered) covered genealogical and other family history; Thomas Melvill was the subject of items 16 through 22; his son Thomas Melvill was covered in items 23 and 24; and so forth. Although the volume's purpose and coherence have been lost, the documents themselves have been placed in appropriate boxes holding the collection.

3. ALs, Allan Melvill to Thomas Melvill, March 11, 1822, G-L, box 216; quoted in part in Leyda, I, 10, and Rogin, pp. 24 and 29.

4. Garner, "The Picaresque Career of Thomas Melvill, Junior," pp. 1–10. "Major Thomas Melville," in Smith, II, 398–400. See note 134.

5. ALs, Thomas Melville to Catherine Gansevoort, July 14, 1867, G-L, box 216.

6. ALs, Allan Melville to Catherine Gansevoort, June 22, 1868, G-L, box 216.

# Appendix D
# Melville's Relations with His Parents, Principally His Mother, and Hers with His Grandmother

To EVEN SUGGEST THAT ONE CAN EFFECTIVELY address oneself to the thorny question of any child's relationship with its parents is presumptuous. To do so in the case of Herman Melville is nearly if not actually absurd. Nevertheless, in this attempt to examine relations between the generations, some comment should be made, especially about his relations with his mother, Maria; the father, Allan, died so early in Herman's life that speculations about the writer's thoughts and feelings, even those inferred from obviously autobiographical writings such as *Pierre*, in the final analysis can only be speculations. There is, however, some evidence to suggest that Herman was a dutiful and attentive son, regardless of whatever hostilities, anxieties, or reservations may have seethed beneath his outward posture. For instance, there are numerous records, in volumes such as *The Melville Log*, of Maria's being a frequent, long-term guest of Lizzie and Herman, and at times a resident in their home. In one letter during the mid–1850s Susan Gansevoort, Maria's sister-in-law, writes her daughter, Kate. She reports that Herman's mother is leaving Susan and Peter's Albany house, where she has been visiting, and is "tomorrow morning on her way to [Herman's] Arrowhead & will remain until the day after[.]"[1] Almost a decade later, when Herman's mother was ill, Augusta writes Kate Gansevoort that he "came on Wednesday bringing with him many delicacies to tempt her appetite." Augusta goes on to report that her mother "has been improving ever since his arrival, the effect of seeing him she said."[2] If nothing more, Herman was a dutiful son who cheered his mother's spirits. This is also evident in the spring of 1868, when his brother Tom was being married, a family event that is well documented in surviving correspondence.[3] In early May Maria wrote Kate before going to New York City to attend Captain Tom's nuptials; she had been ill for about a year, and her sons were quite concerned about her health, as she reported to Kate: "Tom writes me that I must get strong, & Herman & Tom have sent me strengthening cordials. Allan sent me a bottle of rare French Brandy brought out with him from France, & fresh fruit & every thing to make me strong & active." Herman was not simply joining with his brothers in comforting their ailing mother. Maria concludes the letter by noting that she "shall go to New York & take Hermans advice, to come on at least one week before the 4$^{th}$."[4] Maria wrote Kate again on May 15 to report, among other matters, that she was continuing her regimen to strengthen herself for the journey to attend Tom's wedding. She was to stay at Herman and Lizzie's, as would others, including Kate herself, and the arrangements for making the trip to Sailors' Snug Harbor on Staten Island were, of course, of concern to her sons: "About going to the Island on the 4$^{th}$ Tom wrote me that I should have no fatigue on that day, for a Carriage would be at Hermans door, which would take me to the Church door at New Brighton, & after the Ceremony would take me to D$^r$ Bogarts."[5] The courtesies were not limited to their mother, though. Maria continues, "Now I have no doubt that you will be provided for in a similar way by the Cap$^t$ [Tom, the groom] altho perhaps nothing may have been said about it."[6] Later in the year, back in Gansevoort, Maria again wrote Kate and, amid a lot of familiar family and related gossip and conversation, reported that she "had letters from Tom & Katy [Catherine Bogart, Tom's bride] since they left Albany" where they had visited Uncle Peter's household. Katy, Maria's new daughter-in-law, had already secured a firm place in the family: "We were much pleased with Katy, & feel as if our acquaintance must have been of longer continuance than a few months." Maria planned to visit them on Staten Island: "Tom & his wife are very desirous to have us all . . . come to pass the winter with them." And the matriarch makes a strong point that Tom and his new wife are not alone in extending invitations: "But Herman & Lizzie put in a claim too, & Augusta will make her first visit to them." Maria's use of the word *claim* suggests vying for the honor. One should not forget that whatever the outcome, it was Augusta (the most intellectual of Herman's siblings and his favorite sister) who was to stay at East 26th Street. "Fanny & I," Maria continues, "shall go with Tom who will be at the depot to meet us, Herman will be there for Augusta." And lest the small gathering of the clan be incomplete, Maria takes the liberty to urge Kate to "come down to New York this winter while I am there, & make Tom & his wife a visit."[7]

Such letters suggest that Herman was most respectful and solicitous of his mother and that he and his relatives were more than willing to be involved in the busy life of their extended family. The significance of their gestures is made all the more apparent when one recalls that all this was occurring scarcely eight months after Malcolm's suicide and a year after the crisis in the Herman Melville household that almost led to Lizzie's separation from her husband shortly after he had begun his job with the Customs Service. Again, whatever suspicions one may have of serious tension between Herman and his mother, it did not—if it actually existed—spill into his overt relations with her. He was fulfilling the expected role of dutiful, caring, obedient, and respectful son according to the precepts of the Melvilles and Gansevoorts.[8]

Herman's behavior toward his widowed mother was learned from a variety of sources, principally within the family. One of the more obvious and important was his mother herself. Maria's fundamental attitude is stated unequivocally in her correspondence—for example, in a letter to Kate Gansevoort early in 1866. The occasion for her remarks on the trials, tribulations, and duties of the child toward the parent was the recent death of Dr. Howard Townsend.[9] Regarding his wife, Maria comments: "This poor widow, her loss is irreparable; he was her pride—her loved companion her wise counsellor, the Father of her children, one so competent to direct their education & to bring them up to be useful members of Society. No other than a widow ↑ with her sad experience ↓ can feel for a widow, oh the loneliness the emptiness of this world when a woman has buried the husband of her youth, & is left alone to bring up their children, without a loved fathers care & experience to help in the training them to fulfil lifes duties & to point the way to heaven by his Christian example. Poor dear Justina may God in his mercy be with you to comfort & sustain you."[10] How vivid the memories were almost thirty-five years after her own sore loss. It is little wonder that she thought that the burden she had borne as a widow, and for the most part successfully, entitled her to certain considerations from her children.

But this is not the only reason for her claims upon them. There was the fact of her relationship with her own mother, Catherine Van Schaik. Maria and her siblings held their mother in great esteem. In anticipation of her inevitable death, her portrait was being painted, and the last sitting took place in early April 1823.[11] But there was more than what may be construed by the more cynical reader to bind Maria to her mother. She was deeply concerned about her mother's health in mid–1823, as she demonstrated in a letter to her brother, Peter.[12] The mother had been ill for some time and was to continue to be until her death in 1830. In an 1825 letter from New York City to Peter in Albany, Maria (who reports that she herself is ill) is nearly incoherent at points; she wants desperately to visit and help tend to her parent but must wait until the ice on the Hudson has broken so she can travel, a circumstance she keeps repeating. Her sense of duty is simply expressed: "Our good mother has sacrificed the best part of her life to her Childrens Comfort & Welfare & she richly ↑ deserves ↓ every & all possible care & attention from them, allow me again to repeat my request that you would ask Mamma whether it would be agreeable to see me if I could come up with little fatigue, If the Boats should commence running the next week which in all probability may happen." Maria is more than anxious to get to her ailing parent: "it would be a great consolation to me to ↑ be ↓ with Mamma if only for a few days"; and she reports that her brothers are also worried about their mother. Of equal if not greater significance is the gratitude she expresses to Peter and his wife for the care they are giving the sick woman. "Give a great deal

of love to Sister Mary [Peter's first wife] & tell her I rely much
on her kindness & attentions to Mamma, her capability if She is
well & any way enabled to bear ↑ the ↓ fatigue is well known to
me & has always ↑ been ↓ a source of satisfaction <to
me[?]>since my unavoidable separation from my infirm & aged
Mother—Pray write soon & by every stage for I am very un-
easy[;] may my fears be groundless, God grant they may, & in
his infinite mercy restore a beloved Mother from a sick bed to
convalescence & her Children." If redundancy is any signal,
Maria's letter borders on the hysterical. She proceeds, "Remember me with the most sincere affection again & again to my dear
Mother if the Boats were running entirely to Albany nothing
should prevent my embarking with Herman[13] this evening—my
situation is all that prevents my going up in the stage with him."
In the end, she reaches into her resources of religious faith:
"The Almighty ruler above disposes all things as he thinks fit,
Tis is our duty to be resigned & patiently acquiese in his dispen-
sations—my most earnest prayer is that I may be enabled so to
do[.]"[14] Maria's children could not have had a more effective
model of filial respect and the implied punishments meted out
to the undutiful. While one might hear Maria's pleasure as she
planned visits to her children (for example, the arrangements
for the trip to Tom's wedding) and her joy in receiving them,
one must not be deaf to the demands she made. She expected
deference. In 1868 Augusta wrote Kate Gansevoort that her
mother awaited a letter from her; Kate had not been in touch
"since Mrs Bogart[15] & Lizzie were with us," presumably in Gansevoort, from where Augusta was writing.[16]

# Notes

1. ALs, Susan Gansevoort to Catherine Gansevoort, November 20, 1855, G-L, box 245, album 1.

2. ALs, Augusta Melville to Catherine Gansevoort, February 29, 1864, G-L, box 215. The visit is mentioned and another part of the letter is quoted in part in Leyda, II, 665–66; and in Metcalf, p. 202.

3. There are numerous documents concerning the wedding in G-L, box 216.

4. ALs, Maria Gansevoort Melville to Catherine Gansevoort, May 6, 1868, G-L, box 216.

5. Dr. S. V. R. Bogart, the bride's father, was the staff physician at Sailors' Snug Harbor; the wedding took place at the Brighton Heights Dutch Reformed Church. Boies, p. 25.

6. ALs, Maria Gansevoort Melville to Catherine Gansevoort, May 15, 1868, G-L, box 216.

7. ALs, Maria Gansevoort Melville to Catherine Gansevoort, December 27, 1868, G-L, box 216.

8. See, for example, the unflattering portraits of Maria and what is best described as Herman's ambivalent relationship with her in Lewis Mumford, *Herman Melville* (New York: Harcourt, Brace, 1929), pp. 14–15, who goes so far as to write, "Both Melville's father and mother were monsters" (p. 15); in Newton Arvin, *Herman Melville* (New York: Viking, 1957), pp. 17–18, 29–30; and in Miller, pp. 56, 65, and 88.

9. Dr. Townsend, a physician who resided at 15 Elk with his wife, Justina (*The Albany Directory for the Year 1866. . .* [Albany: Sampson Davenport, 1866]), died on the morning of January 16. *Albany Evening Journal*, January 16, 1867, p. [3].

10. ALs, Maria Gansevoort Melville to Catherine Gansevoort, January 17, 1866, G-L, box 216; quoted partially in Kenney, p. 187.

11. ALs, Peter Gansevoort to Allan Melvill, April 7, 1823, G-L, box 33.

12. ALs, Maria Gansevoort Melvill to Peter Gansevoort, June 26, 1823, G-L, box 33.

13. Maria is probably referring to her brother, not her son.

14. Maria Gansevoort Melvill to Peter Gansevoort, March 8, 1825, G-L, box 34.

15. Thomas Melville's mother-in-law of a few months.

16. ALs, Augusta Melville to Catherine Gansevoort, October 9, 1868, G-L, box 216.

# Appendix E
# The Patrician Posture:
# Notably Allan Melvill

HERMAN MELVILLE'S FATHER WAS A MERCHANT who tried to be as practical in political matters as he was in his commercial life. There are a number of incidents of his political involvement that demonstrate the point, but few are more revealing than his elation as a result of the reelection of DeWitt Clinton as Governor of New York in 1824.[1] On November 9, he wrote his brother-in-law Peter from New York City to

> most cordially congratulate [him; Peter was an ardent Clinton supporter] on the glorious result of the Election—the political Capital & the commercial metropolis[2] have indeed achieved wonders, while *'the Lion of the West'* has confounded the hopes of the Young-lings[3] — 'the immortal seventeen' are defunct, King Caucus & the Regency[4] prostrated Root & branch, & the sovereign People again 'Lords of the ascendant'———it is at once a great moral victory, & a noble example of public virtue & retribution ———I rejoice most heartily in the overwhelming majority of our friend Mr Clinton, whose re-election to the chair of state, to which he is entitled as its chief benefactor, disproves the proverbial saying of 'the ingratitude of Republics,' must be peculiarly grateful to his feelings, after the impotent persecution of evil Rulers, & will be a source of exaltation to all generous minds throughout the Union, indignant at his outrageous exclusion from the Presidency of the Canal Board.

Allan was not simply ingratiating himself with his brother-in-law. He had himself been active in the campaign in New York City: "having always entertained a strong personal attachment to M^r Clinton, I exerted myself in his cause. . . . & no man in the community more truly exults in its splendid success, which I consider as the redemption of the Commonwealth[.]"⁵

Herman Melville's father possessed a vision of what the American Republic was, which he effectively, if a bit floridly, expressed in a letter to Peter somewhat more than a month before the election. He had ended with some observations about the impending election:

> I sincerely congratulate you on the nomination of our friend M^r Clinton to the chief magistracy, which should he accept as he probably will, the People will doubtless elect him by a triumphant vote, & thus redeem the character of the State from the stigma of its Legislature, whose exclusion of M^r Clinton from the Canal Board is regarded by all honest men, as the most vindictive act of political persecution & moral ingratitude which ever disgraced the annals of party, but the effect will inevitably recoil upon themselves with retributive vengeance, & elevate his fame above the reach of envy or malice throughout the Union, over whose high destinies I trust in GOD he will be called to preside, if not in 1825, in *1829*.

Allan saw Clinton as presidential timber; Clinton's reelection as Governor was "the most eligible avenue to the presidential chair into which I think he might even now be carried if we [*sic*; that is, he] had a little more time as the 'Peoples Candidate.' " He promised "to use [his] utmost influence to bring my mercantile acquaintance to the Polls," but as a businessman who did not want to offend his fellow merchants, he added, "though I shall still habitually avoid taking an *open* part in political warfare." Allan would do his politicking "in *private* by urging forward the indolent though well disposed, & if each are in favour of the cause would do his duty in this quiet way, more could be effected than by all the declamatory Demagogues of the Regency & Caucuses[.]"⁶ Unlike his son Gansevoort, who was a successful stump speaker fewer than two decades later, Allan would engage in no overt political activity. As was the case with all these politically involved people, Allan did not lend support for nothing. At the start of the new year, they cashed in. Clinton paid his debt to the Melvill-Gansevoort supporters by writing to ask

John C. Calhoun's[7] help in gaining admission to the United States Military Academy for Peter L. Gansevoort, Leonard's son and the grandson of the Hero of Fort Stanwix.[8] The next day Allan's brother-in-law himself wrote his own letter of endorsement to Major C. Vanderventer, chief clerk of the War Office.[9]

To understand Allan's practical political activities here, one must consider the context of these September remarks. No venal political activist, he saw a moral dimension inherent in the process. His comments on Clinton follow a long and somewhat eloquent (though occasionally flowery) response to Lafayette's[10] visit to the United States, which was then in progress. His concern with the Revolution was not merely to promote his or his wife's family position; in fact, he reveals that he makes a sharp distinction between real giants of the Revolution, such as Washington and Lafayette, and his and the Gansevoorts' Revolutionary forebears. And however dubious he may be about the potential vulgarity and ill judgment of the so-called "mob," and "mobocracy," his sentiments are not aristocratic but rather conservative republican. The statement is passionate and revealing of Allan's fundamental political values:

> I have seen La Fayette frequently in the crowd since his arrival, without following the countless throngs who have tendered their personal respects, the mere ceremony of shaking hands with such a Man without the privilege of conversation had no charms for me, but I shall endeavor to make him a more interesting visit on his return from the southward—I have however enjoyed the felicity of beholding the moral triumph of the two most exalted Men of modern date, whose names alone soaring in native dignity above the region of titles, require no epithets to increase their lustre or monuments to perpetuate their fame; Washington and La Fayette are imperishable appellatives, synonymous of immortality, the great master pupil of political virtue & private worth, without parallel & beyond praise—the gorgeous titles & heroic deeds of the Emperor Napoleon & the Duke of Wellington, may dazzle & confound the eyes of posterity, but the simple grandeur & sublime devotion of Washington & La Fayette, the god-like champions of rational freedom in both hemispheres, will subdue & purify their hearts—
>
> I observed with pleasure that the "Guest of the Nation" rec[eived] a most cordial & dignified welcome in our political

metropolis, his rapid march through the Country displays the magic of a perpetual jubilee, & will constitute a new epoch in republican annals, all persons & all places are alike emulous to do homage to the Man, whom "*the people delight to honour*," while gratitude, enthusiasm, loving-kindness & hospitality showers upon him unexampled favours, until this stern abode of liberty is transformed by his wonder working presence into a fairy land, where generous freemen have forgotten their local feuds & presidential idols, to unite with one accord to worship the Benevolent Wizard who seems to have united all hearts——in such a state of public feeling nothing is too extravagant for the creative genius of a free & sanguine people, at whose nod a dismantled Fort becomes an enchanted Castle, the halls of legislation are metamorphosed into a Temple of revelry, court rooms change to presence Chambers, subscription houses swell to Palaces, theatres expand to Ball-rooms, refectories extend to Canals, steam boats dwindle to hackney-coaches, & even our Country's proud emblem the wild eagle of the mountain, stoops from his throne of clouds to perch upon the humble arch, in exultation at the spirit of the times, which recals [*sic*] into active service the superannuated remnant of the Revolution, inspires our martial youth with the real yankee doodle spirit of 75, & enacts over again for the edification of the Words Bunker Saratoga & Yorktown—It is delightful to witness these magnificent carousals of national hospitality, but I much fear that the honest zeal & warm hearted emulation of the sovereign People will carry us to excess, "there is but a step from the sublime to the ridiculous," & we have already gone too fast & too far, as I at first predicted, it is, bad taste to be over eager & precipitate, & as the illustrious object of all this popular excitement will probably revisit us again & pass the four seasons in his adopted Country, there will be time & opportunities enough to evince our respectful good will, & to exhibit ourselves with advantage & decorum, without committing those exuberant excesses which are too oft to distinguish us on most occasions, & must in the end prove irksome if not fatal to our modest & noble minded Guest—the Inhabitants of Bristol Pennsylvania through which he was to pass at night, devised a novel & ingenious contrivance, when they retired to their respective homes, after erecting an illuminated arch with this simple yet emphatic motto at once apposite & complimentary, Here "*let expressive silence muse his praise.*"[11]

The level of idealism, actual hero worship, and awe of institutions expressed in this letter should be considered in light of the republican views of Judge Lemuel Shaw, the attorney and jurist who had long-standing relations with both the Melvill and Gansevoort families. Writing to Peter, his colleague in Albany, in mid-November 1821, about a professional matter, his crisp certitude is expressed forthrightly: "I do not send you the enclosed report of a trial on impeachment, solely or principally, because I had some share in conducting it; but because it is the first serious trial on articles of impeachment which has been had in this Commonwealth, & because a good many interesting points were considered & discussed. Our Governments are all still to be regarded as new, in a course of experiment, and any solemn proceeding which tends to fix and establish principles, or even to settle forms, must be interesting both to the American Statesman & lawyer."[12] Shaw's professional practicality in these remarks to a fellow attorney provides a striking contrast to Allan's citizen-patriotism. Shaw's remarks are almost an anticipation of the no-nonsense pragmatism—lacking, however, the intensity of commitment to the "forms, measured forms" that Melville would use to characterize Captain Vere.[13]

But we should return to the substance of this part of Allan's remarks on the distinguished visitor to America. Allan's adulation of Lafayette also had its rewards. Reiterating his high praise for the French leader, in a letter to Peter in June 1825, he was pleased to learn that Lafayette had paid his mother-in-law "respectful attention";[14] Allan's strategy of not forcing himself upon the visitor during the enthusiastic reception the preceding September had proven effective. Timing the encounter perfectly, he was sure that when it occurred, it would be more than perfunctory. A few days earlier Peter had written Allan and mentioned that Lafayette had also visited the Albany Gansevoorts.[15] (The Gansevoorts, including Maria, had a long-standing interest in the French. In a letter to her brother in 1823, she suggested he read for amusement a new book, *Memoirs of Marie Antoinette* by Madame Campan, "Sister of Our Old Friend, Monseuir [sic] Genêt."[16])

It might be useful to compare Allan's serious concerns regarding the decline of aristocratic privilege (to paraphrase

Dixon Ryan Fox)[17] with the more casual views of Abraham Lansing, Kate's husband. There was no one in the family who possessed a more secure position among the New York Dutch elite, no one we might expect to be more disturbed by the changing times, the new political arrangements he witnessed unfolding in his lifetime, the dissolving of the old ways, and as a result the diminishment of personal and family prerogatives. Born to the manor, patrician to the core, Abe was no liberal. Yet he had a healthy perspective, in part due to his steady temperament (what better testament to this than his patience during his extraordinarily protracted courtship of Kate Gansevoort?).[18] He was in New York in September of 1867 when he wrote her. (The visit apparently had nothing to do with Mackie's recent suicide.) Abe was disappointed in the city: "The Hoffman House[19] is an excellent establishment (for millionaires,) but rather a poor place, as are all other hotels from which I write letters." What is less predictable, more interesting, and even surprising is his sophistication; he tells Kate, "When you are here, go & see Joseph Jefferson play Rip Van Winkle at the Olympic Theater[20] as I did the other Evening. It will repay you with fine tableaux & good acting & a hearty laugh even at the expense of a representative of that ancient Holland race to which Albanians are proud to trace their origins."[21] His patrician security allowed him to observe with such calm the comic treatment of his ancestry and, more important for us, the passing of the old order. It is hard to imagine Allan Melvill exhibiting such a response, but not his son Herman who, late in life, would write appreciatively of Rip "By Jefferson acted true to life."[22]

# Notes

1. DeWitt Clinton (1769–1828) served two terms as governor, beginning in 1817, and did not run in 1822. He had been a New York State Canal Commissioner since 1810, and as governor had promoted the project to link the Great Lakes with the Hudson River. As a result of his declining to run again for governor in 1822, the "Albany Regency," led by Martin Van Buren, gained power and removed him from his Commission post in 1824. This galvanized Clinton's supporters, and he won the fiercely contested race for governor in 1824. *DAB*. For more detail on his removal as Canal Commissioner, see Dorothie Bobbé, *DeWitt Clinton* (New York: Minton, Balch, 1933), pp. 263–67.

2. Allan is here referring to Albany, N.Y., and New York City, respectively.

3. *Lion of the West* was one of the popular designations for DeWitt Clinton. The Young-lings were supporters of one of his rivals, the politician Samuel Young. Bobbé, pp. 266–67.

4. The "seventeen" and "Caucus" were instruments of the Regency Party which had dismissed Clinton from the Canal Board, a body he had been connected with from the start of his efforts to build the Erie Canal. Bobbé, p. 267.

5. ALs, Allan Melvill to Peter Gansevoort, November 9, 1824, G-L, box 34.

6. ALs, Allan Melvill to Peter Gansevoort, September 28, 1824, G-L, box 34.

7. Calhoun (1782–1850), the powerful South Carolina statesman who, when Clinton wrote him, was finishing his term as President Monroe's Secretary of War and was about to be inaugurated as Vice-President in the administration of John Quincy Adams. *DAB*.

8. ALs, DeWitt Clinton to John C. Calhoun, January 26, 1825, G-L, box 34.

9. Draft ALs, Peter Gansevoort to Major C. Vanderventer, January 27, 1825, G-L, box 34. On the back of this draft Peter calls Peter L. his nephew, so he is probably his brother Leonard's son. Vanderventer is mentioned a number of times in *Memoirs of John Quincy Adams, Comprising Portions of His Diary from 1795 to 1848*, ed. Charles Francis Adams, 12 vols. (1874–77; rpt. New York: AMS Press, 1972).

10. Marie Joseph Paul Yves Roch Gilbert du Motier, Marquis de Lafayette (1757–1834), the French statesman and military man who served the Americans during the War for Independence. He was on his second visit to the United States since returning to his native land after the Revolution to pursue an active and brilliant career. *Webster*.

11. ALs, Allan Melvill to Peter Gansevoort, September 28, 1824, G-L, box 34.

12. ALs, Lemuel Shaw to Peter Gansevoort, November 16, 1821, G-L, box 32. In a notation on the fold-over sheet of what serves as the envelope, there is a notation—it does not appear to be in Peter Gansevoort's hand—that reads:

"Taken from: Report of the trial of impeachment of James Prescott, Esq., Judge of the Probate of Wills, Middlesex Co., Mass. Boston, 1821." Judge Shaw was appointed by the United States House of Representatives as one of the managers of the impeachment which was tried before the Senate. Although his adversary was Daniel Webster, who was defending Prescott, Shaw, leading the prosecution, held his own; Prescott was found guilty of two of the fifteen charges, but the proceedings were complicated and protracted. Frederic Hathaway Chase, *Lemuel Shaw: Chief Justice of the Supreme Judicial Court of Massachusetts, 1830–1860* (Boston and New York: Houghton Mifflin, 1918), pp. 88–106.

13. *Billy Budd*, pp. 128 and 195–96.

14. ALs, Allan Melvill to Peter Gansevoort, June 18, 1825, G-L, box 34; quoted in part in Leyda, I, 21.

15. Typed transcription of ALs, Peter Gansevoort to Allan Melvill, June 14, 1825, G-L, box 34. The original manuscript is not in its chronological place or anywhere else in the box, and we do not know the name of the transcriber.

16. ALs, Maria Gansevoort Melvill to Peter Gansevoort, November 21, 1823, G-L, box 33; quoted in part in Leyda, I, 16; and in Kenney, p. 193.

Unknown edition. According to the *National Union Catalogue*, the two English translations closest in time to Maria's writing this letter were issued in 1854 and 1869, and two French editions of Jeanne Louise Henriette Campan (Genêt), *Mémoirs sur la vie privée de Marie Antoinette* . . . were published in 1867: Paris: Didot; and Paris: Firmin, Didot. Her husband was fluent in French, and there is no reason not to believe that Maria herself read French and was referring to a French imprint. Madame Campan was the sister of Edmond Charles Édouard Genêt (1763–1834), a French diplomat in the United States during the 1790s who later became an American citizen. *Webster.*

17. *The Decline of the Aristocracy in the Politics of New York*, Studies in History, Economics and Public Law, Edited by the Faculty of Political Science (New York: Columbia University Press, 1919).

18. Kate and Abe were not married until 1873, although they had been engaged intermittently, beginning in 1862. Kenney, pp. 253–58.

19. The Hoffman House opened in 1864 at the corner of Broadway and East 25th Street. M. Christine Boyer, *Manhattan Manners: Architecture and Style, 1850–1900* (New York: Rizzoli, 1985), pp. 56–58.

20. Dion Boucicault's 1865 stage adaptation of Washington Irving's "Rip Van Winkle" was the central piece in the repertoire of the American actor Joseph Jefferson (1829–1905). *DAB*. The play had been running at the Olympic for three weeks. *The* [N. Y.] *Evening Post*, September 23, 1867, p. [4].

21. ALs, Abraham Lansing to Catherine Gansevoort Lansing, September 24, 1867, G-L, box 216.

22. "Rip Van Winkle's Lilac," *Collected Poems*, p. 292.

# Appendix F
## Paternalism and Authority:
## Uncle Peter and His Children

IT IS USEFUL TO ASK IN WHAT DEGREE the relationships between parents and children of one generation of a family affect those of subsequent generations. The relationship between Peter Gansevoort and his son, Henry, is a good case, as we have already seen. Peter's formality, his distancing, is evident, for example, in an 1846 letter to his son. Following a scant six lines of conventional courteous remarks, Peter proceeds to the purpose at hand, Henry's life at the boarding school run by Cornelius Chase in Chatham, Columbia County, New York, which he is attending: "I feel, my dear Henry, that you are now in a situation, altogether more advantageous to your improvement, than if you had remained here, attending the [Albany] academy[.]" When a conflict arose between a serious education which promised future advantage and the nurturing a child would enjoy at home, the former prevailed. Peter explains his thinking on the subject of schooling: "But to ensure to yourself of the benefits of this change, you are called upon to exsert [sic] yourself in all respects—You are not so much in a school, as in a family for your improvement." This statement is extremely important, for it reveals the father's conception of the school as equivalent to the family, and, more important, his views about the role and function of the family in the process of childrearing; the child was effectively a vassal. He amplifies: "Each member of this family is your friend and teacher—You are in all things, whether relating to your conduct or your studies, to yield to every one of them, the most perfect obedience and respectful regard and attention—If you hope for improvement, you are to do every thing, however particular, as they think best." In short, obey. Peter continues, expressing his views about curricular matters and reminding the lad about his duty to write to his parents. He then turns to one of Henry's educational deficiencies—his composition—and the way to correct it. "We expect of course, that you will sometimes make mistakes in your spelling; but if you will, when in doubt, refer to your dictionary, you will soon correct these errors[.]" The details of Peter's admonishment—it is more than advice—should be read carefully: "For instance, in addressing your letter to me, you say 'Dear Farther'[.]"[1] Of all words to misspell!

The formality of the arrangements Henry and his father made on certain matters—the most glaring is that regarding Henry's behavior and the regimen he was to follow while attending the Albany Academy—continued long after Henry had completed his schooling. In late 1860, the young man himself, who was at the time temporarily in New York City, wanted to enter a more formal agreement concerning financial assistance from his father. He drafted a letter to Peter in late October, which is revealing for the conditions it sets forth, and even more so for the care with which he composed it. It is marked heavily with deletions and insertions, evidence that Henry, like his father a trained lawyer, was being meticulous about what he was proposing: a $5,000 advance.[2] Peter accepted his son's proposition immediately; his answer is as interesting for its tone as its content: "Last evening I rec$^d$ yr two letters of 24$^{th}$ ins$^t$ & have given to the matters presented by them, the consideration their importance required. Under the inducements expressed & the promise made in your letters to support yourself entirely by your own exertions & the profits of the sum of money you ask me to advance to you; & the hope & expectation that your <real> ↑true↓ & permanent interests may be secured by a compliance with your request, I have concluded to advance you the sum of $5000 ↑Five Thousand dollars↓ ." Peter the father offers his son the opportunity to make his own way while restricting him, and Peter the attorney protects his investment: "For your greater security & to save you from importunities hereafter, I shall require your written promise not to indorse, become security on bail, nor loan your note to any person[.]" As was his custom, he signs the letter "Peter Gansevoort,"[3] a formality reminiscent of the signature "H. Melville" with which Herman ends many of his letters, including those to his children; but whereas Herman usually said "Thine," Peter prefaced his name with formulaic phrases such as "Yr affectionate father" or "Yr true friend & affectionate father."[4] Fastidiousness in such matters is even more evident in Peter's letter of a few days later:

> You ask me to "advance to you a small sum of money (about $100) to defray such expences as arose before *you made the offer to accept* said sum ($5000) *instead of an allowance from me*"—
> I really supposed, when you first applied to me; that you requested an advance of that sum, for the purposes mentioned in your conversation & stated in your letters to me—
> Had *you offered to accept* so large a sum of money, as stated in your last letter, I certainly would not have granted it.
> In my letter to you of 26th Ult[a] to which your letter is in answer, I say that I had concluded to advance you the sum of $5000. under the inducements expressed by you & the promise made in your letters, to support yourself entirely by your own exertions & the profits of the sum you ask me to advance to you & the hope & expectation that your true & permanent interests may be secured by a *compliance with your request.*
> I did not then, nor do I now *make* you an *offer to accept the* money.
> Inclosed is my check N° 361. on the Bank of the Interior for $100, as you request, payable to y[r] order.[5]

It would be unfair to view such a transaction between father and son solely as an illustration of cold formality. While there is no evidence that we have discovered to suggest that Henry Sanford Gansevoort was anything other than a decent and useful citizen and son, with a sense of responsibility and respect for his parents (for that matter, all the institutions his life touched), Peter, it appears, was simply acting according to the understandings of parenthood that he had received from his own father. And we also call attention to the fact that Peter expresses warmth in other letters to his son from this period.[6] Henry had not been a child starved for affection or deprived of the privileges that his family, specifically his father, could afford him. In fact, he had just enjoyed a trip abroad, a grand tour if you will, the generous gift from his father. Appreciation and regard are evident in the many letters he wrote home from Paris.[7] However, while we call attention to this balance, the fact remains that Peter was fundamentally an authoritarian parent behaving according to the standards of child rearing to which he and members of his social and economic class subscribed.

Henry's personality appears not to have been seriously scarred by whatever severity he suffered by Peter's authoritarianism and his insistence, in the Gansevoort fashion, that the lad be aware of the tradition to which he was heir. When Henry was studying law at Harvard, he wrote Kate a witty, pleasant letter (one among many) in which he showed his love for family and friends, and in his own ebullient fashion described some of the historical associations he discovered in the Boston area. One hears little if any solemnity: "I suppose you would like to hear something regarding Cambridge, my present home. Well it is quite a pleasant place, (connected with Boston by a rail road) *and* rendered classic by reminiscences of the revolution[.]" There is none of the unbending reverence about such matters that one finds in Allan Melvill's correspondence as he tried to establish his father-in-law's place in history. Henry continues, "Here is the house which served George Washington as a headquarters before the Battle of Bunkers Hill. Here is the oak tree under which in the presence of the American army he first drew his sword in defence of his country." There is similar lightness when he refers to the leaders of Brahmin literary culture: "here Longfellow, Holmes Emerson and other planets of literature live." The same offhand tone prevails in his description of the campus, the students, and the academic garb they wore, or were required to wear: their "Oxford caps, very broad at the top, with a tassel[.] Their appearance is quite classical but the cap ill suits their Yankee faces." Although he is clearly happy and possesses a good sense of humor (his joke was probably inspired by his having graduated from Harvard's rival Princeton and his being a Yorker in the citadel of the Yankees), he is studying the law seriously: "Around me are numerous law books, lecture books &c. . . . I hasten to finish [this three-page letter] that I may return to my studies[.]"[8]

Whatever tensions may have been created by his upbringing, Henry appears not to have been embittered, nor were the relations between father and son damaged seriously. Consider his Aunt Maria's comment to Kate in a letter of about a decade later: she assumes her brother Peter is quite proud of Henry's having been promoted to the rank of general.[9] One inevitable conclusion the reader of the Gansevoort-Lansing Papers draws is that the constant flow of information among family members provides strong evidence of their concern about each other. An illustration, from a few years after Maria Melville's letter just cited, is from Allan Melville to Kate. He was writing from his New York City home, which had been redone, and had just returned from the South; in New Orleans he had seen Henry who, travelling along the Gulf Coast, was on his way to his post at Pensacola via Mobile. He reports, "I did not visit Pensacola, but did see Apalachacola where I was detained by business for five days. I trust the former is a more agreeable place than the latter for Henrys sake. But then the latter has the variety of the Chattahoochee river[.]"[10]

Our observations regarding the concern of members of the family circle for each other are not meant to minimize the severity of Gansevoort child-rearing practices. Rather, we wish to place their practices in the broader perspective provided by the documents on file in the Gansevoort-Lansing Collection. This balance is captured nicely in a pair of letters from 1855. In September Susan Gansevoort wrote her daughter Kate, who was attending Mrs. Sedgwick's school[11] near Pittsfield, that "Henry left yesterday morning for Buffalo where he intends to commence his studies [in law] if he can find an office that suits him." He was evidently striking out on his own, not taking advantage of the aid his father would certainly have been willing and able to provide. Neither parent was pleased with the young man's decision. "I was very anxious he should remain at home & pursue his studies for one year, but he has an idea that Albany air does not agree with him & would prefer settling some where else[.] Your father seems quite reconciled & we hope the change may be of service to him[.] God grant it may be so! He left in good spirits & with great hopes of success." But even at this juncture the parents were not cutting Henry loose, despite his desire for independence. They planned a trip that would allow them to visit Buffalo.[12] Kate had been invited on the sojourn but declined. Henry wrote to his sister about his parents' visit to him. They had arrived on Wednesday, the week before, "and on Thursday by their invitation I accompanied them to Niagara Falls. We staid at the International Hotel." He describes their touring during the following twenty-four hours, then their short trip to Lewiston, Canada. The point is that there is no tension at all in his account to his sister, one of the correspondents with whom Henry was most frank. There is even a rather enthusiastic account of a favorite family subject: "The monument of Gen'l Brock which was destroyed by the Canadian Rebels during the last insurrection is now being rebuilt by the British Government in a liberal manner. It presents a striking appearance from the entrance to the Lewiston Suspension Bridge below, as it rears its well proportioned outline far above ↑ against ↓ the horizon <above>. It stands on Queenstown Hights [sic] marking the identical spot where the General . . . received the fatal lead."[13] He continues, offering further evidence that all the lessons in the importance of American history—one might say the "experiment" itself—had taken: "Lewiston is a place full of years and horrors. Not much of a specimen of American villages for John Bull to judge of, from the opposite banks."

Henry's wish to leave Albany caused his parents' discomfort, but their acquiescence and the good spirits that afterwards prevailed are evident. He was happy in his new situation: "I am pleasantly situated here and although it is true I miss some home comforts still I am much pleased with the city and the citizens. I am in the office of Sprague and Fillmore[14] and find enough to do and considerable more if I wish it." He concludes with a reference to Herman Melville, not unexpected since Kate was boarding so close by, more evidence of fondness within the extended family: "Give my love to Cousin Herman and all the family. Tell *him* that Father expected him at Albany according to his promise and would have insisted upon his journeying with him west if he had arrived."[15]

Kate Gansevoort's relations with her father and brother reveal that she too was the subject of parental authoritarianism. Surviving documents repeat patterns of parental and sibling behavior that make the case. For example, when Peter Gansevoort was abroad in 1853, he wrote home frequently. His late August letter to Kate is representative in substance and tone. Praising her for what he assumes is her good behavior—he also mentions the same pleasure in hearing similar reports about Henry—he offers her, in light of her youth, reasonably detailed accounts of his doings abroad, inquires about what is happening at "Home, sweet home," and gently asserts his parental authority. What is most telling is the gentle tone, a marked contrast to so much of his correspondence with his son. This, like other letters to his daughter, is tender.[16] He tempers firm paternal authority with a kindly tone in his letters to her during one of the crisis periods in her life: her beginning boarding school at Mrs. Charles Sedgwick's in Lenox, Massachusetts, near cousin Herman's. Kate was dreadfully homesick, as attested to by the letters she exchanged with one of her closest confidantes, Anna Parker, daughter of the Gansevoort family friend and associate, Judge Parker.[17] Peter's response to his daughter's dilemma, as stated in a letter to her of July 1855, reveals yet again that he was a loving but firm father. His is markedly different from his wife Susan's much more understanding response.[18] In any event Kate stayed at the boarding school. (There is, by the way, further substantiation of the close links between the Peter Gansevoort household, as well as those associated with it, and the family at Arrowhead, in Anna's letter to Kate of early August in which she says that "Your mother told me before I left Albany that you were to spend that Sunday with your Aunt, Mrs Melville—Give my love to her when you see her. I have dreamed of her for the last two or three nights, & I hope my dreams will come true & that I shall see her very soon."[19] Recall that the Herman Melvilles were being helpful to Kate in this difficult period.) Kate's receiving the education which her parents—indeed, the family generally—thought appropriate for a young woman of her station (and future responsibility) took precedence over the pangs of homesickness. Henry, for instance, no matter how much one may infer he may have suffered from the demands placed upon him, was not above giving his sister advice about responsibility and the larger frame in which she should see her circumstance.[20] Nor was he above teasing her about a variety of matters, including women's suffrage. While his views are good-humored, they are equally important for our understanding how ingrained paternalism and male dominance were in the Gansevoort family, not to mention the Melvilles. In late 1856, he wrote Kate from Buffalo (she was at home on vacation) and devoted a considerable portion of his letter to the impending presidential election that James Buchanan of Pennsylvania would win. Henry jibed, "I suppose you take something of an interest in the approaching election—They say the ladies are the source of suffrage and of will—for they control their husbands ↑ political ↓ action—This I know not whether true or false but I have heard ↑ and know ↓ that <illegible word> instead of depositing votes they deposit voters—not in the ballotbox but ↑ in ↓ the cradle— They say the ladies are unanimous for Fremont and judging from their presence at his meetings I should think they were— You I hope give your sympathies to the Pennsylvania Statesman—for your Father and brother both desire his success."[21]

# Notes

1. ALs, Peter Gansevoort to Henry Sanford Gansevoort, December 5, 1846, G-L, box 163. There is a large gap in the correspondence between the father and son from 1849 to 1855.

2. ALs, Henry Sanford Gansevoort to Peter Gansevoort, October 24, 1860, G-L, box 163.

3. ALs, Peter Gansevoort to Henry Sanford Gansevoort, October 26, 1860, G-L, box 163.

4. For example, the former phrase closes the letter cited immediately above and the latter concludes ALs, Peter Gansevoort to Henry Sanford Gansevoort, November 1, 1860, G-L, box 162.

5. ALs, Peter Gansevoort to Henry Sanford Gansevoort, November 1, 1860, G-L, box 163.

6. ALs, Peter Gansevoort to Henry Sanford Gansevoort, January 11 [or 12], 1859, G-L, box 163.

7. A number of letters from the son to the father are located in box 163.

8. ALs, Henry Sanford Gansevoort to Catherine Gansevoort, October 20, 1856, G-L, box 215.

9. ALs, Maria Gansevoort Melville to Catherine Gansevoort, July 5, 1865, G-L, box 215. Maria was somewhat ahead of herself. Henry, a Democrat who vigorously supported the presidential candidacy of General George B. McClellan, left the Civil War a colonel. "Henry hoped to share his grandfather's ultimate rank of general, but though his father's friends procured him a nomination as brevet, or honorary, brigadier general, a Republican Senate refused to confirm it." Kenney, pp. 240–42.

10. ALs, Allan Melville to Catherine Gansevoort, May 14, 1867, G-L, box 216.

11. Elizabeth Buckminster Dwight Sedgwick (1791–1864), the wife of Charles Sedgwick who was a son of Theodore Sedgwick (1746–1813), conducted a boarding school in Lenox, Massachusetts. *Appleton's*.

12. ALs, Susan Gansevoort to Catherine Gansevoort, September 5, 1855, G-L, box 245, album 1.

13. Sir Isaac Brock (1769–1812) was killed by American forces near Niagara, New York. He was buried at Fort George, and a dozen years later his remains were placed beneath the Etruscan column that had been raised as a monument to him. The monument was blown up in 1840, but a column topped with his statue was constructed shortly at a cost of £5,000. Another marker is at the spot where Brock actually fell. *Appleton's*.

14. The E. C. Sprague and Millard Powers Fillmore law firm was located at 190½ Main in Buffalo. *1860 Commercial Advertiser Directory*. Millard Powers Fillmore was the son of ex-President Millard Fillmore (1800–74). Robert J. Rayback, *Millard Fillmore: Biography of a President* (Buffalo: Henry Stewart for the Buffalo Historical Society, 1959), pp. 46–47.

15. ALs, Henry Sanford Gansevoort to Catherine Gansevoort, September 23, 1855, G-L, box 245, album 1.

16. ALs, Peter Gansevoort to Catherine Gansevoort, August 21, 1853, G-L, box 215.

17. Amasa Junius Parker (1807–90). *DAB*. For the girls' intimacy see Anna L. Parker's letters to Kate, June 26, July 14, and August 4, 1855, G-L, box 215.

18. Draft ALs, Peter Gansevoort to Catherine Gansevoort, July 31, 1855, G-L, box 215.

19. ALs, Anna L. Parker to Catherine Gansevoort, August 21, 1853, G-L box 215.

20. ALs, Henry Sanford Gansevoort to Catherine Gansevoort, June 4, 1855, G-L, box 245, album 1; and June 11, 1855, G-L, box 245, album 1.

21. ALs, Henry Sanford Gansevoort to Catherine Gansevoort, July 27, 1856, G-L, box 215.

# Appendix G
# The Lemuel Shaws: A Contrast to the
# Melville-Gansevoorts

JUDGE LEMUEL SHAW'S OUTWARD IMAGE among many modern
legal historians and Melvilleans is somewhat forbidding, to say
the least. His reputation as a lawyer and jurist, public servant,
and activist involved in many causes dominates to the point of
obscuring his roles as son, husband, parent—in a phrase, as a
member of a family. True, as a public man he was stern and
formal, if not intimidating, a man of seemingly uncompromis-
ing integrity who was dedicated to his profession and the institutions to which he gave himself. However, little attention has
been paid to him as husband and, especially important for our
discussion, father. Without suggesting that the conventional
perception of him as a public figure is distorted, we wish to
explore the neglected personal side of his life.

His interest in his family is evident in a short letter of 1830
to his second wife, Hope, in which he rather matter-of-factly
announces that he has accepted the nomination as Chief Justice
of the Massachusetts Supreme Court—a major achievement by
any measure—and reports that "We are all well. My mother,
Oakes[,] Elizabeth & self all dined at Mr. Melvill's today."[1] In
general, such communications to his wife were business-like, occasionally brusque, even before they were married. But they
frequently concerned family matters in some measure. Several
years earlier, for instance, he wrote from Boston to Barnstable
(on Cape Cod) a less-than-ardent letter and managed to devote
more than half of it to news about his family: "My mother &

children are quite well. My mother considering her age, and the severity of season, has enjoyed good health through the winter." He reported on his son Oakes's progress at the school he was attending at Jamaica Plain: "He is between six and seven, is an intelligent & good tempered boy, & quite a favorite at the school. This I suppose results partly from the consideration[?] of his being the smallest & youngest, & therefore entitled to be a pet, & partly from his constant good nature." A widower, Shaw had placed the boy in boarding school. The modern reader, however, should not interpret sending a child away to school at so tender an age as an act of callousness, much less a sign of parental indifference. He also reports on Elizabeth: "My daughter is between 4 & 5 . . . amiable, intelligent & enga[ging]. . . .² She goes to school constantly, & h[as] already made considerable proficiency. She can read very well, ordinary pieces both in prose & poetry. Perhaps you may think I am influenced by my partiality. It may be partly so, but I think I cannot be [undeciphered word] as to the leading & predominant truth of this characterizing[?]."³ However occupied he may have been in his profession and courtship during this period, the Judge did not lose sight of the centrality of his children in his life.

This continues to be so even after Hope and he were married. The manuscript reader must not allow these sensitivities, these genuine concerns, to be obscured by Shaw's businesslike tone, reinforced by his aggressively open and sprawling penmanship, the sign of the man of affairs with little time to waste on trifles. In a letter of April 1834 to his wife from Worcester, Massachusetts, he is almost all business but near the end says that he is "very[?] anxious to hear from home, as often as your engagements will admit. Do ask Oakes & Elizabeth to write to me, & expend their best faculties, in giving me an account full [of] the news, domestic matters & incidents. Samuel & Lemuel I must be content to hear from by deputy, at present. I hope the latter little gentlemant [sic] will not forget me. I long most to see him. It gives me great pleasure to learn that my mother seems so[?] well[?], is able to be abroad so much." The Judge was riding circuit with the Court, but the distractions of his professional duties did not diminish his interest in domestic matters. He closes this letter, "Do let me hear from you often."[4] In 1830, when he had also been in Worcester, he revealed the same concern. About half of a three-page letter is devoted to his wife and the children; he begins the family portion in a manner he used when ending that just cited: "I hope you will write me frequently. I have the most anxious desire to hear often from my dear wife & children. Tell my mother she need feel no anxiety for my health at present, though I am grateful to her and all my friends for their Solicitude. Tell Oakes that I hope by the time I return, I hope he will be quite satisfied with his school, that though he may find it hard now, I have no doubt that before long he will find it quite easy and agreeable. That I hope he will become better acquainted with his school-mates, that I advise him by all means to form an acquaintance only with those who are good.—Tell Elizabeth that I feel the utmost anxiety on her account & nothing would afford me more pleasure than to hear that she is kind, affectionate, obedient & good tempered. Tell Lemuel that father loves him dearly, longs to see him & hopes that he will be a good[5] boy. . . . I hope you will write me often."[6] Seven years later, on circuit in Springfield, he wrote his wife, filling about a quarter of his report on business with family concerns. The children were ill. "I have received two letters from you since I arrived here. . . . I am very glad to hear from all the children, as well those who can write as those who cannot. I was led to believe from Elizabeth's letter that Lemuel unquestionably had the whooping cough, & I suppose it highly probable that Samuel would have it too. I shall not much regret it; it is an uncomfortable & trying disease, but one which they probably must have, & could hardly hope to have at a more favorable season of the year. I am anxious to hear whether it is the whooping cough or not. I hope you will continue the practice of writing me daily, be assured I feel a deep interest in every thing tha[t][?] occurs in family, or affects the interests or feelings of any single[?] member of it. I shall write to Elizabeth in a few days, & I hope also to my mother."[7]

Nor did the passing years diminish his attachments to home and hearth when riding circuit. In 1840, he again wrote Hope, this time focusing on not being available to help Lemuel, as well as articulating his concern for the entire family.[8] Such expressions of solicitude reveal his conscientious sense of duty to his children. This is illustrated when, writing Hope in 1833, he expressed the pleasure he received when one of the family's letters arrived and stated how anxiously he anticipated turning his "face homeward." He reported that he had gotten "the letter of the children" and had immediately written Oakes: "I feel anxious about him but hope his illness is not serious. I think he wants relaxation and exercizing, & if he goes to school at all that his evening lessons ought to be dispense[d][9] with for some time." But then he continues, "I think I mark[?] a great alteration in his hand-writing, but I presume he will be obliged to practice a good deal, after he has finished his lessons, to [undeciphered word] & his [sic] improve his [sic] newly acquired hand." Nor was Lizzie neglected. The Judge promised "to write to Elizabeth [when] she has returned to Uxbridge."[10] This same combination of tenderness and authority is present in an 1831 letter to his wife, in which he says: "I hope Oakes & Elizabeth are both improving in health &[?] character, & enjoying this fine season in the country Give my love to them; & tell them how anxious I am for their improvement in all respects. . . . [and am] desirous of seeing them."[11] There was also humor in the parents' perceptions of their children. Writing the Judge in 1833, Hope reported in a postscript that "Elizabeth told me, that Lemuel requested to *marry her* when *he was a man*; but— then ↑ *she* ↓ *was not to mention this engagement to any one.*"[12] Several years later she reported, among other matters, that "Lemuel has written a little letter to you & I think that I shall copy it as it is short. I mentioned to Sam[l] your wish respecting him. He says 'I do not know what to say,' but with a little assistance respecting arranging his sentences—Tell Papa the Martins have got into their house—& tell I have not had the black mittens on, or the *fools cap*." And here Hope transcribes the child's letter to his father, written the previous week, dated "Boston Sunday 23." One sees here the pleasures sensitive parents can find in their children. The letter also provides a glimpse into young Lemuel's adaptation to the easy atmosphere of Bronson Alcott's school, which he was attending, and it offers some insight into the boy's notion of what was in progress at the institution which his parents had carefully selected for his early education: "How do you do? <I have> I have been very well since you have been gone except having a ↑ large double ↓ tooth out. I have given up my theatre. And to replace it, I have got a shop from which I expect to gain some profit[.] Mr Alcott expects some new scholars if he makes his price lower. And he must remove to a nother room it is in the Masonic temple at the little gate in the temple place. I believe I have got the whooping cough. Mr Alcott is agoing to take little children of Samuel's age for five dollars ↑ 5. years old & *15 dollars* ↓ a quarter, till they are 7 years old[.] all other age 25. dollars." The boy signs the letter "Yours affectionately," and Hope adds that "I write this just as he did—in sealing it, he burnt his letter—but I will keep the original for you."[13]

Lizzie demonstrates tenderness toward her father in correspondence such as that of early November 1843, an omnibus letter (by family members and house guests) from Boston; the Judge was in Salem, Massachusetts, and down with a cold. "After what has been said by our illustrious guests, any thing that I could write would probably appear tame and unmeaning, nevertheless I here offer you my heartfelt sympathy for your sickness increased, doubtless, by separation from your family and friends. Earnestly desiring your speedy return, I remain your affectionate daughter, Elizabeth." Similar ease of relations is evident in the notes of the others who contributed to this letter. Perhaps the feelings were best summed up in the lines with which Hope concluded the letter: "As its [*sic*] uncertain when you return I am afraid to wait for the children to write, after receiving so much love & sympathy. I hurry with this Letter to convince you how *dear you are* to us when *with us* and when separated from us." And she adds, "With much love—and impatience for an answer—truly most truly."[14]

The views of Judge Shaw and his wife, Hope, on parental responsibility and child rearing are reflected in their thinking on education. Substantial information on this subject appears in the Lemuel Shaw Papers collected in the Massachusetts Historical Society. A good avenue to follow is their concern for Lemuel Shaw, Jr.'s schooling.

Judge and Mrs. Shaw had a profound interest in education,

not only their own (and Hope's stepchildren), but generally. The Judge expressed himself forcefully on the value of education in the letters he wrote his children. Those to Lemuel are representative.

Addressing the boy, who was away at boarding school in 1842, the Chief Justice's letter voiced his concern for Lemuel's educational progress, which was no different from that he displayed for his other children, and provides a broad statement of his philosophy, laced with practical advice, the sort of wisdom many parents feel compelled to give to the younger generation. The father concentrates on the content rather than the practical advantages to be gained from education and reveals a sensitivity to the subject as well as his son:

> I have been reflecting, with the deepest anxiety, almost ever since you was last at home, upon the future course of your education. You know we had some conversation about, but nothing by any means definite. I have in this matter, no one object in view, but to promote your own best interests. The great purpose of all education is, to enable one, most effectually and certainly to accomplish the great objects for which life is given, to be useful, honorable, virtuous, & happy, to perform most efficiently & completely the duties of the present life, & be able to look, with a humble hope & a firm confidence in the wisdom & mercy of God, to the joys & blessings of a future state of existence. But this, we shall I hope have time & opportunity to discuss <this> more hereafter. The object now is, rather to consider the means than the objects of high & liberal education. I think you are now old enough & manly enough to look at this subject, with the steadiness and sobriety, which its importance demands. You are old enough, & have reflected enough to understand & appreciate the value of a useful and thorough education; and yet you are still young enough, & have time enough before you, to accomplish all the great purposes of education, with care & certainty. This is to be done, not by occasional efforts & violent exertions, but by steady & pressing[?] industry. It is not necessary, indeed it would not be beneficial, if you were disposed, to worry & fatigue yourself, by *very* hard or *very* long study, at one time; it would do more hurt than good. But the great object is to have a systematic distribution of time, to study as *many* hours each day, carefully & diligently, as are allotted for study, &

which can be done without fatigue. It is this steady industry, which accomplishes every thing elevated, honorable and useful. It is indolence and frivolous and idle pursuits, which wastes our time & our faculties, to no purpose.

I have been long of opinion, & you know I have often stated to you, in conversation, that for the earlier years of a boy's education, before his mind is sufficiently mature for the higher branches of philosophy and science, there is no system of education so useful, so beneficial, so well calculated to cultivate the young man, & [undeciphered word] for the great subjects of inquiry which are to follow, as a careful, exact & systematic study of the latin & greek languages. The reasons for this opinion, I will give you more fully hereafter. You have now arrived at an age, at which I think it will be for your benefit, to devote yourself, for some time to these studies with vigour and perseverance, and with a determination to master them. This I desire, not on my own account but solely on yours, & because I think it the best mode of training, to which you can devote yourself, not however wholly omitting such other branches of study, as are necessary to a complete liberal education. But for some time at least, latin & greek, I think, are to be the leading objects. Then the next inquiry is if you agree with me in this view, what is the best situation in which you can be placed in order to prosecute these studies with the best hopes of success. To continue where you are To come into Boston & go to the latin school or to go to some academy or other school in the county?[15]

Clearly, the Judge was a devoted believer in the study of the classics as a foundation for education. But one should also note how he engages his son in consideration of the subject. Absent is the extreme authoritarianism one hears, for instance, in the assertions and demands of Peter Gansevoort when discussing such matters with his son, Henry. Judge Shaw is as persuaded, we suspect, of the correctness of his views as was Peter. His style, however, is more congenial; he engages the child in discussion rather than ruling by fiat. He seeks to persuade and encourages the boy to participate in the decision rather than making him the subject (or victim) of it.

Young Lemuel was at the time attending a school run by Joseph Allen,[16] a situation in which he was sometimes pleased and comfortable but frequently unhappy. Burdened with cares and responsibilities, the Judge found time to communicate with his son, especially about his schooling, on what appears to have been a fairly regular basis. In an earlier 1842 letter, he began somewhat apologetically, "I believe it is a good while since I have written to you, but be assured it is owing to my constant engagements, not to a want of deep interest in your welfare & prospects. I believe you know me well enough to believe that whether I write to you or not, I think of you often, love you dearly, & most constantly wish you well, happy, & good."[17] The Judge was not spare in expressing the emotional bonds he felt with his children. He continues in a rhetorical fashion often employed in his correspondence with them—mixing mild censure with affection and understanding: "I believe you have not written to me during the present term but am not certain." He then turns to the lad's studies, as usual to promote his work in the classics. "It gives me great pleasure to hear that [you] like Virgil, and that you are getting on sucessfully in the study of that delightful poet. You may find the study of latin & greek as I have often told you, a little dry at first, yet I now repeat the assurance which I have given you before, that upon the fullest reflection & considerable experience I am convinced that the study of the latin & greek, languages, affords the [undeciphered word] basis of a useful & elegant education. I advise you therefore to persevere & let no impediments dishearten you. There are no difficulties which thousands before you have not overcome." Having more to say on a subject evidently so dear to him, Chief Justice Shaw promised, "When I see you I give you my views more fully on these subjects. I do not think it necessary to set your self great &[?] endeavor by extraordinary exertions to do a great deal in a short time."[18] (One might infer that Judge Shaw would be pleased by the interest in the classics of his future son-in-law, Herman Melville. He might also have been disappointed that Melville had small Latin and no Greek.)[19] The boy's father exhorts him to steadiness and industry, as he often did. But he is not merely pressuring the boy. There is an emotional resonance not apparent in the relations between Peter Gansevoort and his son and, judging by some of the key surviving evidence, between Herman Melville and his children. Chief Justice Shaw continues, "I wish you would write

me and give me an account of your studies ↑ & ↓ progress[?][.]
I write to forewarn you in season, that in fitting for college, it is
extremely desirable not only to be just fit, so that you can square
in, that you be fully & abundantly fitted so you may not only
enter with ease & certainty, but be able to take a high stand.
. . . In this matter, I speak from experience." And here the
father is signally honest with his son. "I was very poorly & in-
sufficiently fitted, & felt the ill effects of it, two or three years."
As usual he signs himself "Your affectionate father."[20] As a matter of fact Judge Shaw had failed in his first attempt to pass the
admission examination for Harvard.[21]

In his insistence that the boy study the classics, the judge was
building on foundations he had laid earlier—for example, in a
letter to Lemuel almost a year before, in which he had said: "I
was extremely delighted with your determination to learn the
greek alphabet out of school, that you might commence the
grammar with Mr Allen's son. It was so much the more agreeable as it showed an energy & resolution which if persevered in,
will carry you forward to almost any height of success, which
you may aim at. A vigorous and spontaneous effort of your own
mind can do more for you, than any exertions of others, however much they may feel interested in your welfare and success." One point that should be noted is that rather than forcing
the young scholar to adopt his father's values, the Judge is en-
couraging the child's independence and inculcating responsibility for the decisions being made at these early critical junc-
tures in his life. Nor should we lose sight of Judge Shaw's
sensitivity to the practical uses of education.

The Judge's concerns about curriculum were not limited to
the study of the classics. He continues in this letter: "Next to
your religious moral character, which are [sic] nearest my heart,
I desire that you shall be qualified for some useful and honorable pursuit in life; and to accomplish this object, I wish to see
you making the best improvement of your time and opportunities to get the best possible education. With this you will be in
a good condition to enter on any pursuit or profession, which
your genius and inclination may dictate, when the time comes
for making a choice."[22]

Lemuel Shaw was not stodgy on educational matters, as his

guidance of young Lemuel's early education illustrates. According to tuition receipts in the Shaw Papers, the Judge entrusted his son's education to Bronson Alcott from at least late 1834 until at least early 1837.[23] Alcott, notable for his revolutionary teaching methods and his Transcendental philosophy, was conducting a school at Boston's Masonic Temple at the time. It was the general opinion that "there had never been such a schoolmaster before—and when he ended, there would never be, so far as Boston could help it, such a schoolmaster again." The school, which catered to the offspring of the city's elite, began, as did virtually all Alcott's ventures, with great promise and ended in disaster.[24]

It would probably be unfair to suggest that, in light of the Judge's long-term commitment to the improvement of public education, he was even partially motivated to send young Lemuel to the Masonic Temple School in order to shield him from having to attend a public institution, which, Shepard suggests, was the motive of most parents of Alcott's pupils.[25] The Judge was willing to experiment. The Alcott classroom was not the scene of a free-for-all; rather, "Perfect order and steady concentration upon whatever is in hand is quietly insisted upon."[26] Alcott no doubt "departed" even more than he had earlier "from the English mechanism of the 'Lancastrian' or 'monitorial' system as he had seen it at work at Philadelphia and New York,"[27] the system Herman Melville and so many other future literati had been subjected to at the New York Male High School on Crosby Street.[28] Lemuel Shaw chose as his son's teacher a man already known for radical methods. Yet as eccentric as he may have been, Alcott was a responsible thinker. His personality, ideas, and intelligence were not only sufficient to allow the families of the thirty-seven children enrolled to trust him, but to win him the friendship of the emerging leader of the Transcendentalist group, Ralph Waldo Emerson.

Alcott's was an experiment in what he understood as Christian education. One student of his educational theory and practice describes the goal of the Temple School: "He proposed to turn the mind of the child inward upon itself, that the child might gain a knowledge of the divinity in his inner being, and that he might learn to appeal to that inner principle as a guide to conduct."[29] Punishments were a matter of consensus, and all the activities were designed to promote "social living in accord with Christian ideal."[30] The venture collapsed when Alcott lost the support of Elizabeth Palmer Peabody, who was critical of the school's operation and very visible in the community, especially among intellectuals, and collided with influential figures in Boston, including Dr. William Ellery Channing.[31] Despite the good advice of people like Judge Shaw, who suggested more practicality, the school collapsed with the country's economy in 1837.[32] And so the Judge had to turn elsewhere to continue his son's education.

From early in 1838 to 1842, young Lemuel boarded at a rural school for about fifteen boys in Northborough, Massachusetts, conducted by the Reverend Joseph Allen.[33] And from almost the beginning of his stay, there is evidence that all was not well with him there.[34] For example, in a note appended to one of the boy's letters home in 1839, the schoolmaster, while noting that "Lemuel has conducted himself quite well this term," also observed that he thought Lemuel "has enjoyed himself better than before."[35] Several months later (as indicated by the Judge's note of receipt on the document) relations between the lad and his teacher had deteriorated; the Reverend Mr. Allen told the Judge that he "was mortified & distressed that Lemuel should open the letter I addressed to you—not because I was unwilling that he should see what I wrote—but because I chose you should see it first. & because it is very improper for him to break a sealed letter without leave of the person to whom it is directed."[36] The situation became worse the following summer when Lemuel returned to school after enjoying his vacation at home with the family. He was homesick. Allen himself, however, did not observe his unhappiness but became aware of it indirectly; writing the Judge in August 1840, he began, "I was sorry & surprised to learn from your letter, that Lemuel was not contented." He went on defensively to describe the preference of some of the boys of Lemuel's age to attend school in the city rather than the country, pointing out that his "school was composed principally of small boys," and he asserted that he "had seen no symptoms of dissatisfaction . . . in . . . Lemuel for some time." The teacher said that if such unhappiness should continue, he would not object to the family's decision to have him attend another school, a Boston institution "of a high order of excellence."[37]

The situation illustrates how deeply involved Judge Shaw was in the lives of this child and, we might note, in those of his others. A letter to Lemuel, dated the next month, provides a labyrinthine set of tentative travel plans for both the Judge and his wife and sketches in detail the alternatives for Lemuel, Jr.'s joining either or both of them while they are in transit. One is struck by the Judge's strategy: he outlines the alternatives while allowing the child to make the decision. Yet despite this manner of handling the child, Shaw closes by warning him that "If you go alone in the cars, 'be careful.' "[38] (There is not a little humor in the note on a small slip of paper placed in the folded three-page letter, which is scrawled in a crabbed hand, perhaps Lemuel, Jr.'s, when he reread this letter as an old man: "Lemuel Shaw Jr/all fathers are alike / he urges much care[.]")[39] And, in perfect keeping with this profound sense of family, the Judge reminds him in a postscript, "Remember that this is the anniversary of the death of your dear grandmother, remember her."[40]

It does not appear that Lemuel was having academic difficulty. For instance, one of Allen's progress reports to the family (in either 1841 or 1842) states that "Lemuel has attended principally this term to French & Arithmatic. He has begun Algebra & I think will soon learn to like it. He has finished the Life of Washington in French—and will begin Charles the 12th next term. I think he has studied as well and made as much proficiency as in any former term and his conduct has generally been good."[41] If Allen were pleased with his progress, Lemuel was not. Writing to his parents in June 1842, he began with a description of daily events at school and in the community, then launched into a critique of Mr. Allen's management, based partially on the experience of having attended Bronson Alcott's school for several years. He was quite serious about his education and also perfectly open with his mother and father about matters that many young people, particularly fourteen-year-olds, would prefer not to acknowledge, much less initiate discussion of.

I think I have now found what is the reason this school is not so good for me. It is because I am not stimulated to do enough; I only study six hours and then I dont study so very diligently and it is left to my own pleasure whether I study out of school or not and if I do it all very well and if I dont nobody knows or cares if I go to study this little thing takes my attention and then that and so I do not study much. I think that I need to [go] to a school where there is a stated lesson and where I am spurred on to do something; there is too much *innate laziness* in me. Mr Allen is just the thing for *little* boys. I cant possibly express what I want to in writing. I think I want a stricter master than Mr Allen and one that has more firmness or resolution. He lets me have my own way too much and if that [is] the case my innate laziness prevails over all good resolutions I can make; for a few days I can study dilligently and after that very[?] law quickly[?] some thing[.] I like Mr Allen father writ[ing]⁴² that I wants [sic] me to read a loud in school;⁴³ that for about a week perhaps a fortnight he has the boys read every day and then he leaves off gradually and we dont hear anything more of or reading *that* term: and it is pretty much so with every thing else. He goes by fits and starts too much.⁴⁴

A few years had matured Lemuel significantly. For example, in his letter of July 31, 1839, quoted above, his report had concentrated upon outdoor activities such as berrying, boating, and gardening; he had waited until the last line to report, "I study Latin a great deal here"⁴⁵—this after all the Judge's exhortations about the value of the classics. On the whole, however, there is no doubt that Judge Shaw had a profound influence on him. The tone, posture, and substance of his counsel to his son, as well as his affection, are evident in an 1840 letter to Lemuel, who was having such difficulty adjusting to life at Allen's after his evidently glorious vacation. We quote it in full:

I saw your letter to your mother the other day, in which you speak of your being banished from a home that you love, but in which you are not loved, and much more to the same effect. I am much surprised, or rather I should be very much surprised, at language like this, if I thought it true and sincere, and if you truly believed what you thus ↑ say ↓ . But I am convinced that it is the language of dissatisfaction of natural disappointment, which you feel keenly, and express strongly in leaving home, after a pleasant vacation. No Lemuel, your parents and your family do love you, love you dearly, and you must know it & feel it, and upon a little cool reflection must acknowledge it. You have felt and enjoyed, the ardent, sincere love and devoted affection of your mother too long, to harbour a doubt on that subject. By [*sic*] my Dear boy, we have not only a fervent feeling of affection to gratify, as parents, but a high duty to perform. [Note that the Judge shifts here from the heart to the head, to his sense of duty.] And although it might be more agreeable to us, for the time being, to have you with us, to see you often, and enjoy your society, yet we are bound to look beyond the present hour, and to place ↑ you ↓ in such a situation as aims[?] but calculated to promote your present and future welfare.

Your own welfare here and hereafter, in this life and in the life to come, depend upon the character you may form in your youth, depend upon your education. And by the blessing of God, we mean to adopt such a concern as in our judgment, will be best calculated to promote your good, whether it is the most agreeable at the time or not. You will soon arrive at years of manhood if your life is spared, to take your place in the world, and to stand or fall by your own merits & qualifications. If in the mean time you have established a good character, if you have formed and cherished pious and devout sentiments, a true, thorough and warm[?] love of God, feelings of kindness and benevolence to all Mankind, with high moral and intellectual improvement, you may be useful honorable and happy. You will have the prospect of enjoying all the blessings which this life can afford and of leaving it with the cheering hope of a happy immortality beyond the grave. But if your youth is wasted on trifling amusements, and mere temporary pleasures you will fall into habits of indolence, perhaps of vice, and become a useless if not a pernicious member of society. Now you have an opportunity to acquire good habits, by industry, by determination and persevering resolution, to pursue those studies and those objects, which may assure[?] you real good. There is no obstacle, which at your time of life good resolution cannot overcome. You have now the means in your power. You have friends able and willing to assist you. How long our lives may be spared you know not. You may soon be left a helpless orphan & be compelled to depend on yourself. Save the present moment then take advantage of the present time, see what is before you, & determine now that you will be an industrious useful, honorable man. Your affectionate father,

Lemuel Shaw[46]

From one vantage point, the advice and encouragement the Chief Justice provides his namesake is conventional, at least for the vigorously entrepreneurial ethic then emphasized in American society. In fact, it is almost the same as that we hear from Peter Gansevoort. The difference, however, is in the style, the tone. There is no reason to suspect that the Judge is less than sincere in his assertions of the family's affection and love for young Lemuel; only the most cynical would read the opening of the letter as a clever strategy by a jurist skilled in the ways of argument designed to soften the youngster for the short lecture on the purposes and promises of education and the effective ways of spending one's youth. This letter is only one of many to his children—and to others with whom he felt close ties—that express such emotion and principles openly.

Within a few years Lemuel had indeed outgrown Allen's academy. In August 1842, Judge Shaw wrote the boy from Boston to announce his decision to send him to the Boston Latin School: "After making all the inquiries & getting the best information in my power, regarding Mr Allen's letter & taking into consideration all the circumstances, I have come to the conclusion, that it is best for you to enter the Boston Latin School." This was not merely caving in to Lemuel's complaints about his Northborough experience, but a move made with the boy's best interests in view. The Judge explains: "It will be a most important & critical period in your life, on which your future character and success in life may greatly depend, and I earnestly hope & pray that it may be beneficial to you." Judge Shaw continued in his usual vein: "Many suggestions occur to me . . . in regard to your studies and the regulation of your conduct both in and out of school; but I ↑ shall ↓ have leisure and opportunity ↑ I hope ↓ , to do that fully hereafter. I depend upon your good sense, & your sensible and conscientious regard to the dictates of duty, as the best security for diligence and good conduct."[47] There is a nice balance here between authority and encouragement. He treats the young man as a mature and responsible person in charge of his own affairs while he supports him at another important juncture in his young life, a point where they were making a most important decision about his education and, as they appear to have fully recognized, his future. Lemuel, Jr., took his entrance examinations and was formally admitted to the Latin School on August 18.[48] On October 1, the first "monthly report of [his] rank and deportment" was issued. His studies in Latin grammar and penmanship earned him the twenty-sixth place in a class of forty, and his "Recitations and Exercises" were for the most part of the highest order; when they were less, they were of the second and third highest (on a six-part scale). A congenial, serious, and obedient young man who attended school to work, as his family wished, his rank in conduct was first in the class. The Judge, as he frequently did with such documents, labeled this when he filed it, "Lemuel's character."[49] There was more at stake than academic performance in this matter of education and progress reports. The school placed premium importance on both deportment and studies, which for the Judge added up to that larger category, "character."

As a child in the Boston area, Elizabeth Knapp Shaw, who was to become Herman Melville's wife, attended several schools. That run by Mary Lamb was to be her earliest. She was there from the spring of 1826, probably with little interruption, through late May 1829, at least.[50] The receipts surviving in the Shaw papers indicate that her brother Lemuel had attended Miss Lamb's school from early June through early October 1823, and probably during the winter term of 1822–23.[51] Given the evidence of the Judge's sensitivity in the care and education of Lemuel, for example, it appears likely that Mary Lamb's tutelage, probably the whole atmosphere and tenor of the school, was gentle, at least when measured by standards of the period. But this presumed gentleness was no doubt countered when Lizzie was enrolled in the Monitorial School run by D. Francis, apparently right after she had left Miss Lamb's. The surviving evidence suggests that she attended the Francis School through July 1832, though the lapse in the written record—receipts from the school for the payment of tuition—indicates that she may have missed all of 1830 as well as parts of 1831–32.[52] Perhaps its rigor is suggested by the comment that appears in the small space labeled "General Character for the Quarter" on the first of the receipts: "pretty good, her offences being those of thoughtlessness, and diminishing daily." The Monitorial School followed the same educational theory as the New York Male High School attended by her future husband. Upon finishing her studies there, she was sent immediately to the Uxbridge Classical School kept by Samuel Clarke where she boarded, of course, until late March 1834.[53] Missing documentation is a problem encountered throughout the record of Lizzie's schooling that can be assembled from the Shaw papers. She next began George B. Emerson's school in Boston, thus enabling her to stay at home. She was there for the most part from November 1835 through May 1837, but then there is a lapse in documentation until the session running from November 1840 to February 20, 1841.[54] Emerson's institution was conducted with a certain seriousness leavened with humaneness. This is suggested, for example, in a handwritten form letter sent to the Judge (and presumably all others whose children were in attendance) in July 1836, setting forth the reasons for not having a summer recess of more than twelve weeks.[55] More important, though, is the information about educational theory and curriculum provided by Emerson's memoir and other writings.

One of his early ventures in education was as founding principal of Boston's English Classical School. Its board was served by several distinguished citizens, including Judge Shaw, who from the beginnings in 1820 gave Emerson the freedom to design the program as he chose.[56] As he described his attitudes toward pupils and his views of teaching, he was a gentle yet firm instructor whose principal goal was to "Educate the conscience."[57] In 1823, he was lured from the English Classical School to begin one for young ladies. There is no reason to doubt that he adhered to the same principles that governed his work at the English Classical School. The purpose was to form character. The curriculum emphasized language study: English, Latin except for those whose parents objected (Judge Shaw would certainly not have), French, and Italian. There were also arithmetic, history, and science.[58] It is unclear whether Emerson himself was teaching when Lizzie was enrolled, but he was in control of the curriculum and the selection of gifted teachers, a matter he was passionate about. He was not as radical as Alcott, but his ideas on education appear to have been much more progressive than those at the schools Herman Melville attended.

This is the extent of Elizabeth's formal education, though it included a significant amount of enrichment by private tutoring and organized group activity. A major point that must be appreciated is that she had experiences as a student that in some respects were similar to Herman Melville's but in others were markedly different. The Judge appears to have monitored his children's education more closely than Allan and Maria Melvill. Perhaps more important, Justice Shaw seems to have been more gentle and sensitive than Herman's parents, certainly more so than his uncle Peter Gansevoort. In addition, Shaw had a near professional interest in education.[59] He was man who, however pressed by the demands of his profession and family, made time to learn about subjects such as educational theory and to serve Boston in practical ways.[60]

# Notes

1. ALs, Lemuel Shaw to Hope Savage Shaw, August 25, 1830, LSP, box 9.

2. Some parts of the letter at this point are undecipherable because the paper is worn away.

3. ALs, Lemuel Shaw to Hope Savage, February 14, 1827, LSP, box 8; quoted in part in Metcalf, p. 30. There is the same sort of interest shown in other letters, such as ALs, Lemuel Shaw to Elizabeth Haywood, February 8, 1827, LSP, box 8.

4. ALs, Lemuel Shaw to Hope Savage Shaw, April 29, 1834, LSP, box 10.

5. Shaw deleted one letter here because it was evidently the false start of a word.

6. ALs, Lemuel Shaw to Hope Savage Shaw, October 3, 1830, LSP, box 9.

7. ALs, Lemuel Shaw to Hope Savage Shaw, May 4, 1837, LSP, box 11.

8. ALs, Lemuel Shaw to Hope Savage Shaw, May 22, 1840, LSP, box 12.

9. This last letter is covered by sealing wax.

10. ALs, Lemuel Shaw to Hope Savage Shaw, May 14, 1833, LSP, box 10.

11. ALs, Lemuel Shaw to Hope Savage Shaw, June 4, 1831, LSP, box 10.

12. ALs, Hope Savage Shaw to Lemuel Shaw, April 28, 1833, LSP, box 10.

13. ALs, Hope Savage Shaw to Lemuel Shaw, April 30, 1837, LSP, box 11.

14. ALs, Elizabeth Knapp Shaw et al. to Lemuel Shaw, November 9, 1843, LSP, box 12.

15. ALs, Lemuel Shaw to Lemuel Shaw, Jr., July 25, 1842, LSP, box 12.

16. The Reverend Joseph Allen (1790–1873), Harvard educated, was pastor of the Congregational Church at Northborough, Massachusetts, for fifty-seven years, beginning in 1816. He wrote local histories, genealogies, sermons, and schoolbooks. *A Supplement to Allibone's Critical Dictionary of English Literature and British and American Authors* . . . (Philadelphia: J. B. Lippincott, 1891). The school he conducted was evidently connected with the church.

17. ALs, Lemuel Shaw to Lemuel Shaw, Jr., February 20, 1842, LSP, box 12.

18. ALs, Lemuel Shaw to Lemuel Shaw, Jr., February 20, 1842, LSP, box 12.

19. David K. Titus, "Herman Melville at the Albany Academy," *Melville Society Extracts*, 42 (May 1980), 1, 4–10, establishes that Melville studied Latin.

20. ALs, Lemuel Shaw to Lemuel Shaw, Jr., February 20, 1842, LSP, box 12.

21. Samuel Shaw, "Lemuel Shaw: Early and Domestic Life," *Memorial Biographies of the New England Historic and Genealogical Society* (Boston: Published by the Society, 1885), 204–5. Among other items, this book contains vol. 4 (1860–62), in which the article appeared.

22. ALs, Lemuel Shaw to Lemuel Shaw, Jr., April 15, 1841, LSP, box 12.

23. Receipts, Bronson Alcott to Lemuel Shaw, March 1, 1835, LSP, box 10; November 28, 1835, box 10; February 19, 1836, box 11; May 14, 1836, box

11; July 23, 1836, box 11; October 15, 1836, box 11; and (in the form of an ALs, Bronson Alcott to Lemuel Shaw), February 18, 1837, box 11.

24. Odell Shepard, *Pedlar's Progress* (Boston: Little, Brown, 1937), pp. 164–65. One of Alcott's most enthusiastic supporters at the beginning was Hawthorne's future sister-in-law, Elizabeth Palmer Peabody, who published a complete record of his educational experiment. Titled *Record of a School* (Shepard, Alcott's biographer, drew on it heavily for his account of the school), it points up the orderliness of the classroom Alcott conducted, as well as his desire to develop morally conscious, socially sensitive, and imaginative students.

25. Shepard, p. 165.

26. Shepard, p. 167.

27. Shepard, p. 123.

28. Murray and Taylor, pp. 5–6.

29. Dorothy McCuskey, *Bronson Alcott, Teacher* (New York: Macmillan, 1940), p. 82.

30. McCuskey, pp. 85 and 90.

31. Shepard, pp. 180–208. See note 24.

32. McCuskey, pp. 99–108.

33. ALs, Joseph Allen to Lemuel Shaw, February 22, 1838, LSP, box 11, and Joseph Allen to Lemuel Shaw, March 13, 1838, LSP, box 11.

34. ALs, Joseph Allen to Lemuel Shaw, November 11, 1840, LSP, box 12.

35. ALs, Lemuel Shaw, Jr., and Joseph Allen to Lemuel Shaw, July 31, 1839, LSP, box 11.

36. ALs, Joseph Allen to Lemuel Shaw, November 23, 1839, LSP, box 11. The substance of the letter is unknown; we have been unable to locate it in the collection—if it survived and found its way into it, that is.

37. ALs, Joseph Allen to Lemuel Shaw, August 10, 1840, LSP, box 12.

38. ALs, Lemuel Shaw to Lemuel Shaw, Jr., September 28, 1840, LSP, box 12.

39. Lemuel Shaw, Jr.? nd, LSP, box 12.

40. ALs, Lemuel Shaw to Lemuel Shaw, Jr., September 28, 1840, LSP, box 12.

41. Report, Joseph Allen to Lemuel Shaw, nd, LSP, box 12. Another hand penciled in "1841" at the top right of the sheet. The document was placed near the front of the folder, in the third position when we saw it. The bill is for December 17 through March 1.

42. Sealing wax covers a word.

43. Sealing wax covers a word or two.

44. ALs, Lemuel Shaw, Jr., to Lemuel Shaw, June 29, 1842, LSP, box 12.

45. ALs, Lemuel Shaw, Jr., to Lemuel Shaw, July 31, 1839, LSP, box 11.

46. ALs, Lemuel Shaw to Lemuel Shaw, Jr., July 25, 1840, LSP, box 12.

47. ALs, Lemuel Shaw to Lemuel Shaw, Jr., August 6, 1842?, LSP, box 12.

48. Printed admission announcement, August 18, 1842, LSP, box 12.

49. Boston Latin School Report for Lemuel Shaw, Jr., October 1, 1842, LSP, box 12.

50. Bills, Mary Lamb to Lemuel Shaw, July 12, 1826, box 8; October 5, 1826, box 8; April 5, 1827, box 8; December 16, 1827, box 8; June 1, 1828, box 9; May 26, 1829, box 9. All LSP. Billing was at the end of the term. Mary Lamb's schools were evidently conducted at her home, 2 Harvard, at the corner of Washington. *Stimpson's Boston Directory* . . . (Boston: Stimpson and Clapp, 1826, 1827, 1828, and 1829).

51. Bill, Mary Lamb to Lemuel Shaw, October 3, 1823, LSP, box 7. It is marked "Fee for the Winter."

52. Bill from D. Francis, December 17, 1829, box 9; November 6, 1829, box 9; August 2, 1831, box 10; July 17, 1832, box 10. All LSP. Billing was at the end of the term.

53. Bill, Samuel Clarke to Lemuel Shaw, October 19, 1832, box 10; October 1, 1833, box 10; March 19, 1834, box 10. All LSP. Bills were issued at or near the end of the term. The lapses in the bills covered in this period may be due to Elizabeth's not attending for some quarters or the bills may simply be missing.

54. Bill, George B. Emerson to Lemuel Shaw, February 18, 1836, box 11; July 16, 1836, box 11; December 12, 1836, box 11; July 12, 1837, box 11; February 22, 1841, box 11. All LSP. Bills were issued at the end of the term. The lapses in the bills covered in this period may be due to Elizabeth's not attending for some quarters or the bills may simply be missing.

55. ALs, George B. Emerson to Lemuel Shaw, July 12, 1836, LSP, box 11.

56. George B. Emerson, *Reminiscences of an Old Teacher* (Boston: Alfred Mudge & Son, 1878), pp. 51–52. Emerson (1797–1881) went to Harvard and became a major force in education, connected with schools, particularly the academy Lizzie attended, until 1855. He was a prolific writer and active after his retirement. *DAB*.

57. Emerson, p. 55.

58. Emerson, pp. 64–69.

59. Chase, pp. 72–76.

60. Chase, pp. 71–72, 110–18, for example; for an outline of his broad interests, see pp. 250–55. These claims are substantiated by countless documents throughout the Lemuel Shaw Papers.

# Appendix H
# Kate Gansevoort and the Melvilles

KATE GANSEVOORT APPEARS TO BE A SEVERELY CRITICAL and detached observer of Herman, Lizzie, their family, and the trials they suffered. But one should realize that her acquaintance with them was more than casual, more than what might be expected even between cousins who lived reasonably close to each other.

One illustration of her familiarity with what took place in the Herman Melville family is in a handful of letters, principally from Kate to her stepmother, Susan, in 1855. Peter Gansevoort and his wife had sent their daughter to boarding school at Mrs. Elizabeth Buckminster Dwight Sedgwick's in Lenox, Massachusetts, just a few miles from Arrowhead, where Herman and his family had been residing for almost five years. As might be expected, Kate was homesick. This was her first extended stay away from her parents and native Albany, and she soon let the family back home know how unhappy she was.[1] On June 17, she wrote her stepmother, "I can not agree with you . . . that *my* coming to *boarding school* will be of very great advantage but I know that I shall value my home much more than I ever did." She goes on to admit that she was counting down the number of Saturdays remaining "till I come home which will be in *fifteen weeks*."[2] Writing her stepmother a few weeks later, she said, "I expected you, and Papa to day mother, or else a letter, which I have looked in vain for, for the past week. I feel so home-sick to night—all the girls, have received good news and letters from home, but I am trying to feel better by writing home."[3] Her father, Peter, was not as sympathetic and solicitous under the

circumstances as Lemuel Shaw was in comforting his offspring—Lemuel, Jr., at a boarding school, for instance—when
they were lonely, distressed, or homesick. Her dislocation and
depression are documented in correspondence scattered
throughout the original Gansevoort-Lansing Collection, for example, in a draft of a letter her father wrote her, in which he
appears sympathetic but firm.[4] Kate's stepmother was more re-
sponsive. In a chatty note of early June 1855, full of gossip from
Albany friends and family, Susan Gansevoort relays her stepson
Henry's report of his recent visit to Arrowhead (Herman was
not there at the time) to the effect that the Pittsfield Melvilles
"seemed much pleased to hear you were at M$^{rs}$ Sedgwicks—said
they would visit you soon—which I know will please you[.]" Susan herself "hope[s] by the time you receive this letter you will
feel quite settled & happy—There seems to be such a comfortable home feeling about M$^{rs}$ Sedgwicks establishment that I
think you must be pleased & that you will soon learn to *love* her
very much. Tavel[5] dear Kate has just handed me your letter for
which I thank you sincerely—I can easily imagine your feelings
after our departure & sympathized with you deeply—but you
behaved *beautifully*[.]" She concludes with a further attempt to
ease the young girl through the transition to boarding school:
"In your letter you say nothing about your room—is it pleasant?
does any one sleep with you & if so, who is it? Have you pleasant
companions & let me know all about the arrangements of your
room &c &c—Have you every thing you want? Write as often as
you can." Susan's ending is in marked contrast to those of Herman to his children and Uncle Peter to his: "All unite in love to
you—/God bless you my dear daughter & believe me sincerely/
your attached/Mother."[6]

The intensity of Kate's homesickness, the difficulty she was
having in adjusting, is further documented in some correspondence from her confidante Anna Parker, the child of one of
her father's powerful and well-placed Albany associates;[7] see,
for instance, Anna's letters to Kate,[8] which perhaps express
with even greater candor the anxiety Kate was suffering.[9] As
might be expected, her loneliness abated with the passage of
time. In September, she wrote a long, descriptive letter to Susan

in which she said, "I wish so much that you would come out" to visit.[10] She still desired face-to-face contact with her parents.

During this difficult transitional period for Kate, Melville and his family served her as surrogate for her Albany family. The written record indicates that she came to know the household in Pittsfield well during this summer of crisis for her cousin Herman and those around him.[11] The most informative of the documents are the six letters, principally from Kate to her stepmother, Susan, which document an intimacy between Kate and her Arrowhead relatives, most importantly Herman. She reported in a mid-June letter that the Pittsfield Melvilles had visited: "This is the first Sunday that the sun has shone since I left home. I had a very pleasant visit from ↑ cousin ↓ Fanny, Augusta Herman and the children yesterday they are looking very well. Augusta said that she would have been here before but rain and previous engagements have prevented. She asked Mrs Sedgwick if I could come to Arrowhead and spend some Sunday and she said yes! So I am going."[12] The visit apparently took place two weeks later. "Last Saturday cousin Augusta came for me to spend the night ↑ Sunday ↓ with her. They send the best love to Uncle Peter, and Aunt Susan—&c. Sunday we did not go to church it was so warm."[13] It seems that Gus was the principal instigator of this family visit, and the primary connection with the homesick girl. However, Herman was gracious and hospitable. Kate offers a significant account of some time they spent together: "After dinner cousin Herman, and I went up the hill behind their house, and took a view of the surrounding country, saw Saddle-Back to gether—with various other place [sic] in the distance. About Seven Cousin Herman drove me home ↑ (that is my *present activity* [?] *place*) ↓ and invited me very politely to come soon again."[14] Evidently referring to the same visit to Arrowhead, Susan wrote her daughter on July 17: "I am glad to hear you spent your time so pleasantly at Cousin Hermans[.] I hope this visit will be the beginning of a *series* of visits & that you will learn to love them better than ever."[15] But we have discovered no evidence of her return in the next month. On a Tuesday evening in August, young Kate wrote her stepmother that she had heard from Gus, who reported on family members (the Griggses, and Allan and Sophia and their family, for example) who had been at Arrowhead.[16] And on September 8, she reported that "Aunt Melville [Maria], told me that Cousin Herman had been very sick, but is now very much better, and intended to start with her for Lansingburg on Tuesday night. On his return he may stop and make you a short visit."[17]

Clearly, Kate's Pittsfield family had served her well as she made the transition into boarding school during the summer of 1855. They supplied a family connection and also some good times: there is a delightful description in the early September letter of amateur theatrical highjinks involving, along with Melville family members, the ebullient Sarah Morewood. In this letter to her stepmother, when speaking of returning home, Kate's tone is considerably less distressed than it had been a few months earlier; she says that she "regretted not receiving a letter from you very much last week. When you do write please tell me of Papas plans about my coming home. . . . I am looking forward with so much joy dear mother to the coming vacation when I can see *Papa and you.* Give my best love to Papa and ask him to write me."[18] This is not to suggest that the contact between the Arrowhead household and Kate dissolved these few months. In the period between this September letter and another on November 24, Susan visited her daughter and there was at least one contact: "I hope Aunt Melville made you a pleasant visit. I have not heard from Arrowhead or its inhabitants since you left me here."[19]

All this should be considered when evaluating Kate's reactions to reports about life in the Herman Melville household. They are at times clinical and severe, as when she comments on Malcolm's death or Melville's qualities as a father. Her acquaintance with Melville and the family was more than passing. And so her opinions should not be taken lightly. They may well be among the more reliable that we have for the very reasons that some readers find them disturbing for their brevity, objectivity, coldness, callousness, and judgmental tone.

What we have called her penchant for harsh judgment might be placed in perspective by a few observations about her relations with Herman's brothers, Allan and Tom. About two months after Malcolm's suicide, the family mounted a campaign to have Tom appointed to the superintendency of Sailors' Snug Harbor on Staten Island. Allan served as the center of a strenuous effort to gain support in some high places, including that of prominent politicians from both major parties, some with shady backgrounds. In late 1867, within a few days of Kate's engagement to Abe Lansing,[20] Allan wrote Kate about the matter, admitting near the conclusion of his four-page letter, "I write this in some haste without time to choose my words." He was direct. The letter starts abruptly with an explanation of the conditions surrounding the post, formerly filled by the "beloved Mr Greenleaf[21] who had been treasurer of the institution for 30 years and knows well (and none[?] better) what qualities are most desirable in the incumbent." Allan then states that he seeks "assistance in presenting Toms merits" and suggests that perhaps "Judge Parker[22] might be persuaded to address a letter to [undeciphered word] Hon. John T. Hoffman[23] our Mayor who is one of the board of Trustees advocating Tom's qualifications obtained by his knowledge of sailors <three words> twenty years experience of the sea. His administrative abilities are also of a high order." As might be anticipated, Allan sought his Uncle Peter's support in this exercise in family solidarity: "Your father who I believe is acquainted with Mayor Hoffman might address him a letter also if he is so inclined"—Allan as well as the other children had long since learned not to take Uncle Peter for granted. Allan is stressing that a strong campaign is in order. He continues with the practical observation of a Wall Street attorney: "Such aids are often necessary to present ones claim & to secure such places, and [undeciphered word] offered are seldom obtained without the asking. I therefore feel the less reluctance in calling upon Toms friends to assist in the laudable undertaking of putting the right man into the right place." Still pushing, he adds: "A letter to Gov Fenton[24] asking his assistance would be useful[.]"

Allan knew his cousin Kate well enough to anticipate her reaction: "You see I am disposed to make you quite a politician, a title unknown ladies have failed to secure for themselves, but I trust you will be more successful than they, and earn the name for yourself in this matter at least—though the office is far from what is generally known as a political one—still letters from those influential in politics are useful."²⁵ So Kate's unflinching character, evident when assessing her cousin Herman and the conditions of his household, has a parallel. Allan felt that he could rely on her for tough-minded, clear-headed help in securing the career of one of the family. His request yielded immediate results. The next day Kate forwarded his letter to Mr. Pruyn.²⁶ She is direct, a quality the reader of her correspondence learns quickly to appreciate. Allan, she states, "urges therein my feeble influence in obtaining for his brother Capt. Thomas Melville (who you know we esteem very highly—the position of *Governor* of the *Sailor's Snug Harbor*. May I ask you the favor to address a few lines to Mayor Hoffman in his behalf? *He* is one of the trustees of the Institution. Mr [Allan] Melville wishes Father to write to Mayor Hoffman which he would do were he able [Peter was indisposed at the time]. Father will with pleasure add his signature to your letter (if you consent to write one[.]" Aware that her directness might seem impolite, she adds, "I am sorry to trouble you with this letter Mr Pruyn—, but hope you will not be offended by my *presuming* to ask for assistance."²⁷

The campaign was successful. In a letter to Kate of November 20, Allan reports that the trustees had appointed Tom "Governor" of Snug Harbor the day before. He says, "I hasten to acquaint you with the news knowing that you would rejoice to hear it and be among the first to congratulate the successful candidate upon his success." Allan graciously acknowledges her effectiveness: "Your letter with enclosure reached me Sunday morning (I appreciate your promptness) The joint letter was delivered by me to the Mayor in person and contributed to the general result—very powerfully, as you must believe."²⁸ Kate did not hesitate to describe with satisfaction the part she had played in the appointment of Tom, one of her favorite cousins. She wrote Henry, "Last week Allan wrote me asking if I could procure letters in Toms favor from Father, Judge Parker &c. I applied to Hon. Robert H. Pruyn²⁹ who wrote a strong recommendatory letter, to Mayor Hoffman which he signed as also did Father & Judge Parker—I forwarded it as was desired, but could get no one to write to Senator Morgan[30] *or* Rev—Morgan Dix of Trinity Church."[31] Maria was pleased with the family's successful lobbying, as she told Kate.[32] The following year Tom Melville was married, and Kate and Henry attended the wedding. If there were any tensions between the residents of 104 East 26th Street and their maternal cousins from Albany, they evidently had diminished significantly by June 1868. Susan wrote Kate on the twelfth of the month: "We received Cousin Herman's letter a short time after you left—inviting you to his house—It relieved my mind very much, for I had *heard* some where that Cousin Lizzie was out of town & was happy to hear it was not so[33]—I am very happy you are with them & you have your Father's & My permission to remain as long as you wish." Family affection is reinforced toward the letter's conclusion: "Give my best love to Cousin Lizzie—Herman & the girls—tell them we hope to see them all in Albany this Summer—& certainly expect a visit from them—To morrow I suppose you will spend with Kate & Tom[.] Give them our *sincere* love & an invitation to visit ↑ us ↓ which we certainly expect[.]"[34] The festivities occasioned by Tom's marriage induced a certain euphoria. Writing to her stepmother on June 6, Kate reported that she was "having a very lovely time all are so kind Stanwix Bessie & Fanny are lovely girls [*sic*]—Cousin Herman Allan & Aunt Melville desire[?] their best love."[35] The festivities attending the wedding are also described in another letter to Susan the next day.[36]

There appear to be significant differences in the feelings Kate had toward various Melville family members. Although there is no hard evidence of strain between her and Herman and Lizzie, her relatively remote attitude regarding Malcolm's death, for example, is in sharp contrast to the relaxed quality of her relations with other members of the family, such as Cousin Herman's brother Tom and most notably her Aunt Maria. One indication of these different relations is the paucity of letters to her from Herman, who could be aloof—and, as might be expected, none from her to him that have been recovered. In contrast, a significant number were exchanged between Kate and her more genial cousin, Herman's brother, Tom, to whom she was closer in age. A sampling from the period of less than two years surrounding Malcolm's suicide in September 1867 and Tom's wedding the following June indicates their easy friendship. Writing Kate in February 1867, Tom gossiped about family matters and visits that members were making to each other, including his "hope to have the pleasure of seeing you in a few days[.] I shall probably ↑ leave ↓ here [he was writing from New York City] for Gansevoort Saturday morning." The letter is another of the many instances we have of Tom's being one of the family members more inclined to keep in touch than certain others, such as Herman—although Herman was more engaged and indeed fun-loving than has usually been assumed. Tom continues to relate his adventures in Gotham: "Mr Hoadley[37] was in New York a few days ago & I took him to see the 'Black Crook'[38] he was delighted with it; said that it was the finest piece that he had ever seen produced on the stage." Nor did Tom's constant traveling when in port bring him only to the immediate family. "Last Wednesday I went to New Rochelle & dined at Mr R[ichard] Lathers,[39] he has a truly magnificent house, eighty feet front, with a deep piazza running the whole length, which is enclosed as a Conservatory & filled with handsome flowers; you can imagine how beautiful it must be." Tom attended a funeral and then returned to the City, where he accompanied Lathers' and Allan's daughters, as well as Willie Morewood, to "the French Theatre." They heard to their "great delight . . . the Opera of Il Travitori [sic],[40] the singing & music were splendid & the scenery good. We enjoyed it very much, when we reached home Allan [who had procured the "Box" at the theater] had a fine supper ready Ice cream, Oysters, &c. & we had a nice cosy time." In his best moments Tom's powers of description lack the vitality even of Allan's. But they show a concern about the family, an affection for his cousin Kate (and the other members of her household). They radiate sincerity. The ending of his letter to cousin Kate is typical: "Remember me to Aunt Sarah Miss Annie & the boys. Give my love to your father & to your dear good Mother."[41] The same depth of connection with his cousin appears in his sympathy for his mother when, for example, he reports to Kate on April 29, and July 14, 1867, that Maria had sprained her "ankle" or "ancle." This injury was to plague her for months and was to become a major topic in her letters to the family during this period of crisis for Herman and Lizzie.[42]

Kate's frequent contacts with her Melville cousins, particularly Tom, continued after the disasters of mid–1867. During the spring following Mackie's suicide Tom's and Kate's respective engagements were announced. Maria wrote Kate the following April to congratulate her on having finally accepted Abe Lansing's proposal, at the same time indicating the busy doings of the family: "Last ↑ week ↓ [Augusta, who was in New York City] went with Lizzy & passed a day with the Bogarts, Lizzie was delighted with her visit."[43] Perhaps their mutual regard, quite distinct from the level of emotion of her correspondence with Allan and absent at this time from that with Herman, was best expressed in Kate's being selected as a bridesmaid[44] when Tom married Catherine E. Bogart, the daughter of the resident physician at Sailors' Snug Harbor.[45] Tom also asked Henry Sanford Gansevoort to be his groomsman. The preparations for the wedding were elaborate. Late in May Tom wrote his "dear Cousin Kate" enthusiastically about these arrangements and his delight in the guests who would be attending. Kate would "have to leave Hermans at 3:15 P.M. so as to take the 4 P.M. boat to the Island." And he went on even more enthusiastically to describe the festivities preceding the ceremony.[46] Such events naturally celebrate family affection. In reading the family correspondence, one discovers, not surprisingly, that the behavior here was no exception. On June 3, Susan Gansevoort wrote her daughter who was staying at Herman's and conveyed her "Love" not only to Maria, her sister-in-law, but to "Cousin Herman & family[.]"[47]

# Notes

1. Kate would in time get over the initial homesickness and become an enthusiastic student and supporter of Mrs. Sedgwick's school. In 1863 Kate joined her fellow alumnae in promising to help promote Mrs. Sedgwick's recently published *A Talk with My Pupils* (New York: J. Hopper; Boston: Crosby and Nichols, 1863). Printed Circular Letter from Former Students to Mrs. Charles Sedgwick, August 20, 1863, G-L, box 215.

Almost two months later, Kate writes one of Mrs. Sedgwick's former students, Maria S. Cummins of Dorchester, Massachusetts, the popular novelist, to acknowledge the printed letter and to praise the circulation project for *"our beloved teacher."* She goes on to say that she has a copy of *A Talk with My Pupils* and has "enjoyed reading it" and that "Mrs S. embodies in that volume the principles she so tried to inculcate in her pupils." [Copy of] ALs, Catherine Gansevoort to Maria S. Cummins, October 12, 1863, G-L, box 215.

2. ALs, Catherine Gansevoort to Susan Gansevoort, June 17, 1855, G-L, box 154.

3. Catherine Gansevoort to Susan Gansevoort, July 4, 1855, G-L, box 154.

4. Draft ALs, Peter Gansevoort to Catherine Gansevoort, July 31, 1855, G-L, box 215.

5. A family servant.

6. ALs, Susan Gansevoort to Catherine Gansevoort, June 4, 1855, G-L, box 245, album 1.

7. Judge Amasa Junius Parker (1807–90). *DAB.*

8. ALs, Anna L. Parker to Catherine Gansevoort, June 26, and July 14, 1855, G-L, box 215.

9. Anna L. Parker to Catherine Gansevoort, August 4, 1855, G-L, box 215.

Anna and Kate's close ties, reflective of those between the Parker and Gansevoort families, are apparent in another of Anna's letters to Kate during the period we are concerned with here: "Your mother told me before I left Albany that you were to spend that Sunday with your Aunt, Mrs Melville [Maria]—Give my love to her when you see her. I have dreamed of her for the last two or three nights, & hope my dreams will come true & that I shall see her very soon." ALs, Anna L. Parker to Catherine Gansevoort, August 4, 1855, G-L, box 215. Close relationships sometimes went beyond the Gansevoort extended family to embrace those, such as Anna Parker, who were dear to its members. It is worthwhile to note Anna's affectionate response to Maria which belies the stereotype of the formidable matriarch.

10. ALs, Catherine Gansevoort to Susan Gansevoort, September 8, 1855, G-L, box 154.

11. This was a trying period for Herman, one of significant activity, including plans about publication (Leyda, II, 505–8). Kate reported to her stepmother that some of the family had visited her, at which time Maria "told me that Cousin Herman had been very sick, but is now very much better, and

intended to start with her for Lansingburg on Tuesday night. On his return he may stop and make you a short visit." ALs, Catherine Gansevoort to Susan Gansevoort, September 8, 1855, G-L, box 154. Summarized from another source in Leyda, II, 508.

12. ALs, Catherine Gansevoort to Susan Gansevoort, June 17, 1855, G-L, box 154.

13. ALs, Catherine Gansevoort to Susan Gansevoort, July 4, 1855, G-L, box 154.

14. ALs, Catherine Gansevoort to Susan Gansevoort, July 4, 1855, G-L, box 154.

15. ALs, Susan Gansevoort to Catherine Gansevoort, July 17, 1855, G-L, box 245, album 1.

16. ALs, Catherine Gansevoort to Susan Gansevoort, Tues. eve, August 1855, G-L, box 154.

17. ALs, Catherine Gansevoort to Susan Gansevoort, September 8, 1855, G-L, box 154.

18. ALs, Catherine Gansevoort to Susan Gansevoort, September 8, 1855, G-L, box 154.

19. ALs, Catherine Gansevoort to Susan Gansevoort, November 24, 1855, G-L, box 154.

20. ALs, Catherine Gansevoort to Henry Sanford Gansevoort, November 24, 1867, G-L, box 161, Henry Sanford Gansevoort/Letterbooks 1866–67. The wedding date was put off repeatedly, and they did not marry until 1873. Kenney, pp. 253–58.

21. Joseph Greenleaf was a New York associate of Peter Gansevoort from at least as early as the the second decade of the century, as their correspondence scattered in the Gansevoort-Lansing Collection indicates. According to *Longworth's New York City Director[ies]*, he had offices in Wall Street or the immediate area from the early 1820s until the early 1840s, and then again in the 1850s. *Doggett's Director*[ies] list him as secretary of the New York Guard Insurance Co. in the 1840s. His connection with Sailors' Snug Harbor, which Allan asserts in this letter, is confirmed by numerous New York State Senate documents, which print the annual reports of the Harbor. See, for example, *State of New York. No. 31. In Senate, February 16, 1841.* Annual Report of the affairs of the Sailors' Snug Harbor. To the Legislature of the State of New York . . . *New York, 10th February, 1841*, p. 4. We also call attention to the fact that Priscilla Scollay Melvill, Herman's paternal grandmother, was the daughter of John Scollay and Mercy Greenleaf (Sealts, "The Melville Heritage," genealogy chart), so Joseph may have been a distant relation of Herman's generation of Melvilles.

22. Judge Parker was Peter Gansevoort's associate and friend, the father of Kate's confidante Anna.

23. John Thompson Hoffman (1828–88) served two terms as Mayor of New York City from 1865 to 1868. A Tammany politician, he was associated with the infamous Tweed Ring, which he subsequently repudiated. *DAB*.

24. Reuben Eaton Fenton (1819–85) was Governor of New York from

1865 to 1869. He defeated Mayor John Thompson Hoffman of New York City in 1866. Robert Sobel and John Raimo, ed., *Biographical Directory of the Governors of the United States, 1789–1978*, III, 1085.

25. ALs, Allan Melville to Catherine Gansevoort, November 13, 1867, G-L, box 216; quoted in part in Leyda, II, 692.

26. John Van Schaick Lansing Pruyn (1811–77), the Albany attorney, politician, and statesman, whose two middle names identify him as one of the Gansevoort-Melville clan. In 1865 the widower Pruyn had taken as his second wife Kate's girlhood friend, Anna Fenn Parker, daughter of Judge Parker.

27. ALs, Catherine Gansevoort to Robert Hewson Pruyn, November 14, 1867, G-L, box 216.

Robert Hewson Pruyn (1815–82), attorney and politician, was married in 1841 to Jane Anne Lansing, the daughter of Gerrit Y. and Helen Ten Eyck Lansing. He provides another illustration of how widely the family net was cast in this small community. *DAB*.

28. ALs, Allan Melville to Catherine Gansevoort, November 20, 1867, G-L, box 216.

29. See note 27.

30. Edwin Denison Morgan (1811–83) served two terms as Governor of New York State from 1858 to 1862, and from 1863 to 1869 was a United States Senator. *DAB*.

31. ALs, Catherine Gansevoort to Henry Sanford Gansevoort, November 21, 1867, G-L, box 161, Henry Sanford Gansevoort/Letterbooks 1866–67.

The Rev. Morgan Dix (1827–1908) was the Rector of Trinity Church for almost forty-six years, including 1867. (*Trow's New York Directory, 1867–68*.) Born to wealth, power, and privilege, this Episcopal clergyman was a valuable ally in New York City political circles. *DAB*.

32. ALs, Maria Gansevoort Melville to Catherine Gansevoort, December 9, 1867, G-L, box 216; quoted in part in Leyda, II, 692–93. This part of the letter is omitted in Leyda; it is not that signaled by the ellipsis, which concerns John Hoadley's concurrence in her plans. These events are recorded on the *Log* in two letters of Kate to Henry and the first paragraph of Allan's. Leyda omitted the family supportiveness material, for it was not to his purpose.

33. This may be a cryptic reference to the marital crisis in the Herman Melville household thirteen months earlier. Kring and Carey, pp. 137–41.

34. ALs, Susan Gansevoort to Catherine Gansevoort, June 12, 1868, G-L, box 245. See also ALs, Susan Gansevoort to Catherine Gansevoort, June 3, 1868, G-L, box 245, album 2, which expresses similar sentiments and concludes: "Love" to Maria "& Cousin Hermans family[.]"

35. ALs, Catherine Gansevoort to Susan Gansevoort, June 6, 1868, G-L, box 154.

36. ALs, Catherine Gansevoort to Susan Gansevoort, June 7, 1868, G-L, box 154. It concludes, "Cousin Lizzie & Herman are well & *all* of us desire lots of love to you & Papa."

37. John Hoadley who was married to Tom's and Herman's sister Catherine.

38. The *Black Crook* was being performed at Niblo's Garden. *The* [N. Y.] *Evening Post*, February 15, 1867, p. [4]. *The Black Crook* by Charles M. Barras is usually recognized as the first American musical comedy. Lavishly produced and extremely successful, its plot, the theater manager admitted, "lacked literary merit," and the reviewer for the *New York Times* reported that the show girls, a prime attraction, "wore no clothes to speak of." The first performance was on September 12, 1866. *The Black Crook and Other Nineteenth-Century Plays*, ed. Myron Matlaw (New York: Dutton, 1967), p. 319.

39. Richard Lathers (1820–1903) was Mackie's employer and a friend of Herman Melville and other members of the family. Lathers was married to the sister of Sophia E. Thurston, Allan Melville's first wife, who is mentioned in the Malcolm letter. Lathers also employed Malcolm at the Atlantic and Great Western Insurance Company from early 1866. Leyda, II, 678–79.

40. The performance of Verdi's opera featured Elvira Naddi and Adelaide Phillips, among others, with "Full Chorus and Orchestra." *The* [N. Y.] *Evening Post*, February 15, 1867, p. [4].

41. ALs, Thomas Melville to Catherine Gansevoort, February 19, 1867, G-L, box 216.

42. ALs, Thomas Melville to Catherine Gansevoort, April 29, 1867, G-L, box 216; and July 14, 1867, G-L, box 216. We refer to Herman and Lizzie's marital difficulties as discussed by Kring and Carey, pp. 137–41.

43. ALs, Maria Gansevoort Melville to Catherine Gansevoort, April 23, 1868, G-L, box 216.

44. ALs, Jane L. Melville (Mrs. Allan Melville) to Catherine Gansevoort, May 13, 1868, G-L, box 216.

45. ALs, Thomas Melville to Catherine Gansevoort, April 25, 1968, box 216.

46. ALs, Thomas Melville to Catherine Gansevoort, May 31, 1868, G-L, box 216.

47. ALs, Susan Gansevoort to Catherine Gansevoort, June 3, 1868, G-L, box 245, album 2.

# Appendix I
# Kate Gansevoort and Malcolm's Death

AN UNDERSTANDING OF KATE'S TIES with Herman and his immediate family is necessary in order to comprehend her initial responses to Malcolm's death and her subsequent relations with his parents. She knew them well if not intimately. She had an affection for them based on the fact of kinship and complemented by frequent contact, but this does not appear to have compromised her ability to make objective judgments about them. One would have expected her to come from Albany to attend the funeral, its preliminaries, or its aftermath.

Her responses in manuscript sources are more numerous and revealing than those in printed records. First, there are her observations in correspondence with her mother and brother. (One should note lapses in the correspondence with Henry during this period, omissions that may be as eloquent if not more so for what they leave unsaid.) Second, there is the more personal record Kate kept in her diary during this period. We shall discuss both.

She fails to mention Malcolm's death in the letters she wrote Henry, then an army officer serving in Pensacola, Florida, during the few days immediately thereafter. This omission is hard to explain. Perhaps Herman and those closest to the tragedy were slow to spread the news, possibly hoping to mute the report of the suicide. We learn from her diary that Kate did not become aware of Malcolm's death until September 13. This is substantiated by her correspondence with her brother. Malcolm died early on Wednesday the 11th after having been out very late the night before. In a letter to Henry written on Friday the 12th at 3:30 P.M., there is no mention of the death.[1] Nor is there any mention in a second letter to Henry, dated the 13th, although she does update news from home such as reports on the illness of their father.[2] Certainly, enough time had elapsed for the news to travel from New York City to Albany. Or was this letter composed and posted before she learned of Malcolm's death? In any event, the lapse is curious.

Although she reported the tragedy to Henry on the 15th, as we shall see, it was not until Monday, September 16 (the time of composition is noted as 5:30 P.M.) that she offered details: "This mornings mail brought us your welcome letter of the 7th Sept, & also one from Aunt [Maria] Melville, enclosing letters from Cousin Augusta & Helen, both of whom, are at that sad, sad home, 104 26th Street New York City. Aunt Melville speaks of Malcolm as a promising boy—good, kind, & gentle,—& most aff[ectionate] to all—& says he was in the habit of carrying a pistol & laying it under his pillow at night. & that she has no doubt he was examining it when it when it [sic] went off—& can never believe he committed suicide[.]" Kate's tough-mindedness comes through here; she recognizes the shock of her aunt's bereavement but nevertheless observes that Maria's is "A very natural conclusion for one who loved poor Malcom [sic] so dearly—He was her eldest Grandson, & all last winter was so devoted to her, & so kind ↑ in ↓ his little attentions." Kate proceeds to discuss Augusta's observations and the immediate family: "Cousin Herman she [Augusta] says is quite composed—Cousin Lizzie has not shed a tear but poor little Stanwix seems heart broken." Kate reports on the gathering of the clan at the house on East 26th Street in this time of enormous family distress and then abruptly states: "Enough, of this sad story Henry & do you beware of carelessness with your pistols!" In the very next sentence of what is slipping into a letter of advice for a beloved brother, she says unequivocally, "Suicide seems such a cowardly act." But then she hedges: "I wonder if poor Malcom [she repeatedly misspells the boy's name] [in] reality commited the act or was it an accident—God only knows[.]" Her ambivalence, however, wavers in her next sentence: "May he spare us all from such a dreadful act[.]" Kate at this point is undecided whether the death was suicide or accident.

There is no lack of certainty, however, in her description of Cousin Herman's behavior as a father. After reporting on other family matters, she returns bluntly to the tragedy of Malcolm's death. The blame is on Melville: "Cousin Herman is I think a very strict parent & Cousin Lizzie thoroughly good but inefficient. She feels so thankful she did not scold him or remonstrate as she intended[.] So she cannot blame herself for having induced him from despair, at her fault-finding to put an end to his life." We should bear in mind that Kate is speaking from a well-informed opinion. These stricken cousins were no casual acquaintances occasionally seen, but intimates. Recall the time she had spent in their company when she was attending Mrs. Sedgwick's school in Lenox a dozen years earlier, and consider that, given the tight family structure, the bonds of kinship were strong. With these in mind, consider her next, more general and humane observations: "I sometimes wish we mortals had the power of seeing the heart & feelings of our friends—I believe there would be greater happiness were such the case—we so often distrust & blame where we should not, because we judge wrongly—& mistake the motives of the actions of others." One can infer the same sort of kindness in her urging to her brother near the conclusion of this letter: "I would write a line to Cousin Herman Henry! He will no doubt feel gratified to know you sympathize with him in the loss of his first born!"[3]

The letter she had written Henry the day before—that is, on the 15th—is bothersome. Composed at about 1 o'clock on a Sunday afternoon, this first of the letters in which she reports on Malcolm's death begins with almost two pages of almost random comment, including remarks on the deaths of some of Henry's friends, before coming to the subject of Malcolm Melville. (Perhaps she uses the preliminaries to ease into the subject.) She is matter-of-fact: "Last Friday's papers contained a notice of a sad case of suicide. that of *Malcolm Melville*—the Eldest son of Herman Melville." We note Kate's formality in identifying the deceased and his relationship to the person who was, after all, their cousin. She continues, "I send [she probably means "sent"] you a journal with the notice marked, & hope you have rec'd it. I will however tell you about it for fear the paper may have been mis-carried." It is not clear whether the

account following is a quotation or paraphrase of the article, or
Kate's version derived from whatever printed sources (including that in the journal alluded to), or her understanding based
upon oral and written information from family members and,
perhaps, others: "It seems that Tuesday Evening. Sept 10$^{th}$ Malcolm did not return home to tea as usual—but came home at 3
A.M. Wednesday—Cousin Lizzie who sat up for him remonstrated with him for staying out so late. He promised never to
do so again [If the suicidal act were already planned, he could
with some irony make such a promise]—kissed her & retired to
rest. In the mning he was called & said he would be down
soon—he did not make his appearance during the day & when
Cousin Herman returned in the Eving the door of his room
[w]as opened & Malcolm was found dead, lying on the bed, with
a single barelled pistol firmly grasped in his hand, & a pistol-
shot wound in the right temple—The parents could not asign
[*sic*] any cause for the suicidal act & the jury (coroner's) came to
the conclusion, that deceased, must have been suffering from a
temporary aberation of mind[.]"

Two points should be noted: first, there is no question in
Kate's mind, as there would be a little more than twenty-four
hours later, that the death was a suicide; and, second, the shooting occurred sometime after early morning—probably after,
perhaps shortly before, Herman left for work. Whether Lizzie
or other family members were home at the moment of the
shooting is not known. This will have to remain a consideration
when speculating about why the shot was not heard by someone
in the house; it must be considered in addition to evidence such
as the intensity of the pistol's report, the muffling thickness of
the wood doors and plaster walls, and the very size of the house.
Kate continues: "The above is all we know of his very sad transaction—We have heard nothing from the family at Gansevrt—
It will be a sad sad blow for Aunt Melville who thought Malcom
[*sic*] a very promising young man—& Henry I believe you at one
time saw a great deal of him." Deferring to Henry's greater
knowledge of the boy, she then asks, "What kind of a person
was he—he had a very fine position in Mr Lathers Insurance
Office[.] All his friends were interested in him[.] I pity his those
[*sic*] poor parents—both Cousin Herman & Lizzie are of such

nervous temperaments I should fear for *their* peace of *mind.*"[4]
Given Kate's observation about Henry's greater intimacy with
Malcolm, we call attention to a troublesome lack of documentation in the original cache of Gansevoort-Lansing Papers do-
nated by Kate (granted, put together, and possibly weeded or
sanitized by her servants). Following folder 8 of box 245, titled
"Catherine G. Lansing/Letters n.d./Letters from Henry S.
Gansevoort," there are three albums of letters which are dated
and arranged chronologically, a fact which is contradicted by
the information in the Library's "inventory." The letters from
1867, our critical year, are in the second of the three. We are
puzzled that there is not one letter from Henry between August
20 and October 7, 1867; if Kate's assessment about his relative
closeness to the 26th-Street Melvilles is accurate, then the gap
is worrisome and, more important, must be acknowledged
when we review the available evidence on which sound judgments in these matters might be made. The few extant letters
do not mention Malcolm's death or the Herman Melvilles.[5]

Kate next writes Henry on September 19, beginning this letter also with the sort of routine news that suggests that Malcolm
is not foremost in her mind. She leads into the section about
the boy obliquely—one might even infer, with an eye on smooth
literary transition: "Among the papers on my desk I find a letter from Aunt Melville enclosing one from Cousin Helen giving
an account of poor Malcom [*sic*] Melvilles funeral." The account
she offers is perhaps a composite or based upon one. She suggests to Henry that he "might like to hear about the arrangements—&c—Well the funeral took place last Saturday mrning
Dr Osgood (their Clergyman)[6] read a chapter from the Bible—
the 15*th* Chap. Corinthians the one used in the Episcopal Burial
Service. Made a short address & a prayer—Then after a
pause—the young Volunteer Company to which Malcom [*sic*]
belonged & who had asked the privilege of being present &
carrying the coffin from the house to the cars—filed in at one
door from the hall & out at the other—each pausing for an
instant to look at the face of their lost[7] comrade. Cousin Helen
says they were[8] all *so young* & it was really a sadly beautiful
sight—for the cold limbs of the dead wore the same garments
as the strong active ones of the living—Cousin Lizzie—his ↑ al-

The gravestone of Malcolm Melville in Woodlawn Cemetery, in The Bronx, New York City, is inscribed with the date of his death, September 11, 1867, and lines from a hymn by Frederick William Faber whose hymnbook his mother owned:

> So good, so young,
> So gentle, so sincere
> So loved, so early lost,
> May claim a tear.

He rests beside the grave of his father.

most ↓ heart broken Mother having dressed her eldest son in the new suit he had taken such pride & pleasure in wearing— Four superb wreaths & crosses of the choicest white flowers were placed on the coffin & it was lifted to the Shoulders of six of the Company & borne down the steps, through the street to the Cars (on the Harlem R. R. I think) which Allan had secured for special use." Especially in times of crisis, the family pulled together and did things properly. "The family & mourners followed—They left the car at the entrance of the *Woodlawn Cemetery*,[9] & the young bearers carried the coffin to the hearse— others bearing the flowers—What a sad sight—'The stone was rolled from the mouth of the cave.'—as the scripture saith—& the remains placed in the recving vault. Cousin Herman Lizzie the children, Gus & Allan selected a location & the others marched through this new cemetery which she says will one day rival Greenwood."[10] Kate concludes the letter with the comment that the lives of the survivors will go on as they must, provides some extraneous gossip, and encloses the obituary from the *New-York Times*.[11]

Three days later, on September 22, a Sunday afternoon, at 3 Kate sent her brother a short note, but there was no mention of Malcolm or the Melvilles, just an up-date on matters at home, such as the health of their father.[12] The record one can construct from her correspondence is silent for more than a month. Her next letter is to her stepmother, Susan. In this very short note she reports that she "went to see Cousin Lizzie & Herman this mning between churches[.] They are well & send their love to you & Papa. They speak of Malcome [*sic*] with such pleasure & seemed gratified to see me."[13] Time is passing, pain is easing, and the judgmental substance present in Kate's correspondence right after the death has diminished.

Kate's diary is enlightening for the little space given to Malcolm's death, the family's response, or her own reaction. We have argued the need to understand the context of quotations from documents, for without comprehending and appreciating their context, distortion is likely. Therefore, a few words about the diary itself.

The booklet is not, first of all, a diary.[14] The volume is small, its cover measuring approximately 4½ × 7¼ inches. The pe-

riod from September 12 to November 4, 1867, is covered in a
sparse twelve pages. Kate's entries are on loose sheets approximately the same size as the book's covers. These pages were
originally sewn in between the printed pages of the almanac—
the printed pages being concerned with a given month. Most of
these sewn-in sheets are now loose, the victims of time, and half
of them—six—are numbered; even numerals appear at the top
right of the recto pages, not on the verso where they should,
and she skipped page 48, inadvertently moving, that is, from
page 46 to page 50. One can locate a specific reference in one
or more ways: page number, placement in a given section of the
original diary (between the printed pages for September and
October, or October and November, for instance), or date. The
latter, of course, is critical, while the former two are useful in
helping locate an entry in the small and fragile volume.

As noted above, Kate first heard of Malcolm's death on Friday, September 13, a surprisingly long time after the event. Visiting her friend Anna Parker who was out, Kate writes that she
"then went to Mrs Buels[?] made a call & there heard of Malcom
[*sic*] Melville (Hermans son) having committed Suicide—which
the Eve'g Journal confirmed." She makes no mention in any of
the daily entries for the next eleven days, September 14
through 24, although on this last date she notes, "Henry arrived
Early this morning." Her entries are short and principally concerned with matters of ordinary daily life, such as the visits she
pays to various people. Nor is there any mention of the events
on East 26th Street during the next six days, from the 25th
through the 30th. This silence is all the more puzzling since
there appears a ready stimulus for reflection on what had happened in New York. On the 26th she records going to "the Burial Ground & to the Cemetary," and on the 28th she notes that
her father, mother, brother Henry, and she go "rid[ing] out to
the Cemetary to see the improvements there."[15] One would expect that such an occasion would at least call up some allusion
to Malcolm, which, it should be noted well, she first recorded in
the diary as a "Suicide" and continues to be an option. Malcolm's suicide and all it caused to reverberate through her mind
and within the family were perhaps more than she wished to
confront or possibly of little interest to her. The silence contin-

ues from October 1 through 15, despite two obvious occasions for some mention, however brief. At the end of her October 2 entry, she writes, "I am sorry to have [Henry] go his visit has been so delightful to us all & Father has fully appreciated the devotion of his son." Nor does she mention in the diary Cousin Herman and his family, despite the frequent visits to the cemetery she records during these first two weeks of the month.[16]

On the 15th, "Cousin Gus Melville & Tom arrived this mning in the tain [*sic*] from Gansevoort, Walked up to the grave yard with them. They made arrangements for moving their Father Allan Melville a native of Boston Mass, & their brother Gansevoort. They went to the Cemetary & M. [Mother?] & I walked down to 103 Pearl St. to see them for good bye." Again, no allusion to Malcolm or the survivors amid all this concern with family burial. Almost as puzzling is the matter of good-bys to other Melvilles. Gus and Tom, who were still in town the next day, simply disappear from Kate's diary accounts after the 17th; she herself left town and returned that same day. And there is no mention of Cousin Herman's bereavement or his family's plight through November 3 — nor later, as our perusal of the documents after that date indicates.[17]

However, Kate wrote her brother that she had seen "Cousin Herman & Lizzie while in N. Y. They all feel Malcom's [*sic*] death but the knowledge of its not being a crime mitigates their grief."[18] The issue of whether the death was a crime is critical.[19] Even if Herman and Lizzie, as Kate reports, have persuaded themselves and others that the death was accidental and, therefore, not disgraceful or criminal under New York State law, the phrasing she chooses at the end of the sentence indicates that she is unswayed. The boy was a suicide.

# Notes

1. ALs, Catherine Gansevoort to Henry Sanford Gansevoort, September 12, 1867, Friday, 3:30 P.M., G-L, box 161, Henry Sanford Gansevoort/Letterbooks 1866–67.

2. ALs, Catherine Gansevoort to Henry Sanford Gansevoort, September 13, 1867, G-L box 161, Henry Sanford Gansevoort/Letterbooks 1866–67. This letter is also noted as having been written on Friday, as was the one above. For whatever cause or causes, Kate may have been confused about the dates—rare for her, so as far as we have been able to determine.

3. ALs, Catherine Gansevoort to Henry Sanford Gansevoort, September 16, 1867, G-L, box 161, Henry Sanford Gansevoort/Letterbooks 1966–67. She also reports Augusta's assertion that Mackie should not have slept with the pistol under his pillow and her description that when discovered "the sweetest most placid expression was upon his features his face is perfectly natural & not disfigured—only the slight bruise on the side of his right eye"; and she says that Tom, Allan, and his wife, Milie [their daughter, Maria], and Gus [Augusta] Peebles were present when the door to Malcolm's room was broken down; quoted in part in Leyda, II, 691.

4. ALs, Catherine Gansevoort to Henry Sanford Gansevoort, September 15, 1867, G-L, box 161, Henry Sanford Gansevoort/Letterbooks 1866–67; quoted in part in Leyda, II, 690.

5. ALs, Henry Sanford Gansevoort to Catherine Gansevoort, August 20 and October 7, 1867, G-L, Box 245, album 2. In the latter, Henry, who writes from New York City where he has seen Tom, says he just received hers of September 5, regarding their uncle Wessel's gravestone. There is no mention of any of the Melvilles in his letter to his sister, dated October 11, box 245, album 2. Nor is there mention in another to her on the same day in which he reports that Tom is coming to Albany. Box 245, album 2.

6. Samuel Osgood (1812–80) spent twenty years (1849–69) as the minister of New York's Unitarian Church of the Messiah. In 1870 he became a priest in the Protestant Episcopal Church, so his reading the "Episcopal Burial Service" may have been an anticipation of the directions his calling was to take. Of course, he was friendly with Henry Whitney Bellows of the Unitarian Church of All Souls, which the Herman Melvilles attended before and after their Pittsfield years. *Appleton's*.

7. No word is deleted here but there is a blank space created by her not writing over the impression her blind-stamped logo made on the verso page.

8. No word is deleted here but there is a blank space created by her not writing over the impression her blind-stamped logo made on the verso page.

9. Woodlawn Cemetery is situated in the Bronx, north of Gun Hill Road.

10. Greenwood Cemetery, another landscaped burial park, is situated in Brooklyn.

11. ALs, Catherine Gansevoort to Henry Sanford Gansevoort, September 19, 1867, G-L, box 161, Henry Sanford Gansevoort/Letterbooks 1866–67.

12. ALs, Catherine Gansevoort to Henry Sanford Gansevoort, September 22, 1867, G-L, box 161, Henry Sanford Gansevoort/Letterbooks 1866–67.

13. ALs, Catherine Gansevoort to Susan Gansevoort, November 3, 1867, G-L, box 154.

14. It is a printed paperbound pamphlet entitled *Webster's Calendar of the Albany Almanac for the Year of Our Lord 1867*. At the top of the cover appears: "No. 84. / First Printed, 1784."

15. Diary, pp. [41]–44; these sheets are located between the August and September printed pages of the almanac. See Appendix K for more information on the significance of these graveyard "improvements."

16. Diary, pp. 46–[51], sheets between October and November printed pages.

17. Diary, pp. 50–54.

18. ALs, Catherine Gansevoort to Henry Sanford Gansevoort, November 25, 1867, G-L, box 161.

19. Suicide was not a crime in New York City in 1867.

# Appendix J
# Other Melville Family Reactions to Malcolm's Death

IN THE ALLUSIONS TO THE RESPONSE of Maria Gansevoort Melville to her grandson's death, one can show that she was shocked, crushed. This is confirmed by the correspondence in the Gansevoort-Lansing and Lemuel Shaw Papers. One might assume that the depth of emotion Maria was experiencing could be shared fully with her brother Peter and his wife, who had been so supportive through the years; her children (including Herman and the daughters with whom she was so close); or any other male relative. On the surface this appears true.

On September 14, she wrote Peter and Susan from Gansevoort. (She was at the time confined due to an ankle injury that made getting about difficult.) Enclosing Augusta's letter from New York City, which she had "rec'd this morning," she assumed that they had "doubtless seen Malcolms death reported in the papers," and she commented briefly on the boy's nature and the circumstances of his death: "Poor dear fellow he was a promising boy. Good kind & gentle most affectionate to all, He was in the habit of carrying a pistol, & laying it under his pillow at night." Refusing from the beginning of the ordeal to accept the judgment that the act had been intentional, she asserted her view unequivocally: "I have no doubt that he was examining it, & it went off I never will believe he committed Suicide." Perhaps with an eye toward keeping the embarrassing possibility as much within the family as possible, she told her brother and sister-in-law (did they really need such a reminder?): "I want you ↑ to ↓ return those ↑ Letters ↓ on Monday." Then in what is possibly as revealing of her own agony as that being borne by her son and his wife, not to mention Malcolm's brother and sisters, she reported, "Poor Herman & Lizzie May God sustain them under their severe affliction." The letter concludes "with love to Kate—she must write me," a report that she has "letters from Tom & Allan," and her "hope [that] Peter continues to improve my love to him." She adds a postscript about the boy who was being buried that very day: "On opening my Port Folio to write you the first thing that presented itself was a letter from dear Malcolm written so beautifully, in his own affectionate manner—[.]"[1]

Our perusal of the surviving documents shows that Maria expressed her deepest feelings to her brother Peter's wife, Susan. Writing her sister-in-law four weeks following the event—that is, on Tuesday, October 8—from Gansevoort, she thanked Susan for her "kind & sympathizing letter received last month[.] [It] should have been replied to sooner, but dear Malcolms death, so sudden, was overwhelming to me, we were all so much attached to him, & were looking forward to him with so much hope." She affirmed the departed boy's worth, if you will, by reporting that "Mʳ Lathers was pleased with his conduct at the Office & this fall he was intending to again promote him, but vain are human hopes—& uncertainty to change are stamped upon all earthly things." Putting aside material evidence for the emotional, she returns to the condition of the survivors: "Herman & Lizzie were much gratified to know that you sympathized with them so fully & desire to be remembered." After a digression into some talk of her health and Peter's, she reports, "We heard from Tom this morning he writes that Herman & Lizzie are well, but sad very sad." Concerned as always with the family, she further observes, "Henry was there I believe on Saturday Eveg & that he is looking very well, Henry has been with you a week I hear, how happy his father mother & sister must have been made by the visit."

Maria was not to be deterred from speaking of other matters, despite the fact that her grandson was less than a month in his grave. The living took precedence, as they should. The matters she subjects herself to may seem pedestrian in light of her deep concern about Malcolm. But to address the routine is in itself therapeutic:

> I am glad to hear that Peter is able to ride out daily, give my love to him, As to my ancle it is still weak, & I can walk very little without feeling it. I walked this morning from the piazza to the wood house with the aid of a cane. It is the first time that I have ventured out alone. But the day is perfect & I could not resist walking out to enjoy its loveliness. . . .
>
> As soon as I can walk a block or two without limping I shall be most happy to come & see you all, for a long time has passed since I saw you & brother Peter, & much has transpired since then,
>
> Tom & Augusta could not stop on their return from New York, Maria[2] returned with them, & M^rs Hoadley[3] was waiting for their return to go to Brookline, where they have hired a ready furnished house for six months, or a year, ↑ if they desire it ↓ until they can get a house in Boston to suit them.
>
> Augusta & Fanny are well & desire me to send much love to you—
>
> Did you receive a Boston paper from me with a beautiful obituary & a truthful one written by M^r Hoadley.
>
> Helen[4] is well, she will be near Kate this winter, not quite <a> half a mile & a pleasant walk. They will be together a great deal, M^r Hoadley keeps a pair of horses, they will have many pleasant rides together.
>
> This morning we rec'd wedding invitations from Albany, the envelope & card <were> beautiful, but who is "M^rs Theodore Miller," whose card with her husbands name attached was also enclosed.[5]

And after signing herself "Ever / your / attached / sister/ M G. Melville—" she adds that Susan should give her "Love to Kate she must write me."[6]

In the correspondence to Kate from Herman's brother Tom and two of his sisters, Augusta and Helen Melville Griggs, one factor that stands out is that the tragedy, while naturally important to them, did not supersede their other concerns. Their remarks when read out of context in the relatively short extracts provided by Leyda, for example, make their grief seem more engrossing than it actually was. The full letters place comments on the tragedy in perspective. This need not suggest that they

are being unsympathetic about Malcolm's death or in their relations with Herman and the members of the household. It
seems to mean nothing more than that for most of the family
life continued even after tragedy interrupted the ordinary flow
of events. Further, the family had a penchant for hiding the
unpleasant and embarrassing. (Two exceptions are Allan and
Augusta, who sustained Herman, Lizzie, and the other children
during this hour of need. This is not surprising since it would
appear that emotionally, these two were among his closest relations.)

We start presenting this handful of letters in order to provide
some sense of the developing perspective on Malcolm's suicide.

Writing Kate from Herman's house in New York in late September, Tom begins with an apology: "I would have answered
your letter before but have been traveling around so much &
have had so much to do, that I really have not had time." He
then offers some detail about his business: "After poor Mackis
[*sic*] funeral I returned with Mellie[7] to Gansevoort we went up
in the day boat New Athens & had a delightful trip up the river
reaching home at 7 P.M. Tuesday evening," presumably the
17th, three days after Mackie's burial. He stayed in Gansevoort
for almost a week, traveling to Boston the following Monday,
the 23rd, where he remained with Helen in Brookline for
slightly more than a day. On Wednesday, the 25th, he reports,
he "came on to New York [and] found Augusta still at Herman's.
Herman & Lizzy have been at Allan's making a visit & have just
returned[.] I think the visit has done them both good they feel
poor Mackie's loss deeply. The little girls are well. Gus goes
home tomorrow as Kate & children will leave Gansevoort Tuesday for Boston." The last two pages of Tom's letter trail off into
family gossip, touching, for example, on the handsome Brookline house the Hoadleys had rented for the winter, Tom's own
plans to return to Gansevoort for a month or so, and some remarks concerning the Washington Street house of Uncle Peter,
Aunt Susan, and Kate. At the time this letter was written, less
than three weeks had passed since Malcolm's suicide and more
than two weeks had elapsed since he had been buried. Tom was
neither dull nor unfeeling but had other obligations to meet.[8]

But Helen's letter to Kate of October 6, the first she wrote to her since Malcolm's death, is disturbing. One can understand Tom's distance, but one is unprepared for Helen's so casually alluding to the event (granted, it was almost a month past) or not even mentioning Herman and the family. After beginning with an assurance to Kate that "I had not forgotten my promise, to enquire concerning those 'invalid tables' on my return to Boston; but I had scarcely got home, before dear Mackie's sad death called me to New York, and since then my time has been very fully occupied by household matters." She rehearses these in detail and although there is about a page of discussion of Mühlbach's novels,[9] even this obvious link does not inspire her to some reflection on the suffering of her own novelist brother. She seems insensitive but in the light of the other difficulties at East 26th Street, such as the marital strains that in the preceding May had led to serious talk of Lizzie's leaving Herman,[10] one might interpret her silence as avoidance of unpleasant matters of which she may well have had her fill. There is a further possibility. Helen tended to be superficial and conventional. Such a conclusion is sustained by the quality and tone of her other letters[11] and perhaps by her observations about matters literary in this letter. She admits not liking *Frederick and His Family* much.[12] "But then historical novels are not to my taste; I much prefer taking my history, and fiction, separate." The next sentence is perhaps more revealing of her literary tastes generally than of the novel she is discussing. "One reads a novel to be amused, a sort of agreeable pastime, tho' not a useful one perhaps." How disheartening such a view of fiction would have been to her brother Herman had she ever expressed it to him. Her critique does not stop here, however: "if one reads history, let it be read for improvement, and then the characters must be drawn as they actually were, not poetically nor romantically, or one cannot lay the flattering unction to the soul that one is actually engaged in solid reading, really enlarging and cultivating the mind, which is a pleasantly complacent feeling."[13]

How could the creative, imaginative, intellectually, and artistically gifted Herman have responded to such observations that so clearly flew in the face of his own theory of fiction? Our suspicion is that her remarks, which were not untypical of popular thinking, would have been yet another reason for his turning inward. Negative assessments in published print are vicissitudes inevitably encountered by any author. Such views from one's own sister carried greater weight by virtue of their very source: a family member, a sister, with whom he had shared their parents' roof and whom he had also helped provide a roof for when he was first married. She had been a daily witness to the intense, even enervating, intellectual struggles he engaged in during the composition of *Mardi* and on occasion had worked as his copyist.

One possibility was that Mackie might have been a novice with firearms. There are claims of such inexperience from several quarters, not the least important of which is Augusta. Writing to her brother Henry on September 16, Kate notes that "Cousin Gus says, 'Poor Mackies death is a lesson to all who place pistols under their pillows he must have been handling the pistol, <when> for it was found in his hand—His friend George Starr, had remonstrated with him ↑ several times ↓ , telling him, he would kill himself some day with his carelessness in using fire-Arms." One wonders whether Gus is retailing a story emerging from a grieving and embarrassed family or relating her own version of what happened. How much credence might the investigator give her commentary? Like everyone near the situation, she was somewhat emotionally wrought. Kate's letter continues, confirming Herman's widely known comments regarding Mackie's "last attitude." Still quoting Gus, Kate reports, "She says that the sweetest most placid expression rests upon his features & his face is perfectly natural & not disfigured— only one slight bruise in the side of his right eye[.] & then tells the same story as we have seen in the papers."[14] How to apply this and similar testimony about Mackie's being inept and careless when handling weapons is problematical. Several questions arise, the answers to which are critical to a determination of whether the death was an accident or suicide. For instance, first, what standard was Starr using to judge Mackie's proficiency? One might find it hard to believe that a young man with experience in the militia would not have acquired a sufficient proficiency with his own pistol to have avoided an accidental discharge. These skills the recruit masters in the earliest stage of his training. However, Malcolm appears to have enlisted only a short time before his death (we do not know the precise date), and his training may have been very limited. One wonders how he came to have in his possession a pistol issued by the military company, if indeed it was. Perhaps it belonged to him. Members of volunteer companies often supplied their own arms. Was it given to him, this symbol of manhood, as a present from his father?

But even if one grants that the weapon discharged accidentally, one must ask why he had it positioned right next to his temple. Mere chance seems a less reasonable inference than intention. Further, the person judging cannot have it both ways. Mackie was either awake (or in a stupor) and handling the gun, or he was asleep with it under the pillow when it went off by accident. The answer requires our knowing the angle of the bullet's entry and whether it exited. There are obviously other questions one might ask.[15]

# Notes

1. ALs, Maria Gansevoort Melville to Peter and Susan Gansevoort, September 14, 1867, G-L, box 154.

2. Possibly Allan Melville's daughter and her namesake, usually called Millie.

3. Herman's sister Catherine who was married to John C. Hoadley.

4. Herman's sister Helen Maria who was married to George Griggs.

5. We are no more enlightened about Mrs. Miller's identity than was Maria.

6. ALs, Maria Gansevoort Melville to Susan Gansevoort, October 8, 1867, G-L, box 154.

7. Unidentified, but possibly a careless spelling for *Millie*, the affectionate name of Allan's daughter Maria.

8. ALs, Thomas Melville to Catherine Gansevoort, September 29, 1867, G-L, box 216; quoted in part in Leyda, II, 692.

9. Luise Mühlbach, the pseudonym used by Klara Müller Mundt (1814–73). She wrote social and historical novels.

10. Kring and Carey, pp. 137–41.

11. Both in the original Gansevoort-Lansing Collection and the Gansevoort-Lansing Additions.

12. A novel by Luise Mühlbach (see note 9 above), translated into English in 1867. *Webster*.

13. ALs, Helen Melville Griggs to Catherine Gansevoort, October 6, 1867, G-L, box 216.

14. ALs, Catherine Gansevoort to Henry Sanford Gansevoort, September 16, 1867, G-L, box 161, Henry Sanford Gansevoort/Letterbooks 1866–67.

15. We have been unsuccessful in our search for the minutes of the coroner's jury, the New York City Police blotter book, in which such incidents would have been recorded, and other possibly useful documents. See p. 105, note 116.

# Appendix K
## Family Monuments and
## Malcolm's Death

THE GANSEVOORT-LANSING COLLECTION gives the impression that Augusta Melville was ubiquitous, always there to support, always central to matters that concerned the family in general, especially the Herman Melvilles. As noted above, she was among those who stayed longest with Herman, Lizzie, and the surviving children after the events of September 1867.

Malcolm's suicide paralleled a series of gestures of family solidarity and pride: the restoration of the Gansevoort monuments and work on other family graves in Albany.[1] Both Augusta and Kate were involved. In October 1867, Kate wrote Henry an effusive letter about the care of the graves and the establishment and maintenance of Gansevoort family monuments. She and her parents had visited the site and agreed that "the graves, & the stones above, surrounded by periwinkle looked beautifully." All the Gansevoort family remains are at last together in a location that pleases her; she evidently looks forward to joining them, satisfied with the prospect of resting with her family when the time arrives. She is especially pleased with the stonecutter's work, whose cooperation extends to providing the family with accurate records for their genealogical purposes. She concludes by reporting that "Tom & Gus Melville came down last Tuesday morning from Gansevoort. They spent most of their time at the Cemetery & grave yard."[2] And in her diary for October 15, Kate adds that among the first things her cousins did upon arriving was to visit the grave sites. Tom and

Gus had also "made arrangements for removing their Father Allan Melville [*sic*] a native of Boston Mass. & their brother Gansevoort." The cousins stayed on for another day and made at least one more visit to the Gansevoort site on the day after their arrival.[3] Allan informed Henry of the reburying of father and brother and the commencement of work on their gravestones in a letter to Henry of October 7.[4] Augusta wrote Kate near the end of October, reporting that her mother "has taken the matters into consideration, & having decided to have the monument cleaned and improved according to the proposed plan, would ask you to be so kind as to let Peter tell the man that he can proceed at once to do it. As soon as the stone is ready for the lettering, please let us know."[5] But the refurbishing of family graves did not stop there; Kate's and Henry's Uncle Wessel Gansevoort's stone was also inscribed in early October, within a few weeks after Malcolm's death,[6] which, again, was slipping into the background.

The subject, though somewhat depressing, is another illustration of the family working in concert. If Augusta was always present for such occasions, Kate was there to perform whatever practical services were necessary—a fact acknowledged by Gus: "You were very good Katie dear to make the kind offer you did to do any thing for us in this matter that lay in your power, & we all feel much indebted to you." Kate's kindness extended to Malcolm's grieving grandmother. Gus continues, "And now let me thank you & [undeciphered word] Uncle & Aunt Susan for the very affectionate invitation you sent to Mamma to make a visit at 115 Washington St. Nothing could be kinder." Maria, however, was unable to accept the invitation, because her injured ankle still did not allow mobility, and, alas, neither could Fanny nor Gus.[7] This was followed the very next day by another note to Kate from Gus. On the third page she turned to the matter of the monument: "Mama says that you may lett [*sic*] [the stonecutter] to build the foundation for the monument at the Cemetery, & retain the obelisk in his shop until one of the family can be in Albany to see about the inscriptions." Gus was aware of the work involved for Kate, not, as we have noted, without some enthusiasm; after all, these were matters of serious family concern. The letter continues, "I am real sorry to give you so much trouble about this matter, dear Kate, but cannot well help it."[8]

Before December 2, Tom was involved. In a letter to Kate that day, he wrote, "Enclosed please find Check for $78.18 the amount of [the stonecutter's bill] which you will please give him as soon as he reports the Monument as being in its place & all right."[9]

From the tragedy and embarrassment of Mackie's suicide we obtain insights into the Melville-Gansevoort-Shaw clan. For example, generalizations about monolithic family reaction do not suffice because they fail to take into account the differing responses of its individual members. Yet despite differences, there appears to be a pervading concurrence. Kinship overshadowed personal feelings and produced cohesion, a shield to protect the interest and image of the family. Malcolm's death gave momentum to a family enterprise, the restoration of the monument: the stone proclaimed to the world that this was a family of substance, one to be respected for the prominence it had attained from colonial times. The patriarchal structure and the assumptions on which it was built may have been eroding during Melville's lifetime—they had begun to show signs of stress at least as early as his father's generation—but the family worked hard to at least impede its collapse. And as a member of the family, the one in fact most aware of this reality, and as a father mourning the loss of a son, Herman Melville no doubt sympathized with their undertaking.

# Notes

1. The location of the graves is the Albany Rural Cemetery. Kenney, p. 246. Peter Gansevoort is listed as a trustee of the cemetery, which is located on the Troy Road near West Troy, in *The Albany Directory, for the Year 1867* (Albany: Sampson, Davenport, 1867), p. 245, as well as in the editions of 1865 and 1866.

2. ALs, Catherine Gansevoort to Henry Sanford Gansevoort, October 21, 1867, G-L, box 161, Henry Sanford Gansevoort/Letterbooks 1866–67.

3. Catherine Gansevoort Lansing/Diaries 1860–72, October 15 and 16, pp. 50–[51], G-L, box 255.

4. ALs, Allan Melville to Henry Sanford Gansevoort, October 7, 1867, G-L, box 161, Henry Sanford Gansevoort/Letterbooks 1866–67.

5. ALs, Augusta Melville to Catherine Gansevoort, October 29, 1867, G-L, box 216.

6. ALs, Catherine Gansevoort to Henry Sanford Gansevoort, October 5, 1867, and October 9, 1867, G-L, box 161, Henry Sanford Gansevoort/Letterbooks 1866–67.

7. ALs, Augusta Melville to Catherine Gansevoort, October 29, 1867, G-L, box 216.

8. ALs, Augusta Melville to Catherine Gansevoort, October 30, 1867, G-L, box 216.

9. ALs, Thomas Melville to Catherine Gansevoort, December 2, 1867, G-L, box 216.

# Appendix L
# The Family Circle in
# Times of Joy and Sorrow

ATTEMPTING TO CHART THE INTERWOVEN CONNECTIONS of the various members of the Melvilles and Gansevoorts is surprising and frustrating, as a few unexpected examples will show.

Consider, for instance, some letters to Peter Gansevoort from Herman's Uncle Thomas Melvill in 1818. Allan Melvill was in Europe on business, and his brother Thomas was moved to communicate with this Albany relative-by-marriage. Late in April Thomas wrote "to acquaint you, that we are in our usual health, and to request the favor of you, to let us know from time to time, the welfare of Maria & the Children, of your good Mother, and your own[.]" Thomas reported that he had just had news from his Boston relatives there, including his father, and that he sympathized with his brother Allan, who was separated from his wife and children. He dwelled on Maria's plight without her husband in a nearly incoherent but cordial and well-meaning paragraph. One should not miss the concern for family in Thomas's letter, even if the occasion was the opportunity of having it hand-delivered by a visitor on his way to Albany from Pittsfield.[1] Two days later he wrote a similar note and at the end voiced his fondness for Peter: "we think of you all often, & bear you most affectionately in our hearts."[2] He was equally supportive and warm in another letter to Allan's brother-in-law a week later.[3]

Such expressions of family ties continued over the years. Recall the connection between Herman and Kate Gansevoort when she was attending Mrs. Sedgwick's boarding school in nearby Lenox.[4] Her stepmother wrote her, "I am glad to hear you spent your time so pleasantly at Cousin Hermans[.] I hope this visit will be the beginning of a *series* of visits & that you will learn to love them better than ever."[5] A decade later (1865) her Aunt Maria wrote Kate from Gansevoort to tell her, among other things, about the grand family picnic she had missed because Maria's letter of invitation evidently went astray: "We were very sorry that my letter to you mis-carried, for Tom returned from the Station where he had gone to receive you, & Miss Lansing[6] & Miss Parker[7] we[re] quite disappointed, for we had anticipated a pleasant visit & a merry one. But alas we were doomed to disappointment. We had seated ourselves on the piazza all ready to receive you, the day most beautiful, the broiled chickens most excellent &c, &c & you did not come. Well we must hope on." (The picnic had evidently taken place a few weeks earlier since Maria reports that Tom had been gone a few weeks.) She offers a page and a half of news, then adds, "I wish you could have been here yesterday" for a meeting of "four Sabbath Schools. . . . Herman, Florence Kitty & Lucy are staying here & all went to the Picnic, had a grand supply of iced cakes, sugar-plums, peaches nuts, biscuit &c, quantities left were given to the poor—Fifteen hundred persons were there at least, enjoying themselves." But a storm came up and the crowd dispersed. Herman was enjoying his visit with his mother, and she reported that "Herman just came in—he desires me give his love & regards to Uncle & Aunt Susan." The arrival of the rest of his family was anticipated: "We expect Lizzie with Bessie & Fanny in a few days. Maria[8] is coming home from Helens with Sam Shaw to Arrowhead where he is to make a visit, Maria will probably come here with Lizzie."[9] (The year before, Maria had reported a similar visit by Lizzie who planned to "leave us on Friday next with her four children for New York."[10]) Numerous bits of information testify to the repeated visits and festivities within the family circle, Shaws included, and it is reasonable to assume that Herman participated in them.

The mid-1860s appear to have been a period of busy family socializing. For instance, in March 1866, Gus wrote Kate from New York City that "Herman & Lizzie & all the household unite in much love to you all." Then in an informal postscript over the date on the first sheet of the letter, she added, "We [Augusta was staying at East 26th Street] have just had a charming call from Uncle D'Wolfe. He asked about his Albany friends."[11] And Tom wrote to Kate in September from Brookline, Massachusetts, where he was visiting his sister, that "Herman's two girls are staying with her [Helen], so she has quite a houseful." Tom paid his respects to Lizzie's family while he was in town: "I have called on Mrs Shaw what a lovely old lady she is."[12] Often on the move, he wrote Kate in late September to say that he had "been in New York a week but shall leave for Gansevoort tomorrow night."[13] If Tom were sociable, those who welcomed him as house guest were equally so; family openheartedness complemented, made possible, such visits. And what of the activities that engaged the brothers during their visits? In another letter to Kate, in 1867, Tom tells her that "Herman, Lizzy, & the children are well, they send their best love to Uncle & Aunt Susan & yourself with many thanks, for your kind wishes. Last night Herman & I went to see 'Ristori' in 'Elizabeth'[14] she is a splendid actress, & I had a delightful evening."[15]

We have noted Henry Sanford Gansevoort's curious silence or the gap in correspondence after Malcolm's death.[16] However, one should not conclude that his relations with Herman and his family were strained. In fact the documentation in the Gansevoort-Lansing Collection suggests that there was a special bond between Henry and his cousin. Their relationship appears to have been based on their concerns for each other as kinsmen. Henry seems to have followed Melville's career as a writer and lecturer not from shared literary interest but because he wished him well. He owned a copy of *Battle-Pieces*, Melville's collection of Civil War poetry; as a veteran he would naturally have had an interest in it.[17] Herman and Henry were evidently close over the years. There is no better evidence than in the family's response to Henry's death and their reaction to the mementos his sister distributed. Herman was among the cousins, and their children (second cousins) to whom Kate gave remembrance gifts. A note in an unidentified hand states that "*Henry* requested his sister Kate to send *gifts* to all *Blood-Cousins* and their

The Herman Melville residence at 104 East 26th Street is the first building on the left, with the tree in front. From *The American Architect and
Building News* (December 12, 1890), p. 355.

children and friends who I think will accept them as intended."
The short list includes Herman and his brothers and sisters,
each of whom received a ring, while their children, the second
cousins, got "some piece of jewelry."[18] In a letter to Kate of November 1871, Augusta registered her pleasure: "His ring is on
my finger, & as I look upon it the tears are in my eyes & in my
heart. Tears for him, that his young life should have thus
ended; tears for you my dearly loved Cousin who so mourn his
loss. Bright & pure as the beautiful stone which rays in this fair
light, will be the memory of your noble gallant brother Henry
Sanford Gansevoort." She had started her "hurried lines" by
reporting similar responses from Helen and Fanny and re-
marking on its meaning to her and, we may assume, the other
recipients: "Your sweet note [enclosed with the "precious package"] is before me with its touching memories of your darling
brother. I shall keep it always, dear Kate, in memory of him, &
of that sad night when one so dear to us passed away. The
thought that we were remembered thus by him is very sweet to
me."[19] Herman wrote his own note,[20] and there were similar
acknowledgments from Fanny, Helen, Allan, and Florence[21] as
well as relatives by marriage, or long family connection, such as
Lemuel Shaw, Jr., who was given a pair of sleeve buttons.[22]

For Maria there was a poignancy that more strongly suggests
the profound sense of family and continuity. She wrote Kate in
February 1872 and reflected, "How well we all remembered the
evening when the ring came for my father." So in making this
gesture, Henry, and Kate who carried out his request, were
maintaining a Victorian memorializing tradition. Her aunt continues, "He opened it at the dinner table—and was so much
pleased with it. He wore it, all during his illness ↑ too ↓ and it
was only on the morning of the day he died that I took it off his
hand <and> by his desire and have had it ever since. Mama
says that I am to keep it now. With that ring which I cannot too
highly prize with its double associations, I have now the beautiful gift from Cousin Henry. How beautiful it is—how I wish my
father could have seen it."[23]

Kate arranged for a handsome commemorative volume to be
compiled. John Hoadley edited it and undertook to ensure its
place in the public record by having it deposited in institutions,

which he listed in a letter to Kate of February 17, 1878.[24] The passage of nearly a decade since Henry's death had not diminished their desire to perpetuate his name. His prominence did not compare with that of "the Hero of Fort Stanwix," but he was a Gansevoort. And by the agency of Kate's and Henry's Uncle Robert E. Sanford, it was placed in the library of The Union League Club, located (according to the stationery on which his February 4, 1878, letter is written) at Madison Avenue and East 26th Street, a block from Herman's house.[25] And on January 24, 1878, Lemuel Shaw, Jr., acknowledged receipt and recommended that she send copies to Harvard and the Boston Public Library.[26] For a select group of family members there was to be a bonus. In his letter of February 17, John Hoadley wrote that he had "a suggestion to make [to Kate], which I hope your indulgent kindness may receive without offence—I have a few copies left of that steel plate portrait of your [undeciphered word]. My wife and children would like to have one each in their volumes.—*Perhaps* you, and darling Fanny, and Tom and Herman, would like to have one in theirs."[27] Kate gave her permission and on the 24th Hoadley announced that he would have the plates she had sent "bound up with six of the books[.]"[28]

What the family did to preserve the record of Henry Sanford Gansevoort's life helps the scholar understand Lizzie's efforts shortly after Herman's death to secure her husband's niche in the history of American letters. Although she had the will and motive, Lizzie did not have the financial resources that allowed Kate to ignore the volatile American economy of the 1870s with its Panics in 1873 and 1877. A similar fiscal crisis occurred in the early 1890s and halted the project Lizzie had initiated with the Stedmans to reprint her late husband's works.[29]

But we should return to our principal subject, the relationship between Henry Sanford Gansevoort and Herman Melville, as well as that between Melville's immediate family and the Shaws. There is a well-documented record scattered through the Gansevoort-Lansing Collection. First, some observations about casual visits and interests in common. When Henry was in Europe in 1859, he wrote his cousin Allan and included Herman's family among those to whom he wished to be remembered. In 1861, he wrote Kate, observing that "Cousin Herman

I see has failed to obtain the Consulship at Florence." Nevertheless, he remained hopeful: "I hope he will become successful regarding some other appointment."[30] On the page for June 28, he listed Melville (presumably the family as well as Herman himself) in his "Clayton's Pocket Diary for 1862" as among the seven people to "Visit out town."[31] And writing to Kate in May the next year, he casually asked, "Have you heard that Herman Melville has purchased a home in this city[?] He has sold his place in Berkshire to Allan who intends I believe spending the summer there."[32] Such references continued after Malcolm's death. For example, when Kate was at Cousin Herman's in New York, she received a letter from her stepmother which shows that Henry also was there, and ill: "You say Henry is no better. We do sympathize with him, & I wish he was home. Give him our best love & tell him if he is not better he had better come home again."[33]

We have seen that Henry's interest in Herman appears to have been concerned with the person more than the literary personage. However, there are comments on Herman as lecturer that one should note. He wrote Kate in January 1859, that he had attended Herman's lecture at the New-York Historical Society, but he was negative in his criticism.[34] A month earlier he had seen Herman in New York, as he reported to Kate on December 8: "Cousin Herman has been in town and I believe lectured last night at Yonkers. The subject of his lecture was the 'South Seas.' I saw him at Cousin Allens [sic] on Sunday"[35] Henry had seen Herman when he was on the lecture circuit earlier in the year, this time in Boston; as he wrote Kate: "On Saturday I dropped in to See Judge & Mrs Shaw and staid to dinner with them. Cousin Herman is there at present. He has just returned from a visiting & lecturing tour in the South & West. This week he goes to Rochester NY. All were well."[36]

Henry's following Herman's career as lecturer was largely due to his being in the right place at the right time. However, it shows his loyalty to a relative and friend. We notice that Henry was maintaining his links with Herman's in-laws in Boston, no surprise in the light of his father's long-standing friendship with the Judge. While studying law at Harvard during the 1857–58 academic year, he saw the Shaws regularly. In November he wrote Kate that he had "dined at Chief J. Shaws. We have [*sic*] a very pleasant and elaborate dinner. Herman Melville and his wife and children were present. M^r & M^rs Griggs etc." His comments on the family, particularly the Melville children, as well as the Shaw boys, reveal that he was a perceptive observer.

> Herman has four children. Malcom [*sic*] the eldest is a fine boy but Stanwix the next ↑ to the ↓ youngest is rather sickly, Bessie seems to be a beautiful girl[.] Her features <seem to be> ↑ are ↓ different from those of her parents. She seems a rara avis in terra.[37] Herman lectures in Boston next Wednesday. He seems to fancy the business and I think will succeed. I intend to attend his lecture and will give you an account of it.[38] Samuel Shaw Mr Shaws youngest son arrived here a few weeks since from Europe. He seems to be a little more gay than Lemuel but a very nice fellow. Herman wished to be remembered to you all[.][39]

A dozen years later, a few years after Malcolm's suicide and shortly before his own death, Henry would still be visiting the Shaws. He was then stationed at Fort Independence near Boston and wrote Kate to report that "I saw [undeciphered word] the other evening at Mrs Shaws. She is well and coming down to the Fort to see me next Thursday."[40] Good relations obtained between Henry and the Melvilles, extending to Lizzie's family. This is typical of the common regard and sociality within the family circle.

# Notes

1. ALs, Thomas Melvill, Jr., to Peter Gansevoort, April 25, 1818, G-L, box 30.
2. ALs, Thomas Melvill, Jr., to Peter Gansevoort, April 27, 1818, G-L, box 30.
3. ALs, Thomas Melvill, Jr., to Peter Gansevoort, May 2, 1818, G-L, box 30.
4. See pp. 185–88.
5. ALs, Susan Gansevoort to Catherine Gansevoort, July 17, 1855, G-L, box 245, album 1.
6. It is impossible to identify which Miss Lansing is being referred to here.
7. Anna Parker, Kate's friend from childhood.
8. Either Allan's daughter (nicknamed Milie) or Catherine's (nicknamed Minnie).
9. ALs, Maria Gansevoort Melville to Catherine Gansevoort, August 17, 1865, G-L, box 215; quoted in part in Leyda, II, 675, and in Metcalf, p. 205.
10. ALs, Maria Gansevoort Melville to Catherine Gansevoort, September 5, 1864, G-L, box 215. (This folder should precede the one above in the file box, but we have preserved the Library's order.)
11. ALs, Augusta Melville to Catherine Gansevoort, March 23, 1866, G-L, box 216. John D'Wolf (1779–1872) was married to Melville's father's sister, Mary (1778–1857).
12. ALs, Thomas Melville to Catherine Gansevoort, September 2, 1866, G-L, box 216; quoted partially in Metcalf, p. 206.
13. ALs, Thomas Melville to Catherine Gansevoort, September 23, 1866, G-L, box 216.
14. Adelaide Ristori performed in the title role of *Elizabeth, Queen of England* at Steinway Hall. *The* [N. Y.] *Evening Post*, January 7, 1867, p. [4].
15. Thomas Melville to Catherine Gansevoort, January 8, 1867, G-L, box 216; summarized in Leyda, II, 685.
16. See p. 202.
17. This is the only title that appears in one of his notebooks labeled "Books / Belonging to / Col. Henry Sanford Gansevoort / 5th Regt Artillery." The tan-on-maroon, marbled, soft-covered volume, which is much like a school tablet, contains alphabetical labels, and under the letter *B* we read "Battle Pieces by Herman Melville." On most pages, including the one containing the *Battle-Pieces* reference, there are vertical cross-out lines running through the entries. Furthermore, the top five lines of the *M* section have been cut out, as are the many pages after *M* that are not lettered. For Melville's visit to Colonel Gansevoort's regiment, his participation in a cavalry raid, and the verse that he wrote about it, see Stanton Garner, "Melville's Scout Toward Aldie," *Melville Society Extracts*, 51 (September 1982), 5–16; 52 (November 1982), 1–14.

18. The gifts were apparently ordered from Tiffany & Company. The documents are collected in G-L, vol. 77, "Letters of / Condolence / Upon Death of / Henry S. Gansevoort / 1871–1878." The note lies between the ALs, Abraham Lansing to Catherine Gansevoort, April 11, 1871, and a tipped-in, taped page composed of telegrams to Abe from Lemuel Shaw and G. H. Brewster.

19. Augusta Melville to Catherine Gansevoort, November 11, 1871, G-L, vol. 77, "Letters of / Condolence / Upon Death of / Henry S. Gansevoort / 1871–1878."

20. ALs, Herman Melville to Catherine Gansevoort, November 13, 1871, G-L, vol. 77, "Letters of / Condolence / Upon Death of / Henry S. Gansevoort / 1871–1878." *Letters*, p. 237, and Metcalf, p. 220.

21. ALs, Frances Priscilla Melville to Catherine Gansevoort, November 12, 1871; ALs, Helen Maria [Melville] Griggs to Catherine Gansevoort, November 12, 1871; and ALs, Allan Melville to Catherine Gansevoort, November 23, 1871, vol. 77, "Letters of / Condolence / Upon Death of / Henry S. Gansevoort, 1871–1878." All in G-L. Some women received chains (or necklaces) and some of the men, perhaps the women's husbands, watch chains.

22. ALs, Lemuel Shaw, Jr., to Catherine Gansevoort, February 24, 1872, G-L, vol. 77, "Letters of / Condolence / Upon Death of / Henry S. Gansevoort / 1871–1878."

23. ALs, Maria Gansevoort Melville to Catherine Gansevoort, February 26, 1872, G-L, vol. 77, "Letters of / Condolence / Upon Death of / Henry S. Gansevoort / 1871–1878." We note the confusion in generations here. Maria is clearly talking about the ring received by her father from her grandfather, but her mother had been dead for more than forty years at the time this letter to Kate was penned. Perhaps the explanation is that she was merely confused or flustered. It should be noted that the letter is in her hand and signed "Maria G. Melville."

24. ALs, John C. Hoadley to Catherine Gansevoort, February 17, 1878, G-L, vol. 77, "Letters of / Condolence / Upon Death of / Henry S. Gansevoort / 1871–1878."

This royal octavo volume is *Memorial of Henry Sanford Gansevoort . . .* , ed. J. C. Hoadley (Boston: Franklin Press; Rand, Avery, & Co., 1875). We have seen two copies in the New York Public Library, one of which Kate inscribed in ink on the flyleaf: "Presented to the / 'Lenox Library.' / New York City. / N. Y. / By / Mrs Abraham Lansing. / of Albany N. Y." A penciled note below the inscription reads: "[Delivered by Herman Melville. / See: Melville Family Correspondence. / ed. Paltsits. 1929. p. 54.]"

25. ALs, Robert E. Sanford to Catherine Gansevoort, February 4, 1878, G-L, vol. 77, "Letters of / Condolence / Upon Death of / Henry S. Gansevoort / 1871–1878." He recommended recording the provenance of the volume with an inscription: "Presented to the Union League Club of New York city, or of the city of New York, by Katherine [sic] Gansevoort Lansing."

26. ALs, Lemuel Shaw, Jr., to Catherine Gansevoort, January 24, 1878,

G-L, vol. 77, "Letters of / Condolence / Upon Death of / Henry S. Gansevoort / 1871–1878." He acknowledges receipt of the copies in an ALs to her, September 1, 1878, G-L,vol. 77, "Letters of / Condolence / Upon Death of / Henry S. Gansevoort / 1871–1878."

27. ALs, John C. Hoadley to Catherine Gansevoort, February 17, 1878, G-L, vol. 77, "Letters of / Condolence / Upon Death of / Henry S. Gansevoort / 1871–1878."

28. ALs, John C. Hoadley to Catherine Gansevoort, February 24, 1878, G-L, vol. 77, "Letters of / Condolence / Upon Death of / Henry S. Gansevoort / 1871–1878."

29. Sealts, *Early Lives*, pp. 47–64, 97–115, 149–66; and Kier, 3–8.

30. ALs, Henry Sanford Gansevoort to Catherine Gansevoort, March 30, 1861, G-L, box 245, album 1.

31. Saturday, June 28, 1862, *Clayton's Pocket Diary for 1862*, box 171, Henry S. Gansevoort's Notebooks.

32. ALs, Henry Sanford Gansevoort to Catherine Gansevoort, May 21, 1863, G-L, box 245, album 1.

33. ALs, Susan Gansevoort to Catherine Gansevoort, June 12, 1869, G-L, box 245, album 2.

34. ALs, Henry Sanford Gansevoort to Catherine Gansevoort, January 8, 1859, G-L, box 215.

35. ALs, Henry Sanford Gansevoort to Catherine Gansevoort, December 8, 1858, G-L, box 245, album 1.

36. ALs, Henry Sanford Gansevoort to Catherine Gansevoort, February 16, 1858, G-L, box 245, album 1.

37. A rare bird on earth.

38. We have been unable to locate Henry's "account," if he ever wrote one.

39. ALs, Henry Sanford Gansevoort to Catherine Gansevoort, November 28, 1857, G-L, box 245, album 1. Leyda notes only that Melville attended Thanksgiving at the Shaws.

40. ALs, Henry Sanford Gansevoort to Catherine Gansevoort, September 21, 1869, G-L, box 245.

# Afterword

ON JUNE 22, 1848, Melville bought a copy of *The Vision; or Hell, Purgatory, and Paradise* (Sealts no. 174), Henry Francis Cary's translation of Dante's *Divine Comedy*. Some time later (the date is uncertain because he continued to read and mark passages in it for many years thereafter) he wrote on a blank leaf at the end:

Tu asperges me. 344.

The Latin phrase is from Canto 31 of *Purgatory*, page 344 in the Cary version, a passage Melville marked. Its source, as Cary notes, is Psalm 51, the lines "Purge me with hyssop, and I shall be clean; wash me, and I shall be whiter than snow." This psalm was of peculiar importance to Melville. In his copy of *The New Testament* [with] *Psalms* (Sealts no. 65), he lined the margin of the first and third verses, the prayer, "blot out my transgressions," and the acknowledgement, "sin *is* ever before me," and above the heading he wrote, "This is the chief of Rome seven Penitent[ia]l Psalms." For Protestant interpreters, these verses likewise signify acceptance of guilt. In the *Purgatory* canticle, Dante, after repenting, is immersed in the river Lethe which washes away his sins, and he hears "*Asperges me,*" in the language of the missal, sweetly sung. *Asperges*—literally, to wash or sprinkle—is the Roman Catholic ceremony of sprinkling the altar and communicants with holy water, a purification that precedes the mass. During the ritual, the words "Asperges me, Domine, hyssopo, et mundabor . . ." are intoned.

Why did Melville inscribe these words recounting Dante's allegorical cleansing and remission, which derive from a ceremony of purgation, based upon the psalmist's penitential prayer? Certainly not as a profession of faith, for as Hawthorne understood, Melville could "neither believe nor be comfortable in his unbelief." The words of the *Asperges* articulate a psychological rather than a spiritual progress. They suggest his contrition, and his gradually coming to terms with a history that embraced a Calvinist sense of original sin, a family burdened with the sins of the fathers, and personal responsibility for the death of Malcolm.

# Works Cited

Adams, Charles Francis, ed. *Memoirs of John Quincy Adams, Comprising Portions of His Diary from 1795 to 1848.* 12 vols. 1874–77; rpt. New York: AMS Press, 1972.

Ahlstrom, Sydney H. *A Religious History of the American People.* New Haven, Conn.: Yale University Press, 1972.

*The Albany Directory for the Year 1865.* Albany: Sampson, Davenport, 1865. Also for the years 1866 and 1867.

Aldrich, Mrs. Thomas Bailey. *Crowding Memories.* Boston and New York: Houghton Mifflin, 1920.

*Appleton's Cyclopaedia of American Biography.* Ed. James Grant Wilson and John Fiske. New York: D. Appleton and Company, 1887–1889. 6 vols.

Arvin, Newton. *Herman Melville.* New York: Viking, 1957.

Bagger, Louis. "The Sailors' Snug Harbor." *Harper's New Monthly Magazine,* 46 (January 1873), 188–97.

Barbour, Oliver Lorenzo. *Treatise on the Criminal Law of the State of New-York; and upon the Jurisdiction, Duty and Authority of Justices of the Peace, and Incidentally, of the Power and Duty of Sheriffs, Constables, &c. in Criminal Cases.* 2nd ed. Albany: Gould, Banks; and New York: Banks, Gould, 1852.

Barker-Benfield, G. J. *The Horrors of the Half-Known Life: Male Attitudes toward Women and Sexuality in Nineteenth-Century America.* New York: Harper & Row, 1976.

Barnum, Phineas T. *The Catalogue or Guide Book of Barnum's American Museum.* New York: Printed and Published for the Proprietor, 186[?].

————. *The Life of P. T. Barnum Written by Himself*. New York: Redfield, 1855.

Bell, Robert, ed. *Songs from the Dramatists*. London: Parker, 1854.

Bezanson, Walter E. "Melville's Reading of Arnold's Poetry." *PMLA*, 69 (June 1954), 379–80.

Bickman, Martin. "Melville and the Mind." *A Companion to Melville Studies*, ed. John Bryant. Westport, Conn.: Greenwood Press, 1986, pp. 515–41.

Black, George F. *The Surnames of Scotland*. New York: New York Public Library, 1946.

Bobbé, Dorothie. *DeWitt Clinton*. New York: Minton, Balch, 1933.

Boies, J. J. "Melville's Staten Island 'Paradise.' " *Staten Island Historian*, 27 (July-September 1966), 24–28.

Boyer, M. Christine. *Manhattan Manners: Architecture and Style, 1850–1900*. New York: Rizzoli, 1985.

Bracher, Peter S. "Dickens and His American Readers, 1834–1870," Diss. Univ. of Pennsylvania, 1966.

Brakeley, Theresa C. "Bells," *Dictionary of Folklore*, ed. Maria Leach. New York: Funk & Wagnalls, 1972, pp. 132–34.

Brand, John. *Observations on Popular Antiquities*. 1877; rpt. London: Chatto & Windus, 1913.

Brandon, Edgar Ewing. *Lafayette: Guest of the Nation*. Oxford, Ohio: Oxford Historical Press, 1950.

*Brewer's Dictionary of Phrase and Fable*. New York and Evanston: Harper & Row, 1965.

Campbell, William W. *The Life and Writings of De Witt Clinton*. New York: Baker and Scribner, 1849.

Carlyle, Thomas. *On Heroes, Hero-Worship and the Heroic in History*. New York: Appleton, 1841.

Chase, Frederic Hathaway. *Lemuel Shaw: Chief Justice of the Supreme Judicial Court of Massachusetts, 1830–1860*. Boston and New York: Houghton Mifflin, 1918.

Child, Francis James, ed. *English and Scottish Ballads*. Boston: Little, Brown, 1854–57. 8 vols.

*Commercial Advertiser Directory.* Buffalo: Thomas and Lathrop, 1860.

Cowen, Walker. *Melville's Marginalia.* New York and London: Garland, 1987. 2 vols.

Dante Alighieri. *The Vision; or Hell, Purgatory, and Paradise. . . .* Trans. Henry Francis Cary. London: Bohn, 1847.

Davis, Merrell R. *Melville's Mardi: A Chartless Voyage.* New Haven, Conn.: Yale University Press, 1952.

Davis, Susan. "More for NYPL's Long Vaticans." *Melville Society Extracts,* 57 (February 1984), 5–7.

DeMarco, John and Carolyn. "Finding the New Melville Papers." *Melville Society Extracts,* 56 (November 1983), 1–3.

*Dictionary of American Biography.* Ed. Allen Johnson et al. New York: Charles Scribner's Sons, 1927–36.

*Dictionary of National Biography.* Ed. Leslie Stephen and Sidney Lee. Oxford: Oxford University Press, 1921–22.

*Doggett's New York City Directory.* New York: John Doggett, Publisher, 1842. Also for the years 1843–49. Titles vary.

Duyckinck, Evert A., and George L., comps. *Cyclopaedia of American Literature.* New York: Charles Scribner, 1855; 2 vols.

Ehrenreich, Barbara. *Fear of Falling: The Inner Life of the Middle Class.* New York: Pantheon, 1989.

Emerson, George B. *Reminiscences of an Old Teacher.* Boston: Alfred Mudge & Son, 1878.

Emerson, Ralph Waldo. *Representative Men: Seven Lectures.* Boston: Phillips, Sampson, 1850.

Emmers, Amy Puett. "Melville's Closet Skeleton: A New Letter About the Illegitimacy Incident in *Pierre.*" *Studies in the American Renaissance,* ed. Joel Myerson. Boston: Twayne, 1977, pp. 339–43.

Fisher, Marvin. *Going Under: Melville's Short Fiction and the American 1850s.* Baton Rouge: Louisiana State University Press, 1977.

Fox, Dixon Ryan. *The Decline of the Aristocracy in the Politics of New York.* Studies in History, Economics and Public Law, Edited by the Faculty of Political Science. New York: Columbia University Press, 1919.

Frazer, James G. *The Golden Bough.* New York: Macmillan, 1922.

Gardner, Augustus K. *Old Wine in New Bottles; or, The Spare Hours of a Student in Paris.* New York: C. S. Francis & Co., 1848.

Garner, Stanton. "Allan Melvill to Martin Van Buren on Major Melvill's Removal." *Melville Society Extracts,* 47 (September 1981), 4–5.

———. "Melville in the Custom House, 1881–1882: A Rustic Beauty among the Highborn Dames of Court." *Melville Society Extracts,* 35 (September 1978), 12–14.

———. "Melville's Scout Toward Aldie." *Melville Society Extracts,* 51 (September 1982), 5–16; and 52 (November 1952), 1–14.

———. "The Picaresque Career of Thomas Melvill, Junior." *Melville Society Extracts,* 60 (November 1984), 1–10; and 62 (May 1985), 1, 4–10.

Gilman, William H. *Melville's Early Life and REDBURN.* New York: New York University Press, 1951.

Hayford, Harrison. *Melville's "Monody": Really for Hawthorne?* Evanston, Ill.: Northwestern University Press, 1990.

Heimert, Alan, and Andrew Delbanco. *The Puritans in America.* Cambridge: Harvard University Press, 1985.

Herbert, T. Walter, Jr. *MOBY-DICK and Calvinism: A World Dismantled.* New Brunswick, N. J.: Rutgers University Press, 1977.

Hoadley, J. C., ed. *Memorial of Henry Sanford Gansevoort.* Boston: Franklin Press; Rand, Avery, & Co., 1875.

Horth, Lynn "Letters Lost, Letters Found: A Progress Report on Melville's Correspondence." *Melville Society Extracts,* 81 (May 1990), 1–7.

Howard, Leon. *Herman Melville: A Biography.* Berkeley: University of California Press, 1951.

Kelley, Wyn. "Melville's Cain." *American Literature,* 55 (March 1983), 25–40.

Kenney, Alice P. *The Gansevoorts of Albany: Dutch Patricians in the Upper Hudson Valley.* Syracuse, N.Y.: Syracuse University Press, 1969.

Kier, Kathleen E. "Elizabeth Shaw Melville and the Stedmans: 1891–1894." *Melville Society Extracts,* 45 (February 1981), 3–8.

Kring, Walter D., and Jonathan S. Carey. "Two Discoveries Concerning Herman Melville." *Proceedings of the Massachusetts Historical Society*, 87 (1975); rpt., *The Endless, Winding Way in Melville: New Charts by Kring and Carey*, ed. Donald Yannella and Hershel Parker. Glassboro, N.J.: The Melville Society, 1981.

Levy, Leonard W. *The Law of the Commonwealth and Chief Justice Shaw*. Cambridge, Mass.: Harvard University Press, 1957.

Leyda, Jay. *The Melville Log*. New York: Gordion, 1969. 2 vols.

*The Literary World: A Journal of Society, Literature, and Art.* 1848–1853. 8 vols.

*Longworth's American Almanac, New-York Register and City Directory.* New York: D. Longworth, 1820. Also for the years 1821–50.

Macdonough, Rodney. *Life of Commodore Thomas Macdonough, U. S. Navy*. Boston: The Fort Hill Press, 1909.

McCuskey, Dorothy. *Bronson Alcott, Teacher*. New York: Macmillan, 1940.

McNeilly, Dorothy V. B. D. R. "The Melvilles and Mrs. Ferris." *Extracts: An Occasional Newsletter*, 28 (November 1976), 1–9.

Macpherson, James. *Fingal, an Ancient Epic Poem . . . Together with Several Other Poems, Composed by Ossian*. London: Becket and De Hondt, 1762.

Mansfield, Luther. "Melville's Comic Articles on Zachary Taylor." *American Literature*, 9 (1938), 411–18.

Martin, Robert K. *Hero, Captain, and Stranger: Male Friendship, Social Critique, and Literary Form in the Sea Novels of Herman Melville*. Chapel Hill: University of North Carolina Press, 1986.

Matlaw, Myron, ed. *The Black Crook and Other Nineteenth-Century Plays*. New York: Dutton, 1967.

Melville, Herman.\* *Battle-Pieces and Aspects of the War*. New York: Harper & Brothers, 1866.

———. *Journal of a Visit to Europe and the Levant, October 11, 1856–May 6, 1857*, ed. Howard C. Horsford. Princeton: Princeton University Press, 1955.

*For the editions of Melville's works most frequently cited, see the list of abbreviations, pp. xi–xii.

————. *Journal of a Visit to London and the Continent by Herman Melville 1849–1850*, ed. Eleanor Melville Metcalf. Cambridge, Mass.: Harvard University Press, 1948.

————. *The Letters of Herman Melville*, ed. Merrell R. Davis and William H. Gilman. New Haven, Conn.: Yale University Press, 1960.

————. *Pierre or, The Ambiguities*, ed. Henry A. Murray. New York: Hendricks House, 1949.

————. The Writings of Herman Melville, ed. Harrison Hayford et al. Evanston and Chicago: The Northwestern University Press and the Newberry Library, 1968–

"Melville's Milton." *Melville Society Extracts*, 57 (February 1984), 7.

Metcalf, Eleanor Melville. *Herman Melville: Cycle and Epicycle*. Cambridge, Mass.: Harvard University Press, 1953.

Miller, Edwin Haviland. *Melville*. New York: George Braziller, 1975.

Milton, John. *The Poetical Works of John Milton*. Boston: Hilliard, Gray, and Company, 1836. 2 vols.

Mumford, Lewis. *Herman Melville*. New York: Harcourt, Brace, 1929.

Murray, Henry A. "Another Triumph for Maria's Firstborn." *Melville Society Extracts*, 58 (May 1984), 1–3.

————, and Eugene Taylor. "The Lancastrian System of Instruction." *Melville Society Extracts*, 69 (February 1987), 5–6.

————, Eugene Taylor, and Harvey Myerson. "Allan Melvill's By-Blow." *Melville Society Extracts*, 61 (February 1985), 1–6.

National Archives Microfilm Publications, Microcopy no. 432, Population Schedules of the Seventh Census of the United States, 1850. Roll 336. Washington, D.C.: N[ational] A[rchives], 1963. Ward 6, p. 33.

Neumeier, Charles, and Donald Yannella. "The Melvilles' House on East 26th Street." *Melville Society Extracts*, 47 (September 1981), 6–8.

Odell, George C. D. *Annals of the New York Stage*. New York: Columbia University Press, 1927–49. 18 vols.

*Oxford English Dictionary*. Ed. James A. H. Murray et al. Oxford: Clarendon Press, 1961.

Parker, Hershel, ed. *Gansevoort Melville's 1846 Journal*. New York: New York Public Library, 1966.

———. *Reading BILLY BUDD*. Evanston, Ill.: Northwestern University Press, 1991.

*The Penny Cyclopaedia of the Society for the Diffusion of Useful Knowledge*. London: Charles Knight, 1833–1846. 23 vols.

"Pierre or the Ambiguities." *American Whig Review*, 16 (November 1852), 446–54. Unsigned review.

Pommer, Henry F. *Milton and Melville*. Pittsburgh: University of Pittsburgh Press, 1950.

Rayback, Robert J. *Millard Fillmore: Biography of a President*. Buffalo, N.Y.: Henry Stewart for the Buffalo Historical Society, 1959.

Robinson, Henry Crabb. *Diary, Reminiscences, and Correspondence . . .* Boston: Fields, Osgood, 1869.

Rogers, Thomas J. *A New American Biographical Dictionary, or, Remembrancer of the Departed Heroes*. Easton, Pa.: Rogers, 1824.

Rogin, Michael Paul. *Subversive Genealogy: The Politics and Art of Herman Melville*. New York: Knopf, 1983.

Roseberry, Cecil R. *For the Government and People of This State: A History of the New York State Library*. Albany: New York State Library, the University of the State of New York, the State Education Department, 1970.

Rosenberry, Edward. *Melville and the Comic Spirit*. Cambridge, Mass.: Harvard University Press, 1955.

*Sailors' Snug Harbor: Investigation into Charges Preferred against the Officers & Management*. New York: Slote and Jones, 1883.

Sealts, Merton M., Jr. *The Early Lives of Melville*. Madison: University of Wisconsin Press, 1974.

———. "The Melvill Heritage." *Harvard Library Bulletin*, 34 (Fall 1986), 337–61.

———. "Melville and Emerson's Rainbow," in *Pursuing Melville, 1940–1980*. Madison: University of Wisconsin Press, 1980, pp. 251–77.

————. *Melville's Reading: Revised and Enlarged Edition.* Columbia: University of South Carolina Press, 1988.

————. "Thomas Melvill, Jr., in *The History of Pittsfield.*" *Harvard Library Bulletin*, 35 (Spring 1987), 201–17.

Sedgwick, Elizabeth Buckminster Dwight. *A Talk with My Pupils.* New York: J. Hopper; Boston: Crosby and Nichols, 1863.

Shaw, Samuel. "Lemuel Shaw: Early and Domestic Life." *Memorial Biographies of the New England Historic and Genealogical Society.* Boston: Published by the Society, 1885, 204–5.

Shepard, Odell. *Pedlar's Progress.* Boston: Little, Brown, 1937.

Shneidman, Edwin S. "Some Psychological Reflections on the Death of Malcolm Melville." *Suicide and Life-Threatening Behavior*, 6 (1976), 231–42.

Shurr, William H. *The Mystery of Iniquity: Melville as Poet, 1857–1891.* Lexington: University of Kentucky Press, 1972.

Smith, Joseph Edward Adams. *The History of Pittsfield (Berkshire County) Massachusetts, from the Year 1800 to the Year 1876.* Springfield, Mass.: C. W. Bryan & Co., 1876. 2 vols.

Sobel, Robert, and John Raimo, ed. *Biographical Directory of the Governors of the United States, 1789–1978.* Westport, Conn.: Meckler Books, 1978.

Spenser, Edmund. *The Poetical Works. . . .* Boston: Little, Brown, 1855.

*State of New York. No. 31. In Senate, February 16, 1841.* ANNUAL REPORT OF THE AFFAIRS OF THE SAILORS' SNUG HARBOR. TO THE LEGISLATURE OF THE STATE OF NEW YORK. . . . New York, 10th February, 1841.

Stein, William Bysshe. *The Poetry of Melville's Late Years: Time, History, Myth, and Religion.* Albany: State University of New York Press, 1970.

*Stimpson's Boston Directory.* Boston: Stimpson and Clapp, 1826. Also for the years 1827, 1828, and 1829.

Stone, Lawrence. *The Family, Sex and Marriage, 1500–1800.* New York: Harper & Row, 1979.

Sundquist, Eric J. *Home As Found: Authority and Genealogy in Nineteenth-*

*Century American Literature*. Baltimore: Johns Hopkins University Press, 1979.

*A Supplement to Allibone's Critical Dictionary of English Literature and British and American Authors*. Philadelphia: J. B. Lippincott, 1891.

Tanselle, G. Thomas. "Herman Melville's Visit to Galena in 1840." *Journal of the Illinois Historical Society*, 53 (1960), 376–88.

Titus, David K. "Herman Melville at the Albany Academy." *Melville Society Extracts*, 42 (May 1980), 1, 4–10.

Tolchin, Neal L. *Mourning, Gender, and Creativity in the Art of Herman Melville*. New Haven and London: Yale University Press, 1988.

*Trow's Business Directory for Greater New York*. New York: Trow Directory Printing Co., 1867. Also for the year 1858.

Wallace, Robert K. "Melville's Prints and Engravings at the Berkshire Athenaeum." *Essays in Arts and Sciences*, 15 (June 1986), 59–90.

Weaver, Raymond M. *Herman Melville: Mariner and Mystic*. New York: George H. Doran, 1921.

Wharton, Edith. *A Backward Glance*. New York and London: D. Appleton, 1934.

Wheatley, Henry B., ed. *Reliques of Ancient English Poetry*. London: Bickers & Son, 1877. 3 vols.

Young, Philip. "Small World: Emerson, Longfellow, and Melville's Secret Sister." *New England Quarterly*, 60 (September 1987), 382–402.

# Index

An asterisk (*) before a page number indicates that the reference is to an illustration.